Ending the Cycle of Abuse:

The Stories of Women Abused as Children and the Group Therapy Techniques That Helped Them Heal

Ending the Cycle of Abuse:

The Stories of Women Abused as Children and the Group Therapy Techniques That Helped Them Heal

by

Philip G. Ney, M.D., F.R.C.P.(C)

&

Anna Peters

Brunner/Mazel Publishers • New York

Library of Congress Cataloging-in-Publication Data

Ney, Philip G. (Philip Gordon)
    Ending the cycle of abuse: the stories of women abused as
children and the group therapy techniques that helped them heal /
by Philip G. Ney & Anna Peters.
        p. cm.
    Includes bibliographical references and index.
    ISBN 0-87630-752-7
    1. Adult child abuse victims—Case studies. 2. Group
pychotherapy—Case studies. I. Peters, Anna. II. Title.
    RC569.5.C55N49 1994
    616.85'822390651—dc20   94-28150
                                                                   CIP

Published by
BRUNNER/MAZEL, INC.
19 Union Square West
New York, New York 10003

Manufactured in the United States of America
10 9 8 7 6 5 4 3 2 1

Contents

Foreword

This is a book about group therapy, but it is no ordinary book on the subject. It is also a book about adults who have been abused as children, but again, it is no ordinary book about such people. It is extraordinary in a number of respects, but most of all because it offers the reader the perspectives of both the therapist and the patients in the group therapy it describes. The senior author was the therapist and the second author one of the patients in the group.

There have been many books about group therapy. A fair number of accounts have also been written about the process of group and other psychotherapies by those who have been treated in such groups. But it is rare for a book to appear that offers both perspectives on the same group.

Ending the Cycle of Abuse describes the group treatment of eight women from that most difficult category of troubled people—those who were severely abused as children. These women most surely met this criterion. They had experienced various combinations of severe sexual, physical, and emotional abuse, as well as neglect, throughout much or all of their respective childhoods. One had been the victim of severe and prolonged ritual abuse. They were the kind of clients who, presenting themselves for treatment, would cause almost any therapist's heart to sink. "What can I do for these people who have been so damaged from so early in their lives?" "How can these people, who have never experienced the love, caring, nurturing, and affirmation children need, ever feel or become whole?" "How can these terribly injured individuals ever be restored to anything resembling emotional and mental health?" "It's not so difficult if they are still children—and the younger the better—but in adulthood what can be done?"

This book provides partial answers to the above questions, but it makes no claims of magic cures. Indeed, it doesn't claim cures at all. One of the tasks the women in the group were asked to address was that of accepting that they could never be what they might have been had they not been abused in childhood. They achieved much more than that, though. In varying degrees, they addressed and dealt constructively with the guilt, the anger, the rage, the fear, and the despair stemming from their early experiences. They were an unusually intelligent group of people, well able to express themselves. Anna Peters (a pseudonym) is clearly a gifted writer, as well, it seems, as having great gifts as an artist.

The therapy stretched to 30 sessions. Some of the sessions were very long, but all but two members completed the course, and one of those who did not joined a subsequent group with a firm resolve to complete it. The others made good, some of them remarkably good, progress.

I suspect that one of the most valuable things this book will give to many of its readers will be a deeper understanding of child abuse and its effects on the developing child. While there is really nothing new about what it says on the subject, it is seldom, if ever, that I have come across the material presented so clearly, spelled out so graphically. We usually first read Dr. Ney's sober, measured words, then the lucid, telling prose of Anna. Although there are many words from Anna, other members of the group contribute also. Lisa's account of her ritual abuse is particularly moving—in a distressing way.

The model of therapy presented is of interest. In addition to Dr. Ney, the principal therapist and only male, there were three assistants: a family physician who was learning group therapy and two graduates of previous groups. The last played key roles in the therapy process, as well as being living testaments to the possibility of completing the group and having much to give to others.

I believe that all who work with adults who have been abused as children, whether they do so in groups or in individual therapy, will gain much from reading and carefully studying this book. So also, I think, will those who have been abused. Undoubtedly, they will see much of themselves in the women in the group. They will also acquire some understanding of what therapy involves—the issues that will come up, the pain, the turmoil, the hard work, and above all, perhaps, the idea that they are not to blame, that child abuse is a complex thing involving three people or groups of people: abuser, victim, and observer(s).

One of the extraordinary things about this book is that it seems suitable for at least two sets of readers, one the helpers and the therapist, and the other the victims. We should probably also add the third group, the observers, and, of course, all of us fit into at least one of these three groups.

When Philip Ney first told me about this book, he said he thought it would be useful both to therapists and to the victims of abuse. I replied, "No, you must write for one group or the other. Publishers like to know rather precisely what a book's potential readership is. They do not like to risk taking a 'shotgun' approach—aiming widely without being sure if any particular market will be hit." But I was wrong, perhaps not about publishers, but certainly about this book! I do believe that both therapists and the abused will find it useful and that the more sophisticated and curious lay public, and indeed all those with any concern about child abuse and its effects, will find that it contains much of interest to them.

Ending the Cycle of Abuse is an important book that both suggests how those who have been abused may be helped and also offers them hope.

PHILIP BARKER, M.B., B.S., F.R.C.P.(C), F.R.C.PSYCH. (U.K.), F.R.C.P.(ED.)
PROFESSOR, DEPARTMENTS OF PSYCHIATRY AND PAEDIATRICS
UNIVERSITY OF CALGARY, ALTA., CANADA

Introduction

WHY CHILD ABUSE AND NEGLECT BECOME TRANSGENERATIONAL

Why don't we ever learn? One of life's greatest mysteries and humanity's most difficult dilemmas certainly must be why people don't learn from their painful experiences. Why must sad history repeat itself? The most terrible tragedy is that childhood abuse and neglect are passed from one generation to the next. Why do children who have been neglected and abused become parents who do very much the same thing to their own children?

I have spent a lifetime of clinical practice and research trying to understand child abuse and neglect. Having analyzed our data and listened to thousands of case histories, I think it is reasonable to conclude the following:

1. Abuse and neglect are often transgenerational.[1] Depending on the type and extent of abuse, there are (a) significant correlations between the ways in which parents were abused as children and the ways in which they abuse their own children, (b) high correlations between the ways in which a parent is abused by his or her spouse and the way in which he or she abuses his or her children, and (c) many close correlations between how a mother was abused as a child and how she is abused by her spouse. For some reason, mothers and fathers choose mates who help them establish the same kind of experience for themselves and for their children that they themselves experienced as children. This happens even in the face of great determination not to mistreat their children. "It was terrible for me and I will not let it happen to my child." The enormous guilt that comes from recognizing that history is repeating itself only adds to the

fear and frustration, which often increases the abuse. I have found, if nothing else, that parents will go into treatment when they are faced with the realization that their early experiences are being visited on their children.

2.   Victims may contribute to their own victimization. Depending on the type and extent of abuse, children can precipitate and maintain it. Some children appear to have characteristics that incline parents to become frustrated and angry. An example is the hyperactive child who, as a result of his or her constant mobility, distractibility, and impulsiveness, can turn even the most sanguine parents into shouting maniacs. In spite of themselves, they may hit the child, thereby causing the child to become aggressive as well as hyperkinetic.

Children also appear to have some part in sustaining abuse. The idea that they might be partly responsible for their own mistreatment is very unpopular, but the research data and clinical experience support this conclusion. This is not to say they are at fault or are culpable or are to be blamed. Scientific observation shows that children who have been abused seem to set up situations in which they continue to be abused. An example of this is the blue-eyed, curlyhaired, muscular little five-year-old who, having been physically abused, is placed with a loving foster family. The foster parents come to my attention not long afterward saying, "Doctor, you must either help us understand what is happening or remove the child because, in spite of ourselves, we're going to kill him. We've never hurt any of our own children, but he is doing something to us so that we can hardly control our anger."

3.   Various types of abuse and neglect usually go together. Few cases are seen with only one type of abuse or neglect.[2] When we studied physical abuse (hitting, burning, etc.), verbal abuse (condemning, criticizing, demeaning, etc.), physical neglect (insufficient food, clothing, medical care, etc.), emotional and intellectual neglect (insufficient affirmation, intellectual stimulation, etc.), and sexual abuse (sexual titillation, manipulation, fondling, penetration, etc.), we found that in less than 5 percent of the cases was there a single type of abuse occurring. Aggressive kinds of abuse, verbal and physical, tended to clump together. Physical neglect and sexual abuse also went together. Thus any scientific reports on one type of abuse or neglect have limited value.

4.   Verbal abuse can be the most damaging and longest lasting.[3] It appears that the things that were said to children become sufficiently part of their self-image and self-directed repertoire that they continue to use the same epithets about themselves in their adult lives. Verbal abuse also is more difficult to treat because it is often so egosyntonic (so much a part of me that I think it is natural). Parents often don't realize the damage they

are doing because there are no bruises or broken bones that might make them recoil in horror. Visible injury can stop them from hurting their children.

5.   Children often blame themselves for their mistreatment. Self-blame seems to be a function of both the type and severity of abuse or neglect. For physical abuse, the correlation is a straight sloping line between the extent of abuse and self-blame. For mild or moderate physical abuse, a child blames himself or herself. For severe physical abuse, a child blames the perpetrator. It is almost as if the child understands that that kind of ill-treatment could not be deserved. For verbal and sexual abuse, it is a U-shaped line, with the child taking the blame if it is mild, blaming others if it is moderate, and blaming himself or herself if it is severe.

6.   Neglect is probably more harmful than abuse.[4] If neglect precedes abuse, the child's vulnerability and susceptibility to abuse are greater. Children who have been neglected have less ego strength to withstand the impact of verbal, physical, or sexual abuse. Neglected children are more susceptible, that is, they seem to be looking in the wrong places for the nurture they didn't receive as children. It is as if a child who was starved is looking for garbage in the street and will be stopped by nothing, even the most severe sanitation laws.

7.   Children usually know why they are mistreated. We found that the most frequent response of children concerning what they felt caused the abuse and neglect was that their parents were immature.[5] Even children understood that it wasn't so much a problem of their parents' aggression, poverty, or even alcohol, but the fact that they didn't have the maturity to be adults and parents. It wasn't that the parents wouldn't give them what they needed; they couldn't. It wasn't that the parents felt the child really deserved to be beaten; it was just that they couldn't stop themselves.

8.   Mistreatment and unmourned pregnancy losses go together. When we analyzed data from adults, it appeared that there were a number of significant correlations between the parents' depression, their inability to touch and the mother's to breast-feed the child, and later neglect and abuse. Postpartum depression more often occurs if there were previous losses. Thus part of the treatment for abusing families must be to help them mourn the loss of family members, particularly pregnancy losses. Depressed parents don't bond as well to their children. Poorly bonded children are more frequently abused and neglected. It is not surprising that rates of abuse and abortion correlate.[6] They must also mourn the loss of some part of themselves.

9.   When all of these data were put together, a pattern seemed to emerge that I have described as a model for how and why abuse becomes transgenerational (Figure 1).[7,8] Primitive morality describes a one-way cause and effect between perpetrator and victim. The evil perpetrator willfully harms the innocent victim. The perpetrator must be punished and the victim compensated. Unfortunately, there are plenty of data to show that this is a much more complex dyad, with the perpetrator and victim affecting each other. I suggest that it is a triangle.[9] The third point is the observer, the supposedly innocent bystander who is not innocent and often is not simply one person. If you ask either the perpetrator or the victim why it happened, each will point to the other. But after gaining insight, they both will ascribe at least partial cause to the observer. Not infrequently, they ask, "Why didn't they stop us?" The young woman, after some hours of insight-oriented psychotherapy for the ill effects of sexual abuse by her stepfather, begins to express her anger. In my experience, most of that rage is directed at the mother. "I told her and she didn't do anything about it. I can't believe that she was so callous and uncaring."

If one asks the observers, they most frequently state, "I didn't know, and, besides, I couldn't have done anything about it." Is this not the statement made throughout history by any group watching a tragedy played out between two other groups? Yet history really asks not whether the

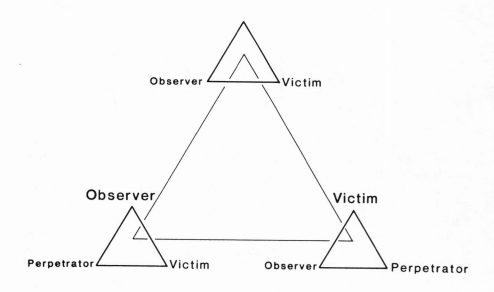

Figure 1. Abuse paradigm

people knew, but what they did with what they did know. Did they try to find out more? Did they follow up on their suspicions? Many did not, and the result was tragic.

The triangle or triquetra of abuse and neglect can rotate with different circumstances and through time. A child who observed a mother and father fighting not infrequently becomes the perpetrator of abuse in his or her own family. The man who sexually molests children, when placed in jail, becomes the victim. The child who was a victim of abuse can become the perpetrator in the next generation. There is a certain arbitrariness as to who is the victim and who is perpetrator or observer. It may serve some function or legal purpose, but this arbitrary assignment does not fit the complex dynamics of human transactions.

If humans keep repeating their mistakes and handing down their problems from one generation to another, is it entirely a tragedy? Is it only maladaptive, stupid, or self-destructive? Or is there some benefit? I began to realize that the human organism was made to be adaptive in almost all of its functions. Perhaps transgenerational abuse has some adaptive purpose.

It appears that people must repeat their problems until they learn from them. Is it possible that they make mistakes recur in order to learn? It seems that having been neglected or traumatized, the child now is host to a conflict that creates a disequilibrium. That disequilibrium will continue until the child can resolve the conflict. One way of doing so would be to carefully pick out other people as an adult who will help him reenact the problems of the past.

It is almost as if the people in a relationship with adults who were abused or neglected as children (boss, mate, children) are given parts to play on stage. Once the action is well in place, the person with the conflict hopes to step off the stage and observe how he or she contributes to his or her own misery. The difficulty is that once one is involved in such a tragic reenactment, it won't continue unless one stays in it. If one did step out, the transaction would collapse. Thus people seldom have an opportunity to watch their own behavior objectively. They rarely receive corrective feedback that could keep them from repeating a tragedy.

Insight isn't everything. Knowing why you reenact tragedy doesn't necessarily free you from it. Those who do learn from their reenactments are still partly bound to continue their behavior because (a) of the fact that their behavior is conditioned, (b) of the pressure of transactions around them, or (c) of the evil and unhappiness in their society. It is hard to contend with social pressure. Too often people in our groups have commented that as they change, there is increased pressure on them by friends and relatives to revert to their old ways.

What is the difficulty with having an unresolved conflict? If people must reenact their problems in order to learn from them, is it worth the effort? Why not just repress it all? Because mental conflict seems to create a disequilibrium, it results in the inefficient expenditure of energy. Like all systems, unless we expend energy efficiently and take in as much as we expend, we will end up in entropy, losing energy and gaining chaos. We cannot just eat and sleep. We must use energy efficiently, otherwise we die, especially in marginal circumstances.

A conflict results in the inefficient use of energy. "Will I?" or "Won't I?" debated all day long can tire a person out without resolving any conflict at all. You are angry at someone who insulted you. The tricep wants to contract to throw the fist at that person's face, but the bicep says "No, he's bigger," and so the two muscles, in opposition, expend a lot of energy and nothing is resolved. To avoid entropy, conflicts must be resolved. To resolve conflict, people tend to reenact it. They subconsciously pick a mate who represents a person from the past. They have children who help recreate scenes from their own childhood. Unfortunately, this reenactment seldom takes place before the eyes of anyone who can (1) give them sufficient insight into the problem, (2) train them in different ways of reacting, (3) point out the social pressures on them, (4) point out the complex transactions in which they evoke behaviors that trigger conflicts, or (5) point out the existential payoffs that tend to make them carry on. If the reenactment did occur with the informed comment, it might allow people to stop behaving in a way that evokes the same tragic consequences.

After many thousands of hours in treatment with only reasonable results, I began to realize that individual psychotherapy was inefficient. Too often it became an intellectual exercise. For disturbed young people, I have been able to develop an inpatient program with good, though not spectacular, results.[10,11,12] I began to realize that many children don't have the ego strength or the support to sustain them during the trauma of intensive treatment. Such treatment should be done efficiently enough to result in an egalitarian distribution among all who need to be treated. I had a very long, and growing, waiting list. So I turned to group therapy.

HOW THIS GROUP TREATMENT WORKS

I was trained in group therapy as a resident and did some afterwards, but not to the extent to which I now use it. I rediscovered its benefit and efficiency. I also realized that there is a natural sequence to the treatment of children and adults as they deal with abuse and neglect.[13] So I put together the scientific evidence, the model, the natural sequence of events in treatment, together with my understanding of groups, and developed this technique. It appears to be effective. It is certainly more useful than the common response of prosecuting the perpetrator.[14]

The first group of adults abused as children that I treated were men. That first occasion was painful for all, but I learned a great deal. The results were sufficiently encouraging to make me want to try again. After many groups of men, of women, and of younger people, I now feel sufficiently confident to describe the process, and even to suggest that it be tried by others. I hasten to add that it is sufficiently difficult and complicated that unless a professional is a well-experienced group therapist, he or she should not try it without first obtaining training and supervision. I have engaged cotherapists as trainees, but realize that this is an inefficient way of training people. Now that the demand is sufficiently great, I am instituting formal training.

Recently I conducted, with a family physician as trainee, a group for women who were so extraordinarily intelligent and verbally adept that I decided this would be the group to describe. I asked them to help me write the book. They all, in their own way, have done just that. I have asked Anna Peters, a woman with a wonderful talent for writing, to be an associate author. She has experienced the whole process as a patient and as a facilitator in other groups. I have great admiration for Anna, who is using a pseudonym to protect the anonymity of her family and the other members of her original group.

I believe that group treatment facilitates the efficient and effective treatment of adults abused and neglected as children for the following reasons:

1. Hearing others emote encourages the expression of a wide range of feelings. Patients who identify with the feelings of another vicariously experience emotions that they might not otherwise have allowed themselves to feel or express.
2. Patients gain insight from each other's hard-won understanding.
3. The statements by other group members about the effects of their maltreatment tends to validate how one felt. As a child, one's loneliness, pain, or hopelessness was seldom communicated. When it was, it was often denied or denigrated by the adults.
4. The group produces a sense of cohesiveness that lessens the loneliness of the individual experience.
5. The group exercises and role plays require the participation of a group of people. Often they do the role plays in pairs. Sometimes the group takes one side of the issue while the person being focused on takes the other.
6. Group therapy makes treatment of more people possible, and therefore it tends to spread the scarce resource of competent therapists more equitably among so many wounded people.
7. Any insights provided by the therapist tend to be received differently by each member of the group. The variety of reactions helps the therapist clarify his or her statements.

This group therapy is quite unlike anything I had seen or read about. It is different, but it contains these recognizable elements:

1. Transactional therapy—with insights as to how one person affects the behavior of another.
2. Behaviorism—with good use being made of rehearsals and increased awareness of contingencies.
3. Group analytic process—where the group is treated as one organism, with its transference being used for insight.
4. Existentialism—where spiritual issues are dealt with.

The framework of the treatment, the assignment of homework, and the group exercises I believe are unique. The group meetings of five to seven members were conducted once a week for two or three hours each. The treatment consisted of eight phases that continued for a total of 24 to 26 weeks. Some groups needed to proceed more slowly, but there was a remarkably constant progression. Two facilitators and one cotherapist were usually present. The facilitators were unpaid volunteers from earlier groups. They benefited considerably from going through a group again because of the change in perspective and because, in reaching out to help others, they were overcoming the self-centeredness engendered by their psychotherapy. The cotherapist was usually a physician or psychologist training to do similar groups.

Each group session consisted of the following:

1. Precheck. The patients were asked to give a report on their present state, telling something about the events that took place in their lives during the past week.
2. Homework. Everyone reported on the process and the results of their assignments. It is important for the group to say "uh-huh" or something supportive in response to someone's expressed distress. A person who is reading from homework cannot see the affirmation in the eyes or expressions of the other group members.
3. Response. There was a freewheeling discussion of the issues that arose from the homework, with explanations and insights given by the therapists.
4. Group exercises. Role plays, rehearsals, and training were used to highlight conflicts and emotions and help people overcome some of their conditioned behavior.
5. Assignments. New homework was given with explanations as to how it could be done.
6. Postcheck. A determination was made of how people felt before they left.

7. Support. Any patients who were not in condition to travel home alone were given some private counseling or taken home by others.
8. Feedback. The therapists and facilitators spent 20 to 30 minutes after each group sharing observations, discussing techniques, and preparing for the next group.

It appears that treatment isn't effective unless all eight stages are completed. Those who drop out or are left behind at some point in the treatment and are carried along without sufficient understanding do not do well and may become worse. It is for this reason that commitment to finishing the whole process is so critical.

ACKNOWLEDGMENTS

While conducting these groups, I have learned at least as much as I have been able to teach. I am very grateful to all of the people in this particular group. The women were candid and did not hesitate to be critical. Nothing has been edited out of this book. From group to group, the process develops and new techniques develop. We have now developed a training manual that is used to teach this type of group therapy.[15]

I am particularly grateful to Margot Ney, who encouraged me and helped with the editing. Thanks also to Dr. Linda Green for her patient encouragement, very wise insights, and amazing ability to support and encourage group members. A very big thanks to facilitators Tasha and Shelly, who were invaluable to each of the group members by describing their own experiences. I am deeply grateful to Sherilyn Thomson, Suzanne Bowen, Adele Wickett, and Jeannine Blumel, who worked on the typing, editing, and research that helped make this book possible. Most of all, I thank God, who has taught, encouraged, and sustained me through all the vagaries of this life, and particularly with the vicarious pain of treating so many wounded people.

REFERENCES

[1] Ney PG, McPhee J, Moore C, Trought P. "Child Abuse: A Study of the Child's Perspective." *Child Abuse and Neglect* 1986;10:511–518.
[2] Ney PG, Fung T, Wickett A. "Combinations of Child Abuse and Neglect." Presented at the annual meeting of the Canadian Academy of Child Psychiatry, Saskatoon, Sask., October 1991.
[3] Ney PG. "Does Verbal Abuse Leave Deeper Scars? A Study of Children and Parents." *Canadian Journal of Psychiatry* 1987;32:371–378.

4   Ney PG, Fung T, Wickett AR. "Child Neglect: The Precursor to Child Abuse." *Pre and Perinatal Psychology Journal* 1993;8:95–112.

5   Ney PG, Fung T, Wickett AR. "Causes of Child Abuse and Neglect." *Canadian Journal Psychiatry* 1992;37:401–405.

6   Ney PG, Fung T, Wickett AR. "Relationships Between Induced Abortion and Child Abuse and Neglect: Four Studies." *Pre and Perinatal Psychology Journal* 1993;8:43–63.

7   Ney PG. "Transgenerational Child Abuse." *Child Psychiatry Human Development* 1988;18:151–168.

8   Ney PG. "Child Mistreatment: Possible Reasons for its Transgenerational Transmission." *Canadian Journal of Psychiatry* 1989;34:594–601.

9   Ney PG. "Triangles of Abuse: A Model of Maltreatment." *Journal of Child Abuse and Neglect* 1988;12:363–373.

10 Ney PG, Mulvihill D, Hanna R. "The Effectiveness of Child Psychiatry Inpatient Treatment." *Canadian Journal of Psychiatry* 1984;29:26–30.

11 Ney PG, Adam RR, Hanton BR, Brindad ES. "The Effectiveness of a Child Psychiatric Unit: A Follow-up Study." *Canadian Journal of Psychiatry* 1988;793–799.

12 Ney PG, Mulvihill D. *Child Psychiatric Treatment: A Practical Guide.* London: Croom Helm, 1985.

13 Ney PG. "The Treatment of Abused Children: The Natural Sequence of Events." *American Journal of Psychotherapy* 1987;46:391–401.

14 Ney PG, Herron JL. "Mandatory Reporting." *New Zealand Medical Journal* 1985;98:703–705.

15 Ney PG, Peeters M. *Hope Alive: A Training Manual for Therapists.* Victoria, B.C., Canada: Pioneer Publishing, March 1993.

Ending the Cycle of Abuse:

The Stories of Women Abused as Children and the Group Therapy Techniques That Helped Them Heal

1

Realization: Knowing and Feeling What Happened to Me

History of Anna Peters

Darkness, time—no memory.

New home, new father, new sibling, a chance to be loved and accepted. Hope and promise. An exciting happy day to begin life. I am eight.

I step out of the classroom. My sister is screaming. She runs frantically past me to the principal's office. I follow terrified. Of what? I don't know. Everyone is upset: teachers, Mommy, my stepdad. The police are called. Our birth father has come to take her. Later no one talks about it. He must be very bad. He didn't want me...I am nine.

"Go to the nurse's room and get measured and weighed." His words rang in my ears like a death sentence. I'd lied, said I was sick so I would miss this class, and now I had to do it alone, in front of everyone. I hate him. I hate me. I hate, hate, hate. Frantically looking to the board, I find the heaviest weight: 155. Mine is much higher. "In front," he demands. Head down, I mumble my lie: 157. I am ashamed. I wish I could die. The familiar tittering of my classmates cuts deep. Hesitantly, I share this experience with my mom, who says, "He's only trying to help." I hate her, I hate me: no one understands. Alone, always alone. I eat. I am 10.

Grabbing, poking, tickling. "Dad," whose touch always makes me uncomfortable. Please, I love you, why do I always have to push you away? Your constant sexual innuendos shame me and keep my few girlfriends away. I can't do anything good enough to please you, "Mom." I am fat and you are uncomfortable. I embarrass you. I am not small, cute, athletic, popular, submissive, quiet, conforming. I want to be heard, understood. I want to think. Let me think. I am growing.

Looking in the mirror, a head on a grossly overweight body stares hollowly back at me. Anger wells up. Fists clenched, I beat my stomach over and over saying, "I hate you, I hate you, I hate you." I am 14.

Boys? No, only the men looked. I want to be loved. Please love me. You want me? I owe you. Beginning to be sexually active. I am 15.

Ravenous! Mom's diet, my diet, stealing lunches, taking money from the cash box at work, using my pay check and baby-sitting money for food and clothes. Look good! Sabotage looking good. Alone, isolated, peering out at a world that judges by appearance and performance. I perform. I owe the world. I am fat and ugly. I am 16.

Graduate, get away. Get married. My choice: a drug addict who uses physical, verbal, and emotional abuse to maintain control while wrestling with his own sexual ambivalence. Two children, full-blown bulimia, and four chaotic years later, I escape. I am 21.

Divorced and living with an alcoholic. Looking good, successfully self-employed, in control, anorexic. Constant tug-of-war between my children and my man. No commitment, day-to-day hoping...(I don't realize he is an alcoholic until therapy 14 years later). I am 24.

Only four months on my own, then I married a workaholic, passive/aggressive, emotionally unavailable father of two. Bouts of emotional, verbal, and physical abuse toward me and the kids left me feeling trapped and helpless again. Fighting bulimia with an endless diet cycle, I was emotionally broken and diagnosed as manic depressive. Found God—or should I say, he found me?

Church support, friends, and hope and strength again. I moved to an isolated community where the church bias was submission. Now I tasted spiritual abuse. I was trying hard to be good: do more, pray, fast, submit, give, love, surrender, support, obey, honor, don't interfere, suffer. I discover that my husband sexually abused our girls. Send them away, protect them, stand by him, keep the boys, uphold our name, God's name. Think: if I do what is right, God will fix everything. I wait. Silence. I am 26 going on 45.

My world crumbling, I can't be responsible any more. I can't hold everything and everybody together any more. I can't function. My body is quitting. I have intense physical pain. I am unable to be the perfect mother, wife, homemaker, Christian, leader, counselor, employee. I can't perform at my usual accelerated pace. I manage the basics only. Friends drop off because I am unable to fix or fulfill their needs. Covered by a shroud of sadness, God whispers to me, "You have never grieved." I begin to grieve for the first time in my life, months of overwhelming sorrow. I don't understand nor do I trust myself to have heard God correctly, and I am too tired to fight. I just let it happen. I can't stop it. Many doctors, many tests, no answers. Am I losing it? I must be losing it. Oh God, help me! The dreaded door, one I haven't tried. I seek a psychiatrist. He must be a Christian. My faith is all I have left. I can't let that be challenged.... He thinks he can help me. He said I could quit going for more tests; I am so tired of tests. Why did I need his permission? Yet somehow I did, and now I feel safe, relieved by just stopping. He says, "It will cost you a lot, more than you can imagine." I am willing. What more can I lose? I am willing to do anything. I am so afraid for my sanity. Four months before the next therapy group starts—an eternity! How will I ever keep it together that long? "You can come back to see me before the group begins if you need to." If I need to? He's got to be kidding. Clinically depressed, frightened, and yet...not without hope. I am 45.

Darkness engulfs me. Fear—lots of fear. Death, darkness, evil. I can't see. I can feel but I can't see. Two hours pass. I am exhausted, yet exhilarated. I hold my hands gently on my chest and feel a warm, secure place deep within, a sense of being. I have been called into life by the Father of life himself. He has a special destiny for me. He told me wondrous and fearsome things. He loves me and created me and called me, and I can face whatever he shows me because I have a safe place deep within where he is. "This really messes up my theology: a womb experience?" I ask him. We laugh together. My Father, God, laughing with his child. I am born.

Again the fear, the darkness. I've been here before. I know where to go. I put my hands on my chest. I feel the warm, safe place deep inside that my Father created. I let the darkness come. I can't move my hands. They are curled in tight against my chest. I can feel saliva trickling from the corner of my mouth. My face feels numb. I hear unearthly moans—oh God, they are mine! I whisper "Jesus" over and over in my mind. I will to trust him and let the darkness cover me. "Daddy! Daddy! Stop. Please don't hurt me!" Screaming, sobbing, curled up, my hands covering my genitals. The memory lasted about an hour. It was like I was there! Three years old. I could remember, feel everything. Afterwards my body was in shock; first hot, then cold, sweating profusely and nauseous. I had been rectally raped. I was three.

Two more months pass. I am not used to the truth of my abuse yet and find myself wandering aimlessly through life. Numb best describes me. I feel like I am living some long-ago movie about someone else.

My husband decided that we needed a holiday. While on vacation, we attended an out-of-province Christian conference. Usually I would have been keen to go; these days it really didn't matter. During the time when thousands of people gathered to worship, I sat, unable to sing. I could feel God's presence all around me, yet I was unable to respond. God seemed to be telling me just to rest and trust. The second day, immediately after a lecture session and the closing worship, I experienced that intense presence again, the one that I was beginning to recognize as preparation for releasing a memory. I was afraid, excited, and trusting at the same time.

I decided to remain seated during the upcoming two-and-a-half-hour break and face this thing, alone if necessary. I was willing. I sat quietly with my eyes shut as the room cleared. I began to hear low moans escaping from deep within me. The last thing I remember before I hit the floor was acknowledging his power and protection and asking for someone knowledgeable and wise to look after me. I felt detached as my body was literally thrown to the floor. I writhed in pain and terror, my arms flailing at some unseen enemy. Cries of torment and despair escaped my lips. Several people helped me out of the room. I could hear them talking and felt their touch, but it seemed filtered, as though from far away. I was unable to see. Apparently, my eyes were wide open; however, I never saw one face. I was terrified of some of the men in the room and filled with rage toward others. Pulling away and hiding, I once even struck out and spat at one young man. The men had to leave before I would settle down. After a lengthy time of fighting my unseen enemies, thoughts began to focus and I again began to recall and relive sexual-abuse memories. Although the person's face never came into focus, I remembered the pain and the raw presence of evil during the abuse. Afterwards I lay bruised and exhausted. I had some kind of heavy vaginal discharge during the body memory and needed to return to my room. I was unable to handle contact with anyone except my husband. I felt violated, dirty, and shaken. After a long bath, I curled up in my bed, where sleep lovingly took me. It was two o'clock in the afternoon.

I was still disoriented as I entered the auditorium the next day. I spent most of the time with my own thoughts, just sitting and thinking about yesterday's darkness and the terror. I was afraid of that sense of evil and intuitively knew it was still a part of who I was. I whispered my fears to God and pleaded for freedom. I didn't want to go on hiding the darkness inside me. I was willing to face it all if only it would go away forever. As I began to moan, my husband had his own battle. Protective of me as a result of watching the horrors of yesterday's memory release, he didn't think it fair or necessary for God to let me suffer any more. He later shared with me that, at one point, he just knew he was supposed to let me be. It was necessary; God would take care of me. Thus began the longest and hardest session of all.

I relived an abuse memory where objects were pushed into my mouth and rectum. I was one year old. Discarded after the abuse like so much garbage, and touched by pain so intense it took my breath away, a swirling maze of terror, pain, confusion, anger, shame, rejection, rage, and hatred consumed me for what seemed like hours. Unbelievable as it seems, I can remember most of it very clearly and understood what was happening almost all the time. Somehow, in the midst of it all, a sense of peace prevailed, allowing me to do the hard work that was demanded. When it was finally over, I knew God's intimacy within me in a way I've never known. I expect it will be like that always when we are with him forever.

❖   ❖   ❖

INTRODUCTION TO WEEK 1

Their pain is acute; their confusion becomes ours. What can be done for them and for their children? These women clearly recognize that they are both hurt and hurters, victims and perpetrators. They also watched their siblings or mother or father hurt, and thus they are also observers. Whether they fill the role of victim, perpetrator, or observer depends on time and circumstance. For now, in this group, they are victims. The object of the first phase of their treatment is to both recognize and realize how they were abused and neglected. They have to remember many painful events.

It cannot be assumed that adults who were abused or neglected as children now realize that they were or are victims. Too often their experience of life is the only one they have ever known. What happened to them as children continues to happen to them as adults. Although they may have seen other families, they had to believe that the children in those families probably suffered the same maltreatment that they did.

Often children and adults, for both practical and psychological reasons, have been afraid to extract themselves from miserable experiences and to view them more objectively. Some never have the opportunity to examine and evaluate what is happening to them because they are so busy just surviving. In some instances, they become such an integral part of a vicious circle that it is almost impossible to state who is abusing whom. As adults, they may be abusing their children. Thus they can't look at their past experience without considering the harm they are doing to their own children.

It is very hard for children to disentangle themselves from the demands of developing and to view their experiences objectively. They depend on the very persons who abuse or neglect them. As adults, they still look to their parents, hoping that somehow they will mature and be able to meet their needs. Or the patients may depend on a spouse who is no better than the parents at meeting their needs. Their continued experience of neglect and abuse may make them even more dependent, but also increasingly skeptical about the ability of anyone to meet their needs.

To remember, and relive, conflicted experience for the purposes of treatment is very difficult and painful. Often traumatic experiences are locked tightly away in memory banks, inaccessible to voluntary recall. The traumatic experience may have occurred when they were too young to have language and thus there may be no way of describing it. The memories may be so conflicted that all the vocabulary the child had at that age cannot do them justice. The memory may be only a feeling, a somatic gut-wrenching experience. Thus the beginning of treatment must be to help patients remember not only the event, but all of the people involved in the event. Most particularly, they need to recall their mixed feelings and the motives surrounding the events. Part of the importance of listening is that it provides validation of what people felt and perceived. If they are validated, then there is a possibility that their expressions of needs are real. If their needs are real and heard by somebody, then it is possible that someone will actually meet them. Adults tend not to listen to children. If they did, they would probably cry most of the time.

The initial stage of group therapy is designed to help patients remember and reexperience those painful, frightening, and confusing experiences. This is more likely to occur when (1) the group members feel they can trust the leaders of the group and trust each other and (2) they feel well supported and encouraged. It is partly for this reason that we have always had nourishment available on the coffee table in the middle of the group room. Although some women complained that they didn't need the calories, most of them found that the atmosphere of camaraderie and food helped them to feel sufficiently well cared for that they could engage in this difficult journey.

In this day and age when so much litigation surrounds abuse and neglect, it is hard even for adults not to feel an involuntary defensiveness. Children know that placement in a foster home may ensue if their parents are not supportive. All the fables and fears associated with being deprived of parents lead them to believe they could be placed in a government institution. Children also read news reports of parents who have been prosecuted and imprisoned for harming their children. Parents feel that if they were to divulge information about their past experience, they would have to talk about their abusing of children, and they too could be reported and prosecuted. Thus there are many fears, realistic and unfounded, that have to be dealt with one by one in order that people can begin to realize how badly they were mistreated.

The deepest pain comes with the realization that they were deprived of a reasonable childhood, a childhood that could have provided the necessary ingredients for building them into the kind of persons they could have become. Although this is a theme that crops up again when the group members deal with letting go of parts of themselves that never properly developed, at this earlier stage, the loss can be felt and given at least a cursory examination.

There are many double binds conveyed by actions that are incongruent with the words. This happens particularly with parents with holes in their superego. They tend to say, "I expect you will become a thief or a prostitute. Don't you dare do it, but let me hear and vicariously enjoy your latest exploits." This and other double binds make it hard for victims to express their distress.

The recognition that they were victims only takes place when they begin to realize the full range of feelings that transpired. Not only did they feel fear and pain, frustration and abandonment, but many of these feelings happened concurrently. To help them understand the complexity of these feelings, the group begins with a technique we call "feeling rehearsal." This involves repeatedly imitating the leader's expression of 12 to 15 feelings. Once they are able to express a wide range of feeling, they are given the opportunity to apply feelings to the appropriate situations and to express them to each other. The homework is designed to help them begin reexperiencing some of these feelings. The therapist has to be careful to monitor how the individuals are doing from week to week. Often there is a sudden recurrence of the defenses and symptoms they previously used to deal with their fears and pains. I reassure the patients that they can have individual time with me if they need it, and particularly if they need help with their own children.

Adults feel a great sense of unreality arising from a lack of confirmation of their perceptions and experience. It is very much like an infant who was neglected. When vital needs are not recognized or met, this produces a sense of impending psychosis in the infant.

With the experience of any pain, there is an automatic response of anger or fear. When children encounter an uncontrollably enraged "giant" three times their size, wielding a stick that could kill them, their pain results mostly in fear and the desire to run away, hide, or disappear. They know they can't run away because where would they find food, warmth, and clothing? Thus they must continually face this huge person, trying hard to swallow their fear. Although it is usually suppressed, there is also anger that expresses itself in many indirect ways. The second phase of the group therapy is devoted to finding useful and appropriate ways of expressing the anger and fear that are the automatic response to the pain.

Children cannot ask their parents for what they know the parents cannot give. They learn to suppress an awareness of their needs and never learn how to ask properly for what they need. When they do ask, they usually ask the wrong person. This happens partly because they are so pessimistic about ever getting what they need. Starving children will eat garbage from the streets (literally and figuratively). Why don't they beg at the doors of wealthy houses? They don't do so because they will be either ignored or shamed. They realize it is better to go to the garbage dump where they can find something by themselves.

Wouldn't it be nice if parental authority and inborn instinct agreed? It is a real tragedy that parents enclose themselves and each other with double messages. They bake cookies for their children and then tell them that they can't have one. If the children do ask for a cookie, they are told that they are bad.

If there is no response to children's most desperate cries to be cared for, they can only assume that there was no one there to hear, that those who were there were incapable of responding, that the cry meant nothing, or that the person emitting the cry was worthless and didn't deserve to be cared for. Children prefer to blame themselves for the nonresponse. The belief that they are ignored because they are bad or worthless has hope in it. They might be able to change and then they will be properly cared for.

Children know that the worst thing that could happen to them is to be abandoned. They will do almost anything to adapt to a pathological situation as long as they are receiving even minimal love and care. In order to help adults neglected as children remember that experience, we do a variety of group exercises that are described in this chapter.

❖   ❖   ❖

History of Tanya

Who am I? The dancer who never danced! The English professor who never taught. I have the usual difficulties: trusting people, beginning new projects, standing up for myself, coping with anger or unpleasantness, controlling my eating…a life of fragments.

My beautiful, elusive mother. Not that she wasn't there physically— she was, but emotionally, sometimes you see her, sometimes you don't. Just when you think you are emotionally close to her, you realize that she has disappeared into the clouds.

I "lost" my father when I was five. He raped me. The sexual things that he did to me before I reached this age I just accepted as the cost of being close to a loving and wise father, but being raped was too high a cost. I couldn't really love him after that, although I went on acting as if I did. My father, myself, I could say. Most of my life, I have been so bound up with my father that I didn't really know where he stopped and I began (much like a relationship I have with one of my four children). My father was everything to me: a patient teacher, a devoted helper, the cheering section for my successes, a handsome and romantic lover, and yet a power-mad and sadistic tyrant. When I was young, as well as sexually abusing me, he teased and tormented me; pinched, slapped, and tickled me; flew into rages or compulsively and angrily argued with me in public. Try as I would, I could not discover what behavior on my part would cause the good daddy to appear and the bad father to disappear.

Both of my parents have tragedy and/or dysfunction in their heritage. When Mom was five, her father lost everything in the stock market crash and never regained his lost "manhood" before his untimely death when she was 16. Dad's whole family was completely and obviously dysfunctional. Very poor immigrants, their lives were marked by years of failure, mental illness, rage, and bitterness, which wasted their obvious academic potential.

Until I had been in therapy for a year at age 39, I remembered nothing of what I am going to share with you. I dissociated every time it happened. By the time I was nine, I knew something was wrong because things happened without my remembering them. I insisted on going to a doctor, but was never able to tell anyone what was wrong, and so they thought I was a hypochondriac. I eventually gave up trying to figure it out.

I remembered that when I was two, I was sexually abused by someone. I am not sure who it was: my mother, my father, a friend of the family, someone my mother knew? From the time I was three, my father touched me and demanded oral sex. When I was five, he raped me. We were in the empty church washroom. When I tried to run away from him because he wanted me to suck his penis, he was angry; I think that is why he hurt me. From then on, he would come to my bed at night. Once, when I was eight, he came to my room drunk and raped me. He did this again after I tried to tell Mom what he was doing. The rest of the time during my eighth year he just touched me or demanded oral sex. I remember that, when I was nine, I came home late one night from visiting friends. My father sent me to my room without supper, but came up later with treats and again fondled me. Later, when I was 12 and we were on vacation, Dad came into my bed and sexually kissed and touched me. I am not sure how old I was—somewhere in my teens—when I did sexual things with my father and his brother, and another time I had intercourse with three of my father's friends. There were other times when Dad and I touched and had oral sex in my later teenage years.

I thought I was abused because I was bad. Three major traumas that seemed to me to be punishment for my badness were my being taken out of ballet at age 12, losing my religion, and failing at the university. Each of these had such devastating effects on me that I am only now getting over them.

I was not sure whether or not I could join the group. I decided that if anyone else had repressed memories to deal with, I would stay. Tonight, two others said they had denied or repressed memories and one of them asked me to stay. I will commit myself to the group.

WEEK 1

That first evening, the members of the group looked around with a mixture of wonder, puzzlement, and fear, enough to make them almost want to run away. But they knew that if they ran, they couldn't run far enough, that the pain would follow them, the confusion would dog their steps, and the tendency to revisit on their children the painful experiences of their own childhood would continue. Every time it did, they would recoil with an even more intense pain and guilt. They tried hard to make sure that they did not become the perpetrators their parents were but every time something triggered a conflict from their past, they were compelled to reenact it. To watch their children become victims of such similar types of abuse or neglect was more than they could take. More than anything, that is what motivated them to embark on the group experience, an odyssey that would take them on a much more painful journey than, at that moment, they could possibly anticipate.

They were an interesting group, considerably more homogeneous than any previous group of this kind that I had conducted. Moreover, they were very intelligent, and, partly because of their own sad experiences, very perceptive. Once their minds were freed of some of their debilitating conflicts, their verbal facilities increased and they became astonishingly adept at expressing their particular difficulties. Although similar in age and background, their experiences ranged from the most abject neglect and sexual degradation to the most painful physical abuse. Their stories would bring tears to this venerable therapist.

From across the small room, my cotherapist, Dr. Green, smiled, and that triggered the beginning: such a soft entrance to a terrible journey, marked with moans, shouts, tears, and screams. I knew what was to follow because I had journeyed this route with others like them. But even though it was familiar territory, I had to gulp. All too well I knew that although they would have to be the surrogate scapegoats, standing in place of all the members of their families and suffering for them, I would suffer with these patients. Could I do it once again? Like the patients in the group, I knew that there was no possibility of avoiding these difficulties.

If they were not dealt with within the group, these problems would rear their ugly heads in the fears and sorrows that would culminate in the psychiatric disabilities of their children. I had learned, if nothing else, that this kind of group therapy was an efficient, effective way of stopping the abuse and neglect from being handed on to their little ones, who were so vulnerable, unsuspecting, and trusting.

I began:

"Good evening. You are very welcome. I want to describe the group process, the difficulties that you will encounter, and the pain and sorrow you might experience. I will tell you the rules that govern the group. We will discuss all aspects of the group, and I will try to answer your questions. Then I want you to consent to this treatment and commit yourselves to staying the full course. After that, I would like you to introduce yourselves to each other. I have met you all, but I want to introduce you to Dr. Green, my cotherapist, and Tasha and Shelly, our group facilitators, who are graduates of a previous group.

"This group will continue for the next 20 to 24 weeks, on Thursday evenings. Each session will last two to two and a half hours. It is important that we begin on time and we will try to end punctually. You must come regularly. The only valid excuse for missing is a major illness or a major family trauma. What you discuss in the group is confidential and cannot be discussed with anyone else unless the group gives permission. There will come a time in the group process when you will be involved with other members of your families, but even then, your discussions must be limited to your own problems and not include those of others. You must not talk with each other outside the group, and for now we don't want you to know each other's family name, address, or telephone number. Within the group, you must try to talk to each other and to us as freely and as frankly as you possibly can. Don't hold back any critical comments, but remember, there is no excuse for bad manners. In order to propel you along the projected course, this group will be quite disciplined. That means that even when you are most reticent, you must participate. When you are assigned homework, you are expected to do it. Please keep a journal for your assignments and weekly observations.

"The group consists of eight phases, and we will spend about an equal amount of time on each. It is difficult, but to gain any real benefit, you must go through them all. The first phase is to cognitively recognize and emotionally realize the breadth and depth of your experience of abuse and neglect. With the realization of that pain and fear, you will naturally want to fight or flee. The second phase, called protest, is to help you mobilize your anger and contain your fear. When you get angry, especially at your parents and those you love, you are bound to feel guilty. The third phase is to deal with the guilt that is both real and unreal. Having dealt with that guilt, you then come to the most difficult phase of all, recognizing that you were robbed of a reasonable childhood. This means that you can never go back and recapture what you didn't get, nor can you reconstruct a childhood in the present. Therefore, you can never become the person you were designed to be. In that despair, you will realize that the people in your life now cannot provide the parenting you needed when you were young. This realization will enable you to develop realistic expectations. Having gained a realistic view of all your relationships, you can now embark on another difficult phase, that of reconciliation. To be reconciled with those who hurt you does not mean that you will have a friendly relationship with them. It does mean that you will engage in the difficult process of exposing your wounds, seeking and giving forgiveness—which may involve gaining some compensation. Once you have worked to achieve reconciliation, you can look for opportunities to use all that you have learned from your difficult experience. The process of rehabilitation means that you can reach out and help others, making something good out of your bad experience. Having achieved that, you can now rejoice in life, experiencing it in all its fullness, the good and the not so good: you can feel the breeze, smell the grass, hear the birds, and delight in the sunset.

"From your own experience, you know that the world is not made up of people in white hats and people in black hats. We are all culpable. For the purposes of this group, I want you to think of your mistreatment as a triangle made up of a perpetrator, a victim, and an observer. These three transact, helping to form the behaviors and attitudes of one another. Each contributes to the ongoing cycle of abuse. Moreover, there is within each of those people another small triangle made up of the same three parts. It depends on time and circumstances to bring out particular characteristics. For example, when some women whine at their husbands, they become victims, and if their children whine at them, they become perpetrators of physical abuse. Or when victims grow up, they become perpetrators, and observers become victims.

"The greatest tragedy of child mistreatment is that although you have tried so hard not to, you find yourself doing to your children what was done to you. Why humans don't seem to learn from their mistakes is a question, an enigma; it is discussed by philosophers, historians, and archeologists, and has been for centuries. I am sure you often ask yourself, 'Why can't I stop? Why do I treat my children as I was treated?'

"The reasons are complex, but simply stated, we will continue to reconstruct our conflicts until we learn from them. These thoughts come from my studies, analyses, and writings. If you care to read my articles, you are welcome to. According to the physicists, the universe may end because it continues to expand. If so, energy would be so evenly dissipated that chaos or entropy would result. The other possibility is that gravity will grasp every particle in the universe and bring it back into one enormous black hole, which may rebound as another big bang. As humans, we are a microcosm. In order to function, we must concentrate energy within ourselves. To this end, we eat, rest, and work efficiently.

"Anything that results in the inefficient use of energy pushes us toward entropy. If we lose or use too much energy, we cannot exist. In order to use energy most efficiently, we must resolve our conflicts. Both interpersonal and intrapsychic conflicts result in the useless expenditure of energy. If we spend a day trying to make up our mind as to whether we should or should not do something, we can become very fatigued without having accomplished anything. If we are absorbed in a conflict with other people, that conflict remains in our heads, even after we no longer see them. We attempt to resolve the conflict in order to conserve energy. We may do this by thinking quietly to ourselves or we may discuss the difficulty with friends or with a therapist, and, by these methods, we learn why we do something so subconsciously. More frequently with severe conflicts, we carefully pick friends, family, and work mates to restage these conflicts. In the middle of the reenactment, we hope to get off the stage while the interaction goes on. Then we can clearly see that when he does this, she does that, and, of course, we tend to respond in this way. The difficulty is that in major conflicts we are unable to get off the stage. We are drawn to the conflict, and kept in it, by the very tensions that demand that we resolve the conflict. And thus the tragedy is repeated from one generation to the next, with few people gaining any useful insight.

"More than you realize, you are here to represent your whole family. In this regard, you are surrogate scapegoats, voluntarily subjecting yourselves to reliving pain and fear in order to stop the tragic history of mistreatment from repeating itself. You have little idea how much this will cost you. Yet your healing will enable many others to benefit. The really great people of history have stood in the place of other people's pain, grief, and sin, and have suffered and died in order that history might stop recycling.

"This sounds a bit dramatic, but once you realize how much you will feel the conflicts of your whole family, you will better understand that you are engaging in a process to help and heal your family, both backwards and forward in time.

"Tasha and Shelly, who are graduates of one of the previous groups, are here to help to encourage you, to reassure you, and sometimes to demonstrate how to accomplish the various tasks. We know that there will be times when your pain and confusion are so intense that you cannot wait until the next group. Do not hesitate to phone. Individual appointments will be made and individual problems dealt with. Now please introduce yourselves to each other with a brief description of yourself and why you are here."

They had all been referred by their family physicians. Though the reasons varied—bulimia, depression, panic disorder—it was soon obvious that they had had many experiences in common. This gave them a sense of camaraderie, but there were reservations.

"Now you must make a commitment to the group and to the process of treatment. This commitment is solemn and binding. You must do this because there will be times when you become so discouraged or frightened that you want to leave the group. It will mainly be your commitment that keeps you going. At times, you will feel there is no end in sight. Sometimes you will think that you are getting worse, but your commitment to each other, to your family, and to your desire to stop the whole process of transgenerational abuse and neglect will see you through."

It was interesting to see how each person in the group, some with considerable trepidation, solemnly committed herself to seeing it through.

"Dr. Green, a family physician, and I have worked together before, and she is joining me with this group. We have different roles. Dr. Green will provide a counterpoint.

"Please tell us your story: what happened, when it happened, and how it affected you. And tell us about your family.

"To make it easier for you, I have asked Tasha and Shelly to describe how it was for them in the previous groups."

Tasha began first by telling a little bit about herself.

"My father was shot and killed, we believe, for gambling debts. For many years, I didn't know what happened to him. I was told many stories, but finally I pieced together information from newspaper reports. Up until that time, I had been his little doll. I was terrified of falling off the pedestal. He always idolized me, but at the same time, terrible abuse and neglect were going on in my family. I found the group extraordinarily hard work. I want you to make sure you do all the homework as we go along. I lagged behind and I had to catch up later. I only wish I had tried harder at the time. I must have become caught up in my feelings. It is easy to become too concentrated on your own thoughts and to forget that this is a process that you must go through. For this reason, it is vitally important that you help each other complete all the work that needs to be done."

Shelly told a story of an alcoholic father and an extraordinarily physically abusive mother who would quote Scripture while she beat the kids. Shelly also had a special place in the family. Her mother confided in her, and as a child, Shelly was not able to express her feelings for fear of letting her mother down. She also had advice for the group describing various processes she had gone through, from abject despair to incredible rage to terrible hopelessness. She had survived and had benefited. The one thing she held out for the other members above all else based on her experiences was that now she was able to relate to her own children and to enjoy their antics instead of blowing up all the time. The little introduction by the two graduates was very encouraging and the group quickly understood that it wasn't impossible to see it through. The example set by the two graduates in speaking so freely about their experiences also paved the way for how the present group members might be able to talk about themselves.

Amy was a tall, slim woman who had always wanted to be a ballerina. She looked shyly around the room, and although she was the youngest there, she wanted to start. "I've blocked out a lot of feelings. It may be because I was criticized so much when I was young. My father drank himself to death. He was never available to me. My mother let the household go crazy. So many times I wanted to talk to her honestly. I wanted to tell her how much I hated my dad for the way he destroyed himself and the way he ignored me. Right now, I'm counting on my mom, though, you see, I have a little girl and I am pregnant."

It was clear to all that although at least some of the members had been sexually abused, there were other kinds of abuse and neglect that had made as great an impact or maybe greater impact, on the group members. Krista was a large, broad-shouldered woman with a great deal of anger and tension. "My father was emotionally abusive. He controls my mother completely, but I am not going to let him control me. I had an abusive brother and a very abusive marriage."

The little vignettes they gave were an introduction to more, but they were testing the waters, watching closely to see how the rest of the group reacted to what they said about themselves. Lisa was a pretty, plump young woman with black hair that stuck out, emphasizing the intense fear in her dark eyes. She had chosen a corner of the softest, deepest couch, and she hardly moved from that spot for the 26 weeks the group was to continue. Lisa sometimes appeared not to be aware of what was going on as she was so preoccupied with her own thoughts, but there was no question but that, given an opportunity, she would speak with a great deal of feeling and considerable insight. "I'm trying to uncover exactly what happened to me. It happened to me when I was very young. My brothers and sisters were taken out of our home because my mother neglected us, and then later I was taken away. During that time, something terrible happened. I think it was ritual abuse. I'm afraid to think about it, let alone talk about it, but I must deal with it. I found my mother. She acts very guilty and afraid. I can't get her to talk about it."

Anna struck me as a person who, having tried many avenues for help, finally decided that she was going to face everything. She was a handsome woman who radiated a certain vibrancy that must have been very appealing when she was young. "Secrecy, all was secrecy. My life fell apart and I've become a basket case. So many awful things happened to me. I believe my mother tried to abort me before I was born. Maybe I will never know."

Shawna was a striking woman with large luminous eyes and very pale skin. "My mother became very sick when I was 12. I became wife to my father. I find I am turning out to be like my mother, and I certainly don't want to. Sometimes I am sick and tired of being an adult at all. I wish I could have someone to look after me."

Certainly all the statements so far hinted at neglect, neglect that had done great damage to them all.

Linda was full of life. She commanded the spot in the corner from which she defended any clear awareness of her struggles with a stream of jokes that would keep everyone laughing. Now she was struggling to be frank. "I was a spoiled brat when I was young. I was sexually abused by two fellows. One was killed by his brother. All my life, I strove to be what other people expected of me. I have had a number of relationships and have been married twice. I want one that lasts. I want to be able to let the wall down, but I don't trust people."

Linda, having said this, reminded Krista of her previous husband, whom she contrasted with a previous relationship. "I can't allow myself to love him because I can't trust him." Krista and all the other members in the group had found that neglect and abuse had damaged their ability to trust people. Still, they knew they couldn't lead isolated lives.

Virginia was gaunt, with deep, penetrating eyes. When she was not perched on the very edge of her seat, she was curled up in a fetal position.

"I don't know if I belong here. I don't know if I can face this. So many awful things have happened to me. Are you sure you want me here? I know I've got to do something. If I don't, Welfare will take my children away from me. I don't know why I keep treating them the way I do. It's so similar to the way I was treated as a child. Why can't we stop hurting those we love so much?"

I noted how interesting it was to see how the group members responded to each other's stories. The other individuals responded with more expressions of distress than did the person who was telling the story. "That's terrible. How could they do that to a child?"

They worried about harming those who had harmed them just by talking about what had happened. I told them, "If you can say something difficult directly to a person, then there is little basis for the fear that you will be talking about the person behind his or her back when you say the same thing in group. But you must maintain confidentiality."

Since I had assessed each of the members before recommending group therapy, at this point I knew more about them than they knew about each other. That advantage didn't last long because they soon gave these histories to the whole group. To follow the process, you, the reader, should also know their background.

"Well, that's my story, but I don't feel anything now. Maybe it is because I have already cried or talked it out. Maybe I am afraid that if I started, I couldn't stop crying." In the years that followed the time when they were abused, they had repressed the memory and, more particularly, the emotions. They had to. Every child must first attend to his or her developmental tasks. To feel all the fear, pain, anger, and despair would make it impossible to carry on. The mechanism of repression is a useful mechanism for growing children. Now they had an opportunity to think and feel about their childhoods, but it was clear that the sadness and confusion were coming back to mind. Once again, they were beginning to feel overwhelmed. Not surprisingly, the first response was to repress it all over again.

"Quite frankly, I'm not so sure I want to relive that garbage. Are you sure we can't just forget it and get on with life?" I didn't need to answer; there was a chorus of "I know I can't; it keeps coming back, often when I least expect it."

"I was beginning to feel better. I'm not sure that I should dig into this again. Maybe I should just forget it and carry on with my life." It was a statement that was to be heard frequently during the early phases of the group, but each person was pushed along by the others. "You know you can't do that. We have to get this fixed up and put away once and for all."

More than one member responded with, "I don't know why I am in this group. Your story is so much worse than mine." Quite clearly, having repressed their own pain, it did seem that their own stories weren't as bad. Many of the stories were awful. There was no way one could say that one was worse than another. Each type of mistreatment had its devastating effect on the development of the individual. Each left turmoil that was barely tolerable.

I believe that verbal abuse has the most overwhelming effect on one's self-image. From our research, I have also found that nearly all mistreated children experience a combination of abuses and neglects. The combination of physical neglect, physical abuse, and verbal abuse has the worst influence on a child's enjoyment of life and hope for a reasonable future. We found that the more extensively a child is abused, the more likely that child is to expect to die young and to die violently. Except for the enormous resilience of children, these mistreated youngsters could not have survived.

"I don't understand why it keeps happening to me. I keep bringing disaster upon myself. I have relationships with the wrong people, then I hurt my children." The explanation of history repeating itself through an individual's desire to reenact it in order to resolve it made good sense to these women. It hardly needed an explanation at all. They understood all too well how frequently they almost wittingly made history repeat itself. There was no question but that they wanted to resolve the underlying conflict. They had to get on with their lives. Although they often had known little but misery, they also knew that there was something better out there. That sense seemed to come from a combination of an innate awareness of what they might have been, plus a brief experience of joy, usually in some other, healthier family. They knew that there was a better life than the one that they were enduring.

The observations made by Dr. Green and myself, with the help of Tasha and Shelly, often coincided. But there were other aspects of a group or an individual's reaction that one or the other would perceive.

Following each group, we would discuss the process and each person's progress. As a whole, the group felt enormous relief in its early stages. Just to be able to share and to know that someone else had such experiences dissipated the great sense of loneliness. The hopelessness that went along with the intense mixed feelings, once shared, also seemed to dissipate. Yet as quickly as they began to hope, some of these women began to suspect that, like other assistance or opportunities for help they had been offered, that this group would also disappoint them.

Relationships quickly developed between group members. Each evening, they would sit in the same places. It was usually the person closest to her with whom each woman formed the closest relationship. This made it easier to help them develop role plays. Often one partner, when trying to back out, would be kept going by a strong nudge from the other.

When they were in greatest distress, they would reach across to touch and comfort each other.

❖   ❖   ❖

Anna's Description

Thursday! It is the first group meeting and my stomach is full of butter-flies. I am so afraid, excited, hopeful, and anxious. God, what can I expect? What will happen? What will I have to do to get well? Can I do it? If this doesn't work, then there is nothing left. I know this will work: God, you are leading me. You promised me months ago when the physical pain was unbearable, and the innumerable tests showed little, when the emotional darkness threatened to consume me, and there were none to comfort me and no answers, it was then you promised, whispered into my pain that if I rested in you, *just rested*, you would do the rest. If I let the horror come up, you would do the rest; let the pain cover me, you would do the rest; let my control go in every aspect of my life, You would do the rest; and now we are here, in group therapy! And less than four months ago I didn't even know that I had been abused. I will *be* and you will do the rest.

As I climb the stairs, I hear people moving and my stomach tightens. They are here already: I am afraid. I enter the room and find a seat, then cautiously look around. No one is talking and most are avoiding eye contact. They are as nervous as I am. After a few uncomfortable minutes and someone's brave attempt at conversation, I escape to the washroom. I don't really have to go and I realize that I am hiding. Shortly after I return, he, Dr. Ney, calls us to follow him. We enter a small room with cushioned chairs and two love seats formed in a tight circle. I like the closeness of it. It feels safe to me. Some of the others are uncomfortable, and one says she would prefer the big waiting room. Not me: too distant, I think.

As Dr. Ney looks at us, he must be able to feel the fear that shrouds the room. He looks like a professor, knowledgeable and distant. He is a medium-built man, with white hair and beard, whose clear blue eyes don't miss a thing. I depended on his wisdom and integrity. Surely his years (over 25 in this field, he said) would enable him to help me. He introduces the codirector, Dr. Green, and I note that her appearance pushes a button in me. She is slim, confident, and relaxed. Dressed simply in black corduroy pants and a plaid shirt, I could easily imagine her speaking for Greenpeace. Then he introduces the two graduates. Oh no! One (Shelly) knows me and my husband. I don't know her well, but I know her. She is small, bubbly, and direct. How can I tell the whole truth and be open and vulnerable when she is here? I don't hear much for a few minutes. I am struggling with her presence. I want to be anonymous. He had said we would be, and now she's here. I want to get well. *Why* is she here? It's not fair. It's starting already: I have to trust her with my horrible truth and trust that she won't share it. I feel so threatened and cornered. I fight with myself. I am attracted immediately to the other graduate, a cute little person with an open, compassionate face.

Dr. Ney explains the rules of the group, which seem easy to follow. We are all quietly listening until he says that we will work through forgiveness and reconciliation, and then there is a lot of protesting. Some are adamant that they will never tell certain people in their lives of their abuse. I can't understand their problem. I just want to get well. (Now I realize that I had no idea of the cost, and these sisters were probably much more in touch than I had ever allowed myself to be.) As he speaks of the tragedy of our abuse and its repetitive pattern, I feel a sense of destiny and affirmation in my courage to face myself and my past. He promises that the healing in my life will help to set both my children and my mother free. I will cling to that promise as a lifeline many times throughout the therapy process. Then we are asked to make a commitment to the group. When Dr. Ney says that we will want to quit and will make up excuses not to participate anymore, I make a note to get my husband to insist that I continue regardless of what excuses I come up with. Some of the group members are really struggling with commitment. I had made a commitment to get well and to follow through with this therapy months ago. I wondered why they came if they hadn't planned to participate. It is my turn and I too have a serious consideration: this person I recognized isn't going to leave the group just because I don't want her there. I have to share my struggle with the identity of the graduate, Shelly, and my fears, especially concerning telling things about my husband in her presence, which, after all, were his to share, except that they touched me too. She responds affirmatively to my need for absolute adherence to the rule of no sharing outside of the group. I am able to commit myself to the group, which was my first big struggle overcome. Wow, this sure is going to be one step at a time.

One woman is really struggling. I really feel good about her being in the group, and I feel disappointed that she is considering not staying, so I ask if I might say something. She acknowledges me, and I tell her that I would really like it if she would continue. I felt drawn to her right away. She is genuinely surprised and pleased at my comment and is encouraged enough to commit herself to the group. Finally, a commitment is procured from each member, and then we, in turn, have to tell our story. The nightmares that we had all lived through! They were horrible: abandonment, physical abuse, emotional abuse, and every form of sexual abuse. As well, each child represented seemed to have been touched by every or almost every abuse category repeatedly. We are truly a group of people who had been cruelly violated. The pain we feel for each other seems to bond us instantly, some more than others. I guess it is both personality and similar pain that influence me to feel a special closeness to Tanya, Lisa, and Virginia.

When I share my story, I feel the support and sympathy of the others in their rapt attention, but more than that, they believe me! The recent body memories that told me of abuse, repeated sexual abuse, and abandonment—things I didn't want to believe happened to anyone, let alone me—this group believes happened and ached with me. I had believed their stories and they believed mine. The session is over already and we are sent out with the first week's homework: to remember our fears, working backwards as far as possible. I don't want to leave. I want it to be Thursday again.

❖   ❖   ❖

"Well, it's now 12 o'clock and you have been working hard for four hours. I can see that you are distressed." Although some were more deeply involved than others, each felt a sense of both dreaded anticipation and relief. "I don't want you to leave here feeling that you are unable to cope, so each one of you must give us a report on how you are feeling. We want a report at the beginning and the end of each group. And, remember, I will see you individually if you need it.

"Your homework for this week is to complete this sentence for as many instances as you can remember: 'I was really frightened when....' This is the time to face those fears and to reach far back into your memories. Use your present fears to help you remember your childhood fears. Trace them as far back as you can. Then finish the sentence. Also, complete the sentence 'I was hurt when....' Don't avoid the details even if they seem insignificant, and do this for as many instances as you can remember. Be as clear as you possibly can. You will find that this will take quite a number of pages."

WEEK 2

Characteristically, Dr. Green and I did a check to see how everybody's week had been and how they were feeling on that evening. On this night, there was a mixture of sorrow and anxiety, but mostly there was relief. Some felt that they had already begun to discover truth in the multitudes of confusing thoughts and feelings that pressed in upon them. Anna mentioned that she saw her mother for the first time in a very long time.

In reporting on their homework, Shawna indicated that she had begun to discover that she was afraid of starving to death. There were fears that she might die alone and nobody would notice what had happened to her. She wasn't too sure why this related to her youth or whether it had come from stories her father had told her. He was, by this time, a very important officer in the military.

Lisa stated that she was having difficulty thinking of fear because that made her even more afraid. In spite of herself, a couple of memories had begun forming in her mind. This was extraordinarily difficult because the real trauma in her life had begun before she was verbal, and to describe something an infant feels before it has words is a very difficult task. With many tears, she insisted she couldn't talk about it, but then began to describe how it was a terrible, evil feeling. Some of this was associated with being in a man's arms and feeling helpless. As she described these feelings, she also mentioned that she was now beginning to feel more in touch and open.

As many others mentioned fears and the clarity with which they could begin to remember some of their early experiences, they wondered about the process of memory. I mentioned that when children are overwhelmed by the rapidity and intensity of conflicting emotions associated with their early trauma, they can't deal with it, and so it is stored away for later resolution. It is a little bit like having a large number of books dumped into the hallway of the library. They are quickly pushed into a variety of rooms for later sorting, but because the librarian is so busy with other tasks, these books, which represent the intense feelings and memories of that particular episode, never do get put away. Children, after all, must get on with life. They are much more intent on surviving and developing than they are on dealing with unresolved conflicts. Yet the mind is constructed in such a way that these conflicts eventually have to be dealt with.

Anna, noticing how much the others were affected by their memories, said something that was true for all of them. "I need someone to hold me while I'm going through this. I hope my husband can do it."

Krista described her older brother. She had been adopted and was told that she was very special, yet her older brother beat her and her father appeared not only to allow it, but to encourage it. "My father allowed him to beat me because my father hated women. His mother and his sister had ganged up on him when he was a child. He told me I asked for it, so for years I was terrified. I tried to confront him with this, but he denied it. Ever since, I've been afraid of being wrong. My brother would humiliate me and my parents would insist that I was bad. Now I seem to reconstruct life in such a way that I continue to prove that I am bad. Somehow I've made it all come true. I'm afraid of authority figures—you, Dr. Ney; my grandmother; those who are teaching me at the university; and many others. I feel I do not belong with these people, but I have always had a strong sense of not belonging. For reasons I don't understand, I give my power away. I allow myself to be a doormat. When I was a child, I had to be cute. I had to entertain the guests when my parents were entertaining. They would like to show me off."

Krista went on: "I still feel God can't love me. I was never allowed to cry. My father was a deacon in the church and he can't face what he has done to me." As Krista was describing this, a look of abject fear and misery appeared on her face. The group sat looking at her intently, not able to move, and yet wanting to reach out. I reassured them that this was something they could and should do, either with words or a hand; they could reassure each other. After all, one of the most terrifying aspects of their mistreatment was that they were alone. They all admitted that even now loneliness was a very terrible experience for them.

Anna looked about the room and began describing how she was having her eyelashes dyed. She found it extremely difficult not to open her eyes, though she had been told of the damage that could occur if she did so. A lot of panic was held at bay by sheer determination, especially when she was going through great pain and turmoil. She was not in control and, particularly now, she was afraid she was unable to stay in control. She had been bulimic for many years. She had lost her upper teeth and had had to have them replaced. In speaking of her fears, there was something related to choking that she could only explain as an experience as an infant following oral sexual abuse. With the extreme fear of choking to death, there was anger, an anger that was now beginning to surface. It seemed to be directed at her mother, mainly because her mother had abandoned her.

Virginia said, "I have equal fears of loving and of being loved. I didn't know my dad until I was 18. All five of the children in my family had different dads. Both of my natural parents were terrible alcoholics. We were taken out of the home and placed in so many foster homes I don't remember. I remember moving a lot and hating everybody. I was hit by a belt and a two-by-four, even while they were telling me, 'I love you.' Eventually, the next door neighbors reported what was happening."

It appeared to Anna, and to many others in the group, that Dr. Green and I were much too remote, that we provided too little reassurance and gave too few answers for their awful experiences. I pointed out that we could not provide quick answers; first, because there weren't any, and second, because we wanted them to discover the answers for themselves. After all, what people discover for themselves is far more meaningful and useful than what others tell them. Much, we did say, was likely to be lost to memory. What they discovered and said to themselves and to others would stay with them. We did recognize how angry they would get because we didn't come up with easy solutions.

What we were there for was to provide a safe atmosphere, to help them re-create certain experiences, to provide reassurance, and, when necessary, to make insightful connections for them that they couldn't easily make for themselves. It was much better if they could discover their own insights. Yes, we did teach and rehearse some interpersonal skills, but it was learning how to analyze and understand their thoughts and behaviors that would be the most useful tool we could give them.

Anna went on to say how she was beginning to get in touch with many early memories and that these were frightening to her. She was feeling extraordinarily raw and vulnerable. I pointed out that children are in such a vulnerable state that they are likely to feel raw and exposed and to take things personally.

Amy, who had been hospitalized for a psychotic experience, spoke of the terror of losing her mind. She also admitted that when she cried, as she was doing now, it was mainly because she was afraid, particularly of going out of control. "I feel so overwhelmed. I'm afraid I could become one of those people who do the hurting. I could hurt my little children. We were yelled at all the time. I never felt safe. I had no faith that my parents would protect me. When I was sick, they never told me that it would be okay. I think my mother was very scared, too. Why didn't she provide any reassurance? Why couldn't she stick up for me?"

I responded: "I can see that you are still struggling to recapture some of those feelings. You can remember the events well enough, but somehow the feelings have become attached to what you do now. Pick a partner and learn how to express your feelings. First, Shelly and I will demonstrate. We are attempting to show how you sometimes can unlock deeply buried feelings by using the words and role playing them with greater and greater intensity."

"I am angry." Then, "I am really angry." Then, "I am so angry I could explode!" Finally, "I am so angry I could kill you!" Or, "I'm sad." Then, "I am really sad," etc.

In pairs, the group members expressed the whole range of feelings to each other with increasing emphasis and intensity. One would encourage the other and provide some sort of feedback regarding how genuine the expressions were. They began with anger because it was the most easily expressed feeling. They also learned to express fear, pain, disgust, and guilt. It was interesting to see how with the role-played expressions would come real feelings. Often, when they were expressing sadness in role plays, they would burst into tears. It wasn't really surprising that a somewhat mechanical expression of feeling unlocked the real feeling. The exercise also served to help connect the right word to each feeling, and this greatly facilitated all types of psychotherapy.

Having spent a considerable amount of time learning to express feelings directly, the group members were asked to say, once again in pairs, as if to one of the perpetrators in their lives, "You hurt me when...." Initially, it was a bland statement but it became very real when the partner was encouraged to respond with, "No, I didn't hurt you. You actually enjoyed it." It took considerable encouragement from the therapists and graduates, together with the courage of these women, to push through the denial.

When they could insist that it really did happen and really was painful, disgusting, or frightening, they could be more frank and open with themselves and with each other.

Having spoken of their pain in pairs, they were then encouraged to use the statement, "You frightened me when...." The response from the partner, playing the role of the perpetrator, would be, "You certainly didn't look frightened." With this kind of response, sometimes the person expressing the statement "You hurt me when..." would give up. Dr. Green, Shelly, Tasha, and I would move from one pair to the other, encouraging them to push through that resistance. The resistance that they were encountering not only was resistance from their partners, playing the role of the perpetrators, but a much deeper resistance from themselves. They had to express, outwardly, those statements that they had so long buried when they were children. They would much rather accept a denial or rationalization from the perpetrator than insist that their pain be heard. It was as if, as children, they had to believe that their parents were good. That hope down deep inside that somehow their parents knew how they felt was what kept them going. They believed that if their parents knew how they felt, they would also meet those deeply felt needs. The struggle to keep going was often based on an illusion, but that illusion was sufficiently good to make it possible for them to put up with intolerable circumstances.

It always amazes me how children keep hoping that their parents are basically good. Their hope impels them, and, therefore, they must keep asking to have their needs met. If they gave up the expectation of something good, their parents could ignore them more easily. So this forlorn hope has survival value. It makes the children keep forgiving their parents and trying to change themselves so that they will be more pleasing to their parents. That desire is even more desperate in our present world in which children know that those who aren't wanted are readily aborted or put up for adoption. "Please, Mummy, I'll be good" is really an appeal to be wanted and, therefore, nurtured. Paradoxically, well-loved and accepted children can afford to be more rebellious and adventurous.

It was often very difficult for an individual to observe her own experience in retrospect with any kind of objectivity. But the stories that the others told could tap those unexpressed feelings and result in deep expressions of grief. Listening to the sordid stories of other group members had cathartic value for all, especially when the stories were told with a full range of feeling.

At this point, Anna bolted from the room and could be heard racing down the hall to the toilet. Tasha followed her and found her cowering in a corner, sobbing her heart out. When Anna returned, somewhat more composed, she said, "I really don't want to do this. I'll read what I wrote, but I can't tell you." Even as she spoke, she was cowering in the corner of the couch. "Somehow I can see myself hiding there as a child and I can't tell you what was happening. I just remember feeling, 'Mommy, don't leave me. I'll be good.'" Later she was able to expand on this memory and the time that she had been placed in a variety of foster homes and the terrible things that seemed to have happened there. Still, the memories weren't entirely clear.

Often the anger or sorrow was almost enough to destroy the shaky equilibrium that allowed them to carry on their present adult lives. That pain became so intense that they felt they would not be able to continue looking after their families or doing their jobs. This feeling was an echo of the shakiness that they felt about their existence as children. They wanted to tell their parents or others how they felt, but were afraid that it would destabilize the family situation on which they depended. They didn't want to hurt their parents because they knew that it was the parents, especially if they were unstable or immature, that they had to protect. If their parents were overwhelmed, who was there to depend on?

It was not only the perpetrator to whom they had to express strong feelings: "I was so afraid...I was so lonely...I hurt...I was so humiliated," etc. They also had to express feelings of hurt and abandonment to the observer, who was often a mother. It was interesting to see how that anger and hurt were more intense when these feelings were directed to the observer than when they were addressed to the perpetrator. "Couldn't you see?....Why didn't you do something?...Maybe I never told you, but I think you really knew....I certainly tried to make it obvious; I was sick all the time."

On this particular night, there was a great deal of fear. It was almost as if leaving the confines and camaraderie of the group to venture out into the early spring night with its dismal rain was too much for them. In anticipation of this, they spoke of their fears and again wondered if this was the right process. Anna, in particular, was terribly distraught. I often asked myself: "Am I doing the right thing?" "Can these women endure this?" "Maybe it is too intense, so should we back off and make the series longer?" But I also knew that those in our earlier groups had endured, and the members of this particular group, although intensely involved, were intelligent, resourceful women. Besides, I was getting an increasing number of referrals for others, both men and women, who wanted treatment. The waiting list for consultations on children referred by family physicians was becoming ridiculously long. Much of the research I was doing was behind schedule. I had a paper to deliver at the annual meeting of the academy. I had a unit of disturbed adolescents to run. No, there was no other way. We had to continue. The group seldom understood how very lonely I felt and how very frightening this work could be. On one or two occasions, I allowed them to see a little of my personal life: "You can be sure that I have earned all this gray hair." But it was better that they didn't know me as a vulnerable human being. For the moment, at least, they had to believe that I was tough, secure, wise, and resourceful. I had to be a parent figure on whom they could depend. In particular, they had to understand that I was not going to take advantage of them in any way. This I could not explain. It was something they had to witness.

"All right. I know it was tough last week, but your homework for this week is just as hard. When you were a child, you not only wanted to tell your parents what was happening, but you also wanted to find out why. Why would they do this to a small child who was depending on them? Why didn't they see the hurt? Why didn't they respond to your needs? So this week I want you to describe those times you wanted to ask a perpetrator the questions, 'Why did you hurt me? Why did you leave me? Why didn't you look after me?' Also, remember the times you wanted to ask the observer, 'Why didn't you see what was going on? Why didn't you intervene?'"

Anna

I've written 16 pages about my fears and their roots and all the people involved with each fear. I had no idea that I was so fearful. How am I ever going to condense this for sharing in the time I have? I'll list the fears and detail only the really significant ones, the ones that I connected emotionally with: I fear fat, mine mostly, someone discovering my weight; the dark; being alone; being deserted by men; not being liked; showers and baths; anger—mine and someone else's; and being held under water. (I remember two near-drowning incidents, one in which my sister and I were caught on a sandbar and the other when a guy was playing around at the lake and held me under considerably longer than my air lasted.) I also fear having no air and small, tight places like stuffy rooms, campers, and cars. I always have to see the door when showering, when bathing, or when in bed. I am afraid of dark water when swimming and of snakes. I have repeated nightmares of snakes and of plunging into the dark off a cliff.

I sometimes fear insanity or losing control. Moreover, being controlled, swallowed up, suffocated, or manipulated by overpowering people not only causes fear, but it panics me. Being bad, wrong, sinful, foolish; people finding out about adult family-shame secrets; anyone mocking or laughing at me; rejection; my mother's or husband's disapproval; not being believed; being naked or seeing nakedness; being examined; others' overemotionalism; being caught relaxing; having my picture taken when unprepared or being videoed—all these cause me great discomfort. During the following two "fear traces," I had *that* sense that I had tapped into a buried memory. I am remembering the stark terror I had when I woke up after having mouth surgery. Full of packing and with an oxygen mask over my face, I had panicked. I couldn't breathe. I felt I just had to breathe and get this stuff out of my mouth, so I tore at the mask and struggled to get up and yet was not able to. All this seemed so out of proportion to the simple procedure I had been through. As I relive this memory, I am crying. I have a horrifying sense of some connection to oral abuse. Maybe it was the time when I was one, but I can't remember. The objects I remember from that body memory were foreign and not human, and yet the deep sense of panic and sickness remains as I examine this fear, because instinctively I know. This deep emotion opened a new fear, one that I had never before acknowledged; that is, the fear of Mom's leaving me. It keeps coming up, but then somehow eludes me. I just can't seem to connect it with anything yet. As I concentrate on the fear, I get really angry. Where the hell were you, Mom? I am afraid of my anger. It feels so bad to swear. It is bad to be angry, and my anger always results in bad things. I am so afraid of this memory. Why?

Thank goodness it's Thursday. I am full of both anticipation and apprehension. When I finally get there, we don't say much more than a stiff Hello as we wait to be called in. They must be as shaken as I am from this first homework assignment. We start right away, sharing in turn our lists of fears. It isn't too hard. I notice that not everyone has written out her work. I wonder why.

Dr. Ney seems to find a tender spot in each person's list of fears and presses it, addressing it directly and making her talk more fully about it. This sure gets her in touch quickly with the pain.

I find myself totally absorbed in everyone's sharing, finding it fascinating. I am amazed at how similar so many of our fears are. Virginia begins to share that she is having a hard time. My heart goes out to her. She isn't prepared, and I see her anxiety and her distancing herself from the group. Dr. Ney pushes her to share her fears and to describe in detail one of the most fearful scenes in her memory. As she begins to share, I feel drawn into her story; I become really connected with her pain. Then she describes her brother's and her being beaten over and over again with a two-by-four. I lose it: I feel the "over and over" thrashing inside of me. I have to run. I have to get out of here. I flee for the door, run to the bathroom and lock myself in. Pain and panic wash over me, and I know that I am beginning another body memory. Oh God, I am so scared. Oh, please help me.

Tasha is knocking on the door and insisting on coming in. I can't let her in. The memory tugs in and out, in and out—I can't think. Yes, let her in. She's in. No, help me. I crouch behind the door. Hanging onto the door, I am terrified. I can't stop the fear. She helps me up and her voice keeps bringing me back. I want to remember; I don't want to remember. Yes, yes, I'll wash my face. Oh God, no, no, the water, something is wrong with the water. I feel the water pulling me into it. She is talking softly. I am here.

It's okay, the memory fades. I am shaken, really shaken. We go back to the room, and Dr. Ney says he's sorry but I need to share what happened for the benefit of the group. I do, but I don't know what I said. Somehow the group ends. I write down next week's homework: to think back on a clear fear memory (who, what color, sounds, taste, touch) and think about the feelings associated with it. As I write it, I feel intense nausea. Dr. Ney says to picture the child saying, "Why are you doing this?" I write over and over in tiny letters, "I am bad, I am bad." I write it six times before I realize what I have written. The meeting ends, and I stumble to my car.

❖   ❖   ❖

WEEK 3

This evening everybody was present and on time and expecting great things, yet there was enormous trepidation. As was the custom, we went about the group in a circle; we began with somebody different each week. Tanya sat in her chair with her legs curled under her, often looking at the floor and almost violently throwing her hair back from her eyes. "I have so many feelings about my father, mostly anger. I can remember, however, there was relief when it happened. Somehow it made things better between us. I remember feeling bad. Where was my mother? Why wasn't she there? I can feel confusion and much loneliness. I was always afraid something was going to happen and I would try to protect myself. I didn't know the rules of this relationship. How could I make it stop? How could I keep my father from doing this and still stay interested in me? If I could only figure out the rules, maybe then I could avoid being hurt again."

Lisa, in her usual position, looked straight across the room as if nobody were there. "As soon as I started writing my homework, I started getting pains in my stomach. Something awful was wanting to come up. With the memory came more pain and more anger. I felt a lot of rejection from my mother, yet the anger was always a power in me. It probably protected me when I was an infant. It probably kept me from...." She didn't finish the sentence. "I've used anger all my life. When I confronted my mother, she wouldn't even look me in the eye. I suspect she abandoned me when I was being abused. I hate my mother. I feel like screaming at her. The more anger I feel, the more fear comes. Within, the pain is more intense at Hallowe'en."

The rest of the group could not fathom the evilness of the ritual abuse of an infant. Somehow it was beyond their experience and they could just look sympathetically at Lisa. It was important that she not feel abandoned. It was at times like this that Tasha and Shelly were particularly useful because they moved in very quickly to surround Lisa and make sure she wasn't feeling abandoned, at least during the group.

It was evident also that the group listened intently to the experiences of the other members. They were obviously picking up expressions and even words, for many of the words were important because, as children, they often didn't have the words to express and explain what had happened to them. To hear the words from other people and add them to their own vocabulary helped them better express some of the feelings they encountered. The words were very useful. It was, after all, a talking therapy, yet it wasn't just a talking therapy. Much of the therapy came from the experiences during the group.

Tonight Virginia looked totally dejected and disconsolate. She said she had done her homework but hadn't written it down. "I feel lost and scared and I have been crying a lot. I don't know if I can do this. It brings up too many awful memories."

It was difficult for me when patients didn't do their homework. Fortunately, I could usually leave it up to my facilitators to urge them for their own benefit, to comply with the homework assignments even if it didn't seem as though it meant much or if it was too painful. That night they didn't let me down. Shelly was adamant. "Virginia, you must do it. I can tell you, from my own experience, that you have to grit your teeth and see this whole thing through."

Krista said she was pleased that hearing others and expressing her own feelings broke through much of the denial that she felt from her parents. When she tried to explain what had happened, there was often an additional thought: "You didn't say it properly." It was little wonder that she was majoring in English at the university. She remembered being utterly humiliated by her father. It was so degrading that she didn't want to go into it. It was almost as if he were saying, "I'm going to crush you."

Krista went on to describe the physical, verbal, and sexual abuse by her brother. "It's just a feeling now. I could never look up to him. I can't defend myself. I feel all this awful anger, but I can't express it. I have the feeling that he was trying to make me feel as small as he himself felt. Sometimes he tried to be nice to me, and when he was, I liked it. It was certainly better than getting kicked and punched. The orgasms that I had I now feel awfully guilty about."

Krista was the first to talk about the enjoyment she received during sexual abuse. Few people would admit it. It is a taboo topic in society, and even very few therapists want to hear about it. I pointed out that the pleasure itself was a terrible trap. It heightened the confusion and the dependency to produce a kind of bond that should not have been there. It stimulated the child's sexuality long before she could deal with it.

The subject having been broached, Shawna was also able to talk about the pleasure she had felt when having sex with her father. "I felt betrayed and guilty, particularly because of the pleasure. I felt there was no control. I cried all night. I remember enormous sadness. It was as if somehow I were being ripped off. Somebody stole something that I could never replace. If this hadn't happened to me, I would have been far less jaded, much more open as an adolescent. My parents betrayed me, yet I'm not sure whether or not I tried to let my mother know about it. She must have known. In many of my dreams I am being chased by bears."

Amy was glancing wildly about. "I don't feel that I belong in this group. When I talk, I feel nobody is listening, nobody reacts. You all seem to be saying that you never really hear anything. I feel so unsafe. It is as if I were high and about to go crazy again."

She was indeed feeling estranged from the group. What she didn't realize was how she tended to alienate herself. She usually didn't listen to others, and when she did, she often misjudged their emotions and made inane comments. Only gradually over time did she begin to realize how little she was able to empathize with people. At this juncture, she was reassured that she did belong and the others did their best to help her realize she was being understood. She spoke more of her parents' immaturity. Even though they had been professional people, they seemed to have very little understanding of what she was going through. I mentioned that parents travel through a child's experience with the child, and if the child cannot mature along with them, the child will have difficulty maturing past the point of his or her parents' own immaturity.

Tonight Linda was not telling jokes. She was looking and feeling abandoned. "I remember feeling abandoned. They were supposed to look after me. I begged my brothers to take me with them, but I couldn't tell them why. I was being used as a sexual toy by two older boys from across the street. My brothers told me I was silly to be afraid. I felt so alone. I felt so smothered. I can remember feeling hot, sick. I remember feeling that I smelled awful. I used a variety of diversions to keep my mind off of what was happening. Even now, my skin hurts when I am touched. When I told my mother, she said, 'I don't believe it.' She never did follow it up. Why didn't she take these men to court like other parents do?"

It was clear that when young children feel their very existence is at stake, they want to tell somebody but can not do so because this would further threaten the security upon which they depend. Somehow children know when their parents are unstable or immature and so they don't threaten them with material or information they can't deal with. Yet these children badly want somebody to know, hoping that perhaps that person might help. They are devastated by the actions of both of their parents. If it is a situation of sexual abuse by a father or stepfather, then enormous anger is directed at the mother. Often it is the other way around. This heightened something that I mentioned at the beginning of the group. This person or group of people that I called observers are also responsible. It is no wonder that victims feel so much anger toward them.

To bring this more to awareness, we did a group exercise in which they paired off and the partners said to each other, representing the child or the observer: "You must have known. Why didn't you do something?"

As Linda and I role played, she responded to me with, "I didn't know. How could I have known? Besides, I couldn't have done anything about it anyhow."

The homework on this particular night was to identify the triggers to their fears and feelings of abandonment from their present experiences. Using these, they could trace them back to early experiences and begin to remember those experiences and use the memories from them.

❖   ❖   ❖

Anna

When Virginia shared last week about her being beaten along with her brother and I fled to the bathroom in panic, I seemed to have picked up the thread that I had searched for all week: the fear of my mother's leaving me. I connected with the hitting over and over. I hid behind the door. I was standing up holding to the door as hard as I could, but inside I felt like I was cowering behind it.

The overwhelming feeling was helplessness. I knew I was regressing but I couldn't seem to get hold of the memory. I knew the water was a link, but I felt as though there were a short circuit. Tasha was there and I kept pulling back to the now whenever she spoke. When I left the meeting, I was really confused and scattered and sleep didn't come for a long time. A weird thing happened. I could see colors when I shut my eyes. I'd never seen anything but blackness before. The next day I was in such emotional turmoil that I didn't know how I could function. Zombie-like, I went to a friend who had recently supported me through one of my few body memories. I shared briefly where I was at and that I knew I needed to finish the work that had been started. We got an experienced person, and within a few minutes after we had started to pray, I regressed to age two and a half. When I regressed, I became the child, physically, mentally, and emotionally, and yet somehow I could hear separately, as if outside of myself. This regression took just over an hour. Maybe this is why it couldn't be completed during last week's session.

The memory was this: I was cowering behind the bathroom door, scared and knowing. It was a resigned, helpless feeling. What was coming had happened before. "Mommy, don't go and leave me. I'll be good," I promised. "I won't talk," I remember pleading. She took my sister; she always took my sister. He was pulling me and pulling and hitting. I remember making a decision: "If I shut my eyes and make it all black, it will go away. It won't be real." He was naked and I could only see his groin. He didn't have an erection. He pushed my face into him again and again. I was choking when he came, it made me throw up, some over the toilet and me and everywhere. He was really mad, and then I remember being in the bathtub and he was yelling and yelling. He was angry. I couldn't tell anyone because he said he would kill me. My head was under the water, up then down again, and I knew I was bad, very bad. I left her there, she looked dead, she was bad. But she wasn't dead, just empty. She was bad and I left her there. At this point, my facilitator's voice somehow entered my consciousness and directed me to go back and get her. I was terrified. I didn't want to. She was bad and it would happen again. Finally, I was able to go, and after quite a battle, I was holding her in a towel and the tub was empty.

In the past few days since the memory, I flash back to the bathtub and sometimes she is still lying there. I probably still have some more work to do. I am overwhelmed with shame. In the other memories, I was unable to stop the violent overpowering. In this one, I felt like I must have participated, and to have had his penis in my mouth until he ejaculated somehow makes me feel responsible. I feel so ashamed. I am not sure who he was. They kept asking me to look but I was so scared. They reassured me that I could tell now, he couldn't kill me, and for a brief moment, I saw a tall, thin, naked man with lots of reddish-blond hair hanging over his forehead. I don't know who it was. I am so ashamed. I abandoned myself. This hurts so deeply, and yet I am so afraid to pick me up.

After I read this at class, there was such support. I could hear the kind and sorrowful responses around the room, but I couldn't look at anyone; I was too ashamed. Later Shawna told me how angry she was at Dr. Ney and Dr. Green because they hadn't stopped me, as she was sure that I wouldn't come back. The reading had made me touch the memory and there were times when I seemed to switch from the past to the present.

On the way home, my self-talk told me I had been far too emotional. I had exaggerated, was out of control, and I had just wanted the attention or to have told the "best story." I felt guilt, shame, foolishness, embarrassment, and I began to determine not to share much the next week, to be in the background. Then I caught myself. I couldn't continue if I didn't tell the truth and give it my all. Right then I determined that whatever the cost, I was in and I would not back away, for my sake and the group's sake.

During the week, Mom phoned. She thinks I am going to the psychiatrist because of my past food disorders. In our conversation, she recounts my whereabouts at age two. It doesn't fit with my abuse memory. I became really scared. It shook me up for days. Maybe I was just making all this up, yet how could I? Maybe I was crazy just like my father. Consumed with anxiety, I got out old photos and tried to piece together the fragments of my life. I just got frustrated; nothing fit, too many blanks. Most of this week, I was very depressed and found anger quickly, but there were several times when I was surprised by a deep sense of well-being that lasted for half an hour or so. It would just be there, an overwhelming sense of life and aliveness that was so intense that it moved me to tears of joy.

❖   ❖   ❖

WEEK 4

This evening everybody was present and ready to go. It was as if they had begun to recognize that there was progress and were eager to get on with it.

If it was bad for Virginia last week, it was even worse this time. "I'm going out to get drunk," Virginia was joking. This was followed by hollow laughter from the group. "I have been drinking a lot. My mother never told me the truth. Whenever she punished me, she always said, 'It only hurts because I love you.' Now the social worker is threatening to remove my children. I've been reported for neglecting them and I don't know what is best. I don't know who to trust." She turned to the group. Faced by the awful prospect of a mother's losing her children, they all turned to me. What could I do? I didn't know her home situation, but I could believe that these children were not being well looked after. I also knew that if the children were removed from their mother's care, it would terribly complicate what we were trying to do for her now.

Over the years, I have begun to realize that the conflicts engendered in the minds of children arise in the first instances of abuse and neglect. It is in the first experiences that almost irreversible damage is done. There is a steep increase in the hurt and harm done to the children, and then it levels off. It seldom gets better, but it doesn't get much worse over a long period. Too much social policy is based on the idea that there is a straight-line relationship between the duration of mistreatment and the harm done to children, thus justifying intervention at any point that abuse is detected. I contend that after the early period, it is better to leave the children in the home even though they continue to get hurt. The reason is that even if they are placed in a foster home, they are taking so much of the conflict with them that they will reenact it. They will set up the foster parents to abuse and neglect them in the same way they were mistreated in their own homes. This leads to a whole cycle of foster homes, which is often the worst experience for children. Repeated attachments and losses make the maltreated even more desperate for nurture and protection, which they seek from adults who take advantage of their desperation or from other young people who, like themselves, have little to give to anyone.

It wasn't hard to identify the triggers. Here are some common ones:

I'm going out.

Try again.

Bend over.

I know what you are thinking.

Take your clothes off.

I'm going to tell Dad.

It's not right.

Come here.

Be good.

The child's response to these triggers was initially, "Why, Mummy?", then "Please don't," and eventually, although buried beneath the thick layer of denial, was a deep anger. "No, I won't."

The parents' response would have been, "Well, if I can't discipline you, then you will have to leave home." The child must, under those circumstances, agree to be punished. It's amazing that children are so easily punished. They always fear something worse. Their greatest fear is of being abandoned. If only the child could say, "I don't mind. If you send me away, I can go somewhere else where I know it is safe." Unfortunately, children don't know about safe places and so cannot easily deal with people who abuse them, much less with those who neglect them.

Anna mentioned that one trigger that had upset her recently was in a phone call from her mother: "Put on weight?" This trigger had always worked with her. She had always seen herself as fat and had struggled with overweight all her life. Now she was struggling with her child's weight. She had some appreciation that being fat was a protection.

Tanya was eager to participate. She knew of all kinds of triggers. "I hate triggers because I lose control. They work. They always work. If somebody says, 'They're lying' or 'You're lying,' I can't deal with it. I have this picture of a man standing over me. There's a critical tone in his voice. There is a hand in the air and something in it and the air is filled with, 'You're lying.' Why do my parents lie? Why do they deny?"

Lisa was looking particularly removed, almost as if she had curled up into a little ball, which wasn't hard because she was very round. "I've had a bad week. I talked to my mother and everything was thrown back into my face. My mother is attacking me. She is abusing me all over again. I feel she is demonized. The triggers that really get to me are 'Liar, sick, it's all your fault,' and any occasion where there is anger and no compassion."

For Amy, the triggers were: "You're just like your Mom." "That's silly." "That was stupid."

For Linda, anyone drinking, not feeling listened to when she needed to be heard, and hearing her baby crying were triggers to which she could not help but respond.

For Shawna, anyone standing too close to her, being told "what's best for you," not being understood when she was trying hard to explain, feeling backed into a corner, and having to defend herself were triggers that always set off deep emotions, particularly here.

For Krista, pretending that it didn't happen, giving advice, and noticing people who didn't intervene for children were triggers she could hardly stand. They always evoked extreme emotions.

The group exercises that took up a great deal of time were having the members respond to each other in pairs. Two basic triggers were "Go away" and "Come here." It wasn't hard for them to imagine the worst responses, and even when they were said fairly calmly, there were extreme reactions. If the individual functioning as the perpetrator shouted one of these phrases, there was terror. Gradually, however, people were able to say, "No, I won't." They said this with greater and greater emphasis.

As homework, I asked them to think of situations in which those kinds of triggers took place and to note what they would have liked to have said to defend themselves. As they left, I experienced a sense of relief. There was no question but that these women were working hard on their own therapy, but most particularly, they were enduring even the most terrible, terrifying memories.

It was necessary that after each group, no matter how late at night, Dr. Green, Tasha, Shelly, and I spend half an hour or so checking our perceptions. We generally agreed, but sometimes there were nuances that one of us had not picked up. We could also express our concerns about various individuals and talk a little about the coming group. Sometimes we would reverse some of the exercises that we would be doing the following week. My three cotherapists were real bricks. Often I wondered how they could drag themselves home at 12:30 or 1 AM after our four or four and a half hours of intense emotion in group therapy and face another day, but they always did.

❖   ❖   ❖

Anna

Many times I find myself sitting quietly in God's presence thinking about the wounded little child inside. The child I didn't even know existed is now constantly on my mind. Her memories crowd into my consciousness and claim me. I feel so afraid of her, of her story. I recognize how weak I am, so weak and afraid. I believe everyone else over her. Me? If someone is lying, it must be me. I've always believed everyone over me. The child says, "He hurt me, she left me, and you left me." I grieve over the abuse and abandonment of this child and I want to promise her that I will always believe her and never leave her again, but I am so afraid. To own it all means it will always be real. Once integrated with her, I will always have her history, her pain, her anguish, her abuse, her body. Apprehensively I surrender myself to my mother's and father's genealogies. I am finally willing to own and accept my history, all of it. God must help me; I cannot do this thing. I promise, "I will not abandon myself any more."

The phone rings. It's Mom....I can't believe her timing. She picked up immediately that something was wrong. Wanting to know what it was, she pushed me to share with her, lacing the conversation with "buck up" and "everyone has problems." Then, teasingly, "I'll come over and give you a kick." I acknowledged that "it wouldn't help." She quickly countered with "a hug then?" It all felt so familiar. I was hurting, she misunderstood, again downplaying and denying my reality, my feelings, my pain! I avoided her questioning and hung up as quickly as I could. More depressed and angry, yet satisfied that I hadn't let her "erase" my truth. I would not abandon me any more. She phoned two more times that day. On the final call, she firmly suggested that I talk to her about what was happening in my therapy group and almost demanded answers—for my own good, of course. We finally agreed, me in tears, that maybe talking over the phone wasn't such a good idea, and when I was ready, we would meet. (We live a day's drive apart.) Exhausted. I don't want to see her. I am afraid.

TRIGGERS

1. *Fat statements*
   - Did you put some weight on?
   - You're still hungry?
   - Should you be eating that?
   - Aren't you on a diet?
   - She'd be pretty if...
   - She's got such a pretty face.

   I can see that my overweight was probably a cover for my sexuality. For me, being thin has always been synonymous with being good, desirable, beautiful, and sexual. Overcontrol and out of control characterize my lifetime diet pattern. When I needed to be held, hugged, or comforted, I ate. Maybe there were no hugs around. I want a man to hold me and to love me and not to be sick or perverted. All my life, I've wanted this. Why does it always escape me?

2. *Anger.* When someone is angry at me, I become obsessed by it until I can "fix" it. I have to get rid of the anger! At any cost to myself or others, I do get rid of the anger. Driven by the fear that anyone who stays angry at me will leave me, I give away my dignity. My own anger brings up feelings of guilt, shame, condemnation, and panic. I feel that my anger is wrong and that I am bad when I'm angry. I am also afraid of the extent of my anger if I were ever to really let it go.

3. *Touch.* Touch that I am not in control of, whether it is a hug, a doctor's examination, or sex, angers or humiliates me.

4. *Criticism.* Unwarranted or exaggerated criticism causes me to become incredibly defensive. Even in simple situations that warrant no such action, I have to prove my innocence.

5. *People.* Pushy, dominating, overpowering, manipulative, or controlling people trigger one of two extremes in me. Either I panic and disappear or I fight with everything I've got. There seems to be no room for balance or calming self-talk.

6. *Being told I'm like my mother, which pushes all my buttons.* Dr. Ney says that to say "I love you" gives up control. Maybe that's why my husband won't say he loves me. Shawna is telling about her father's sexual abuse of her. Where was her mother? Anger

rises up in me, my stomach tightens, and my teeth are clenched before I recognize the incredible rage I feel toward her mother/my mother.

We are reminded that there is a sense of isolation and loneliness that no one can truly enter, that we are scapegoats for several generations of our families. Dr. Ney asks how many of us are the family's "overly sensitive one." Almost everyone nods. We are gently encouraged to "go with the flow" and allow ourselves to trust, to do all the exercises even if they seem stupid or foreign. He reminds us that we can have individual sessions if we need them, but that they *must* be brought back to the room.

My life is in this room; this is the only reality I truly know.

WEEK 5

The group members came in full of grim determination. They knew there was work to be done and they were impatient to get on with it. They quickly began the roll call of their present state. Everybody seemed to be reasonably intact, so we went on to the homework, which was what memories came from these statements: "Come here," and "Go away."

Tanya stated that it was hard to remember. Life was such a puzzle with very few clues. She could remember one night when her mother was going out and she pleaded, "Don't go, Mummy." Her mother responded, "You aren't going to start that, Tanya, are you?" There was a poignancy to this because it almost appeared that the mother was blaming her child for not wanting her to go. The child intuitively understood that the mother could provide protection and nurture, and to be remonstrated with because she needed her mother would strike even a little child as most incongruous. Amy said she didn't have very many pictures in her memory, except of her father slumped in his chair reading a book or falling asleep, sometimes drinking, sometimes smoking large cigars, but always engrossed in something that excluded her. She said, "I never heard, 'Come here.' Our lives were so hard, just one horrible tension. My father was so very depressed and our kitchen was so dirty." On that note, Krista stated, "My life is a mess, and now the sludge is coming to the surface. When I heard 'Come here' it was always from my father, and it always meant that there was trouble and I would get the leather strap. Afterwards, they would send me away, but I was not allowed to cry." The "go aways" that she could remember were of her father going on a trip and she would feel very happy about it, except for the fact that she was left with even stranger relatives.

Linda was very clear about her memory. "Come here for Mummy. Get me my stuff." She always obeyed. She felt like a bad puppy dog. She resented her mother's going out, especially when she complained and her mother said, "Don't be ridiculous." Somehow her mother never picked up on Linda's enormous fears of what would happen when she was left alone in the house. Her brothers would leave and then the two men would come over and she would be sexually used over and over again. Linda could remember once saying to her mother, "Please don't go," but otherwise she felt it was her duty to allow her mother to go out and enjoy herself.

For Shawna, it was, "Come here and do your homework." There were such battles with her mother. She eventually refused to do any. Even now she was so terrified about completing assignments and not doing well that she was afraid to test her remarkable intellect in learning situations. Anna could clearly remember saying, "Please don't go. I'll do anything you want." But her mother would go anyhow. When she talked to her mother about her difficulties without being very explicit, she was hoping her mother would tell her that it didn't happen. She began to feel resigned. Somehow all the whys didn't matter after a while. But she did feel that there was a sign on her forehead, a large recognizable sign that told almost anybody, "Abuse me. Use me."

Linda agreed. "I have the same kind of sign, maybe the same one. Perverts follow me. Maybe they can see my loneliness."

Lisa said she had been thinking a lot. She hadn't written the homework down, but it had stimulated something in her thinking and clarified many issues. "It's been good for me. I never did know why it was always me who had to say goodbye to people. People always seemed to be going away from me and leaving me. When I thought of it, I began crying exactly like a baby and it wouldn't stop. I wanted my mother so much. Now that I have found her, she won't stop abusing me. She phones me and says the most terrible things."

Virginia did not show up for this group. We all wondered what might have happened to her and her children. I knew no more than the others did, but I assured them I would find out.

The homework hadn't taken very long to present so there was plenty of opportunity for the group exercise. When we had gone through the list of exercises, the women were truly exhausted, yet they knew that they would have to go home and they knew that I would give them homework. In this instance, I wanted them to remember all the situations, past and present, in which they had wanted to say, "Stop it" or "No, I won't," or "Listen to me." So they left, clutching their notebooks, with brief goodbyes. There were some who persistently stayed to wash dishes after drinking coffee and tea during the evening. There were always snacks on the table, which helped them feel at ease and also perked them up when their glucose was low. They always had a break halfway through the group, but even so, a four-hour group is a very long one and they became very tired, especially when we would break up at 12:30.

❖ ❖ ❖

Anna

My brother phoned for the first time in ages. He said that something had happened in August. He didn't know what it was, but for the first time in his life, he wasn't afraid to think. Not quite understanding, I questioned him. He shared that he was never able to think very deeply. It had somehow always triggered fear. Explaining that he couldn't even think problems out in school or at work, he had to keep everything on a surface level, relationships included. "Well now," he said, "I am thinking about things—everything—and I am not afraid. Mom told me a while ago that you were having some problems and were going to a therapist. I felt I should phone you but I just couldn't. Now I can hear what you have to say." I shared that I'd been abused and was slowly remembering. A long pause and then, quietly "I've never forgotten. I never admitted this to anyone, not even myself. I've never said it out loud before." He asked me to wait while he went to another phone away from his family's hearing. Tearfully, he told me the details of three incidents of sexual abuse in his childhood. Each had been by a different person. In describing one of the episodes, he repeatedly used the words "hate" and "bad." I could taste his shame. We wept together over the incredible tragedy of our childhoods. Later we rejoiced, acknowledging the freedom my recovery had procured in his life. We marveled at the hope that it had produced in us for our children and the rest of our family. Enveloped in a deep bonding, we eagerly responded to its call of commitment to truth and unconditional support of each other. As I hung up, I knew that I had someone who believed me, really believed me, and would be there in my family, with and for me.

I couldn't sleep. Fear crept around my thoughts. Darkest depression settled over me. Slowly, as the days passed, understanding seeped through. He, my brother, had made it real. It had really happened. Mom couldn't make it untrue. I couldn't make it untrue. There was no way back. Truth was exposed and truth would always be now. I was abused, physically

assaulted, with brutal sexual violation, emotionally battered and abandoned. I'm not crazy; it really all happened.

Homework (groan...)

My inner responses to the command "Come here!" were, "Why? Please
don't, please don't hurt me. No, no, I don't want to. Please stop." The
most horrible of all was just a resigned silence.

I felt overwhelmed, helpless, without hope, and an echo of "I am bad. I
am bad."

When "Come here!" was said by my foster parent, I felt terror and
resignation.

When it was said by my stepfather, I thought, "Why? What do you want?
Don't! Don't! I hate it. I hate it and I love you. Why do you do this to me?
How can I love you if you keep doing this to me? Please stop, let me
love you."

The word "good-bye" I responded to inside with, "Please don't go. Please
don't leave me. I'll be good. I won't talk. Please don't go."

My feelings were fear, loneliness, terror, and sadness.

When the word was said by my mother, my reaction was, "Don't go,
please don't go. I'll be good." This taps into deep sorrow and then rage.

When said by boyfriends/husbands, my reaction was, "Don't go, please
don't leave me. I'll be good. I'll try harder. I'll do anything." Remembering
triggers panic and fear, then shame and anger.

I look around the room. Virginia again is not here. She worries me.
When I drove her home last time, she said that she couldn't stand the
whining. Most of the desperate stories she heard in the room just sounded
like soap operas to her and seemed to make her very angry. She said that
she was going to see Dr. Ney this week about it. I felt really bad that she
wanted to quit and I wished she would keep coming, but I knew I would
understand if she didn't.

When Tanya was sharing about her mother's negligence, not protecting
her from her father's continual sexual abuse, I wanted to scream, "Can't
you see? Why can't you see that you don't need to protect her from the
truth? Mothers are supposed to protect children. Children aren't supposed
to protect their mothers. It's all backwards! It makes me so angry." Most of
us (Tanya, Shawna, Linda, Amy) wanted to protect our mothers. However, Krista and Lisa seemed to want to make them pay.

Amy's life with an alcoholic father must have been horrible, but my
compassion fails me. She's so much like my mother. She always has an
answer or a personal testimony for everyone. I find myself gritting my
teeth whenever she starts talking.

Linda's brothers deserted her. They were supposed to look after her.
When she described the conflict she had with "they were just kids" and
"they shouldn't have left me," I could feel the tug-of-war inside her. The

adult knowing of their innocence; there was no way they could have guessed that when they went out without her, someone would come in and violate her sexually. And yet the child inside her silently screamed for protection, and hates and blames them for not giving it to her. I could see the adult and the child in her body and her face. It fascinated and saddened me.

Dr. Ney rarely teaches us directly, but I have noticed that he drops nuggets of truth along the way for us to pick up if we are ready to hear. Tonight he said, "Anger let out lifts depression." I remember reading somewhere that "depression is frozen rage." This is my answer to the depression that shrouds me, yet I suspect that my incredible fear will prevent me from facing my anger and finally getting rid of my black robe.

We have to role-play again. It makes me really uncomfortable. Tonight we have to say, "You hurt me," and hear back "No, I didn't!"

After a while, most of us were able to get in touch with that inner voice that said and felt, "You hurt me. Why? I am just a little girl. I am innocent. I am helpless. I can't stop you." To hear a firm, loud "No, I didn't" threatened and intimidated us and proved our helplessness. Only after much coaching and listening to the graduates were we able to let the helplessness go and begin to stand up for truth. Clearly stating that we were hurt and that we were not going to "come here" anymore was powerful. Krista was particularly impressed with the power and control it gave. I accepted it because I knew it was right, but I could hear something in our voices that bothered me. Maybe it was the anger that we seemed to need to be able to stand up for ourselves that felt wrong. I don't know. I am tired, so very, very tired. I don't remember feeling so old before.

❖   ❖   ❖

2

Protest: Expressing the Anger and Fear

Professionals who deal with abused children or adults, and the patients themselves, have often wondered why the patients didn't protect themselves, why they didn't stop what was happening, or why they didn't at least protest. The answer is not easy, but it lies in the fact that children will do whatever they have to in order to survive. Survival is the predominant drive, and if protesting might make the situation worse for them, then they will not protest. They will accept the situation no matter how awful it seems. The alternative for most children is for the family either to mistreat them more severely or to reject them. The thought of rejection keeps children from protesting, and it becomes a way of life for the adults.

Having felt the pain and the fear during their phase of realization, there was now growing within each of the patients in the group an anger. The anger was difficult to manage. It was sometimes destructive and sometimes pathetic. Our job was to take that growing feeling and channel it in a healthy way.

When I deal with children, I teach them how to protest in the most effective and, to the parents, the least threatening way. This is for the child's protection. The child has to be able to say to a present or potential abuser, "No, I will not let you do this," and must do so in a way that the perpetrator will be able to hear and respond to. To respond with aggression only accentuates the irritation in the perpetrator and increases the damage. To protest ineffectively makes the victim feel, and seem to the perpetrator, even more vulnerable. The paralysis that some people feel when threatened represents a tendency to protect themselves by shutting down and becoming immobile, hoping that the aggressor will not recognize them. Unfortunately, it is impossible to become invisible. The helplessness tends to evoke worse aggression by sadistic perpetrators.

A child's earliest expressions of anger are probably the healthiest. When these are blocked, the child elaborates other, more destructive, more indirect ways of expressing that anger. Curiously enough, these are permitted

44

by the parents and thus allowed to continue. For example, it is all right for the child to express anger by being sick rather than by writing on the wall.

It is interesting that in the animal sphere helplessness invokes sadism. If a healthy gull is tied by one leg, the rest of the flock will attack it simply because it is helpless. Two large dogs that come into contact with each other will circle, growling, pawing the dirt, and baring their fangs. As long as one does not run away or attack, they will eventually tire of facing off and stride stiff-legged away from each other. When one dog runs, the other will attack it. If one dog attacks, the other must defend itself. Thus passivity and aggression can lead to further violence or abuse. What young children and adults abused as children need to learn is how to assert themselves in such a way that they can stop the potential abuser.

Although it might seem strange, the best way for a woman to deal with a potential rapist is to say, "All right, buddy, so you want sex. Let's go and talk about it over coffee." What the person has to do is to invoke in the perpetrator the maximum humanity. One must not be afraid, must not be ashamed, and must not attack. Screaming or running invites attack. To face the perpetrator with clear eyes and a direct look and make a quiet, assertive response is the best way to prevent further violence.

When I explained this to the group, there was a certain recognition on their part that they needed both to vent the anger and to learn how to assert themselves. However, they were afraid. They had so often interfered with their own aggressive responses that they were afraid of what might happen. When I urged them, they began to protest about protesting.

Adults are afraid to protest for these reasons:

1. If they protest to their parents, their children will do the same to them. To release some of that anger at their parents might allow their children to express the anger they feel.

2. The anger now (which had been so repressed for such a long time) might be such an intense emotion that it might overwhelm their psychic structures and result in regression or psychosis. Indeed, a number of them began to complain about their hearts racing, nightmares, headaches, and other expressions of high levels of anxiety associated with allowing feelings to surface. This heightened anxiety made many of them begin to feel that the only thing they could do was return to their previously defended and denied state.

3. If they began to express strong anger, they might find out how fragile their parents were. Th y always suspected that the parents were both immature and fragile. If they expressed anger, they might destroy them, but even if they didn't destroy them, the parents might be so wounded that they could not depend on them.

The adults abused as children had learned not to trust their parents' emotions. Their parents got carried away. The unpredictability and volatility had made their children afraid that if they began expressing their emotions, they might become even worse in the way in which they treated their own children. They controlled their emotions to protect their children. If they began expressing some of that anger, it was possible that their children would be hurt. Unfortunately, as they protected themselves from the expression of their anger, this tended to subvert and suppress all of their emotions, even the occasional joy that came with insights.

It was difficult for me to recognize that as these parents became better able to express their emotions, it would not always result in control of the situation. Their children could be exposed to it. In fact, a number of the parents began reporting that they were shouting at their children more as they were better able to express their emotions, particularly anger. All the years of pent-up anger, having been released by the exercises we were doing, could not be easily recontrolled in situations in which the children might be at risk.

To help these women practice the expression of their anger and learn how best to do it, I generally asked their husbands to cooperate. I would see partners after the first five or six groups to acquaint them with the process. I asked them to participate by being the object of the anger, a surrogate object for the anger the women felt toward their parents. The husbands would have to play a role. Soon the women began to realize how easily the husbands could carry out these roles. Then they began to wonder whether underneath, they might really be like the parents they had left. I pointed out to them that it was easy to trigger in their husbands the kind of response that they had so often experienced from their parents. They knew this, and they had to be careful. That is why they would have to follow my instructions very carefully; otherwise, they could find themselves being attacked by the very husbands they had learned to trust. It was good that in this group almost all the husbands understood the process, were willing to participate, and realized the dangers.

In looking forward to the next phase, it is understandable that my anxiety was associated with any expression of destruction that the members of the group might feel toward their parents. They were strictly warned not to express that feeling directly to the people who had harmed them or to communicate with them until they were ready to do so. This would take place much later. In the meantime, their fantasies of revenge began to flourish, and with those feelings of revenge came the guilt that would have to be dealt with in the next phase.

They were certainly the surrogate scapegoats for many generations, and now that they were beginning to experience the full extent of that, they were realizing what a huge burden they were taking upon themselves. It was small wonder that they were beginning to wilt under the pressure of it all. They also began to realize, however, that they were changing, that they were healing. They felt guilty about surviving and improving. Again, this would have to be dealt with in the next phase.

WEEK 6

The next evening, it was easy to see that people were even more tense. There were memories, impressions, and feelings crowding into their lives that they had sat on for many years.

Again, Virginia didn't show up, and the group was very anxious. I had heard from the social worker that there was great concern about the welfare of her children. I asked the social worker to try to reconsider taking the children into custody, at least until we had had an opportunity to engage Virginia in effective treatment.

Krista was quick to respond to the homework. "I asked my brother to stop a million times. I asked my father to stop strapping me. My parents still don't listen to me. My mother always makes excuses. Now I begin to see it happening to a lot of people. I'm glad to be able to talk about these things. I've had a pretty good week. I'm feeling more energy."

Shawna quickly followed: "There were lots of times that the two statements somehow went together. Somehow I kept repeating relationships in which I always wanted to say, 'Stop it. No, I won't.' And when I did, the relationships broke."

Linda and Shawna had become good friends, and one always provoked the other. "I was too afraid to say, 'No, I won't' or 'Stop it,' but I thought it many times," Linda said, "especially when I saw my father being so violent with my brother. He implied that my brother had done something to deserve it, but I couldn't understand what it was. So often I wanted to say, 'Stop it. Stop hitting my brother.'"

Anna stated, "I never remember saying, 'Stop it,' but I wanted to so much, especially when my stepfather went on and on telling dirty jokes. I was screaming 'Stop it' inside. I was teased so much at school. I kept saying, 'Stop it' to myself, 'Get out of yourself, don't react,' but I would like to have told all those kids to stop it, if only I had been able to. I also wanted to shout to many people, 'Please believe me. Please hear me. Agree with me. Be nice to me.' Now I am beginning to see how selfish I am."

With all of the various bits of homework and group exercises, it was beginning to become clear to these women that their feelings and their conflicts were very mixed and very complicated. Part of the tragedy of child abuse or neglect is that the conflicts it engenders are complicated, and that is why children cannot figure them out. It takes them an enormous amount of time and effort. It detracts from other essential developmental tasks, and that makes school much harder. When I pointed this out, the women began to heave sighs of relief. They had all thought that their own complicated thinking was peculiar to themselves. Nobody else could have so many conflicting thoughts.

Tanya: "In a dream, I saw myself being left alone. I was screaming, 'Don't leave me,' but the sound wouldn't come out. It was so rare for people to believe me. One of my previous therapists couldn't believe that sexual abuse had happened to me as a teenager and that I did nothing about it. They didn't want to hear it. I didn't want to hear myself saying it. I've just remembered something too that I hadn't admitted to myself. Three men raped me. When it was happening, I thought to myself, 'This is fun.' People would never believe me if I said it, but it was quite exciting."

Lisa, even before she began talking, was in tears. "I ripped up my homework. I couldn't talk about it. Okay, go ahead. Say I am a freak. This spirit keeps coming to me in the night. I keep fighting it off. It is real. It is not just a memory. It sexually abuses me, and sometimes I enjoy it. Can you imagine: I actually enjoy being sexually abused by a demon. I think it is a demon, but I am not sure what it is, but I know the pleasure it can give me."

People in the room couldn't believe her. Lisa had to repeat it, and this time she said it somewhat more sincerely, and many did begin to believe her, but it all sounded so horrible. From that point on, various members of the group began to doubt the things that Lisa reported. They wondered if she weren't making it all up.

Amy had once had a psychotic breakdown that required hospitalization. She had become so disturbed that they had put her in intensive care. She was trying to help Lisa feel more relaxed by saying, "I also felt like a freak. There I was in intensive care, but I'll never go back. So many times I wanted to say 'Stop it' to my father's drinking and his sloppy habits. I wanted to say 'Stop it' to the crude jokes and to the criticism. How I wish I had been able to."

I said, "From pain comes anger. If I stand on your toe, even by mistake, the pain transmitted to the mind results in a strong biological reaction that prepares you either to flee or to fight. Your decision will depend on the circumstances. As a child, even if you generally hid in fear or wandered away, there was also some anger there. Now you can realize and express that anger. For the past two weeks, you have felt mostly the pain and the fear. This week we will start mobilizing your anger. Watch Dr. Green and me role-play a situation of physical and verbal abuse."

"Why, Mommy? Why, Mommy, did you hit me? Why did you keep hitting me?"

"Because you deserved it. You were very naughty."

"No. I did not deserve it. I was a child. I did not deserve it. Why did you keep hitting me?"

"You were a bad child. You know you are a bad child."

"I'm not a bad child. You kept saying I was a bad child. I am not a bad child. Do you hear me? I am not a bad child. You told me I was stupid. I am not stupid."

"You were stupid. Your grades were abysmal."

"I wasn't stupid. Please don't tell me I am stupid. Don't you see that I'm not stupid? Please don't tell me that."

"Shut up! Don't tell me what to do. You were stupid. Now finish your work."

"Please stop it! I can't take it!"

"You don't have any choice. I am your parent. Now do what I say and be quiet."

"I won't let you say those things about me."

"Don't be stupid. You can't stop me."

"Stop saying that right now or I will ... (tell somebody, run away, etc.)"

"You will take this. You will do what I say or you will get something worse!"

"You can't frighten me any more. Now stop!"

"Okay, if that's the way you want it, then good-bye. Good-bye forever."

"All right. I have tried to restrain myself, but now you will bear my anger!"

"No! Please don't! Don't say that to me! Don't do this to me!"

After the role play, I said, "Okay, now you try it, starting with the first statements and getting the tone, facial expression, and posture right before going on to the next. That's good, Shawna, but lower your eyebrows. You are making a statement, not pleading or asking a question."

For those who have experienced various combinations of abuses and neglects, it is important that they go through each one. Evidence shows that some combinations have a greater impact than others. From our studies, it appears that a combination of physical neglect, physical abuse, and verbal abuse has the most devastating effect on young children. The reason is probably that physical care and nurture are such necessary ingredients of child rearing that without them children feel that their whole existence is threatened. On top of that, if they are beaten by the very person who is supposed to care for them, they feel even more vulnerable. If, in addition, when they try to get some physical care, they are berated, this must have an overwhelming effect on them and their views of themselves and the future. This has been corroborated by the research we have done.

All the group members found this phase extraordinarily difficult. They began to protest about protesting, "I want to, but I can't. A deep fear wells up within me." When they were children, they wanted to protest but they were afraid. They thought:

1. They might destroy the parent—the very source, or at least potential source, of nurture and guidance upon which they depended.
2. If they ran away, how could they survive? As far as they knew, the world outside was full of evil animals, ghosts, and monsters from which only their parents could protect them.
3. Maybe their parents were right. Maybe they were at fault, and then they would have to really be punished. This is akin to the deep anxiety felt by children in countries where children were used as sacrifices to appease the angry gods or to appeal for rain and fertility.
4. They had fantasies of revenge, and to express them would reawaken the guilt that had kept those fantasies suppressed when they were children.

Others expressed an anxiety that could be summarized in this way: "If I do this to my parents, my children will do this to me. After all, I have abused or neglected them in ways similar to those I experienced." The group members had made strong efforts to control their impulses, but they knew all too well that they hurt their children. Now, if they expressed the protest, surely this gave license to their own children to express the fear, anger, and pain that they were feeling. If the children were going to express anger with the same intensity that the group members were being encouraged to express toward their own parents, they would not be able to endure it. They would dissolve in guilt.

Many of the group members felt a wide range of psychosomatic sensations during this time. Their hearts raced, they had headaches, and in the time between the sessions, they had insomnia and nightmares. The powerful effects of repression were being loosened. As this happened, new memories popped into their minds, first into their subconscious mind in the form of dreams and vague sensations, and then clearly into their conscious mind. At other times, they experienced a sense of lightness and energy as the effort to keep memories and sensations submerged became available for other activities. At still other times, they experienced the fear of changing. As the memories began to recur, they had to return to some aspects of stage 1 and experience the intensity of those feelings.

For this evening, the exercises were for the group members to learn to assert themselves with "Listen to me" when the person with whom they were trying to talk said, "I'm not interested," or "I am afraid to," or "I don't want to hear what you have to say." Another exercise involved teaching them to assert themselves appropriately and say, "Stop it," even when the people who were using or abusing them said, "But you deserve it," or "I can't stop it," or "I don't want to." They soon began to realize that saying these things to each other with increasing vigor and conviction was making a strong imprint on their minds. They began to realize that they would be able to use this in the real world, and use it they did.

After the exercises, when everybody had cooled down, they checked out. I assigned them homework again. This was now becoming so routine that by the time I said the word "homework," out would come the pencils and notebooks. "I want you to allow yourselves to reflect on the full extent of your anger. Don't hesitate to picture the fantasies of revenge and destruction. Picture who it would be and how close you ever came to expressing it." It wasn't hard for them to understand what I was talking about. Every child in a difficult situation fantasizes at some point about getting even. However, for children who were abused and neglected as these people were, those fantasies were hateful and very destructive. The problem was that they couldn't admit how destructive those fantasies were.

❖   ❖   ❖

Anna

We were asked to think about all the times past and present where we would have liked to say, "Stop it!" or "Listen to me!" I am finding that it is taking much less time to get in touch with the memories and feelings that connect with the homework assignments. As a matter of fact, I seem to be constantly musing on the assignments. I have burned meals, missed appointments, lost my thought in the middle of sentences, forgotten names, and caught myself lost for hours in daydreams. I seem to have quit functioning at my once "perfect" performance level and am on automatic pilot. It is as though I have to give up one realm of consciousness and control to get in touch with the other. I wonder if I will ever be able to fuse the two distant Annas. One seems so scatterbrained, yet feels so deeply and yearns for truth, while the other is so efficient and productive, and yet exists in a world made up of pretense and lies.

STOP IT (PAST AND PRESENT)

I would like to say, "Stop leering at me. Don't touch me that way. Quit joking, tickling, confusing, hurting, scaring, and using me." I'd like to say this to all the men in my life, because any man with whom I have been intimate has either sexually, emotionally, or physically abused me or neglected and abandoned me. As I imagine myself saying this to each of them, I feel such sadness, some shame and anger, but mostly a deep sadness.

I would like to tell my mother to stop fixing me for my own good. Stop manipulating, advising, nagging, complaining, ignoring, controlling, and being so ashamed of me. I want to cry and then scream at her, but I know she won't hear me. She never hears anything except the sound of her own wishes.

I want to tell my husband to stop constantly picking on our daughters—white with anger; yelling; shaking them; occasionally hitting; constant nagging about posture and picking up after themselves, length of skirts, makeup and boys; and then finally sexually abusing them—God, how I wish I'd made him stop it. I am filled with guilt and rage.

I also want to tell my husband to stop looking at other women, to quit criticizing me and others, to stop lying, and to stop making me invisible. Fear wells up inside when I think of confronting him. He might not want me anymore.

I wish I could have said "Stop it" to my mom, sister, brothers, relatives, the school kids, a few teachers, and the other adults who teased, tormented, harassed, or "corrected" me about my weight problem. I feel so ugly and sorry for myself when I think of my body and continual weight problems. The years of incredible cruelty of the kids scarred me deeply. Having no one to comfort or understand my pain marked me even more profoundly.

I'd like to say "Stop it" to my children's anger, disabilities, pain, neediness, childishness, or anything that makes me feel helpless or out of control. I want to let them have responsibilities and independence, but I don't know how. I find myself wanting to control them or push them out. I do not have natural instincts to rely on. No middle ground to trust.

LISTEN TO ME (PAST AND PRESENT)

"Listen to me, Mom." This is a cry that seems to have always been. "Mom, believe me, hear me, love me, protect me, help me, want me, be pleased with me, be proud of me, understand me, want to understand me, let me be me, love me, please."

To my husband, "Listen to me, LISTEN to me!" Listen to me means hear me, know me, respect me, love me, treasure me, accept me, be like me, agree with me. I am amazed and appalled at the progression of thought that came from this exercise. To listen to me I discovered really means don't challenge me. Agree with me or I'll know that you don't believe me, and maybe you do not even love me.

I realize that I accept being needed as a substitute for being loved. I produce to be accepted and valued. I want to be cherished. Maybe I'll never be cherished by someone; therefore, I'll always have to perform to win them. Hardly anyone phones any more. I can't "help" them, so they've gone away. I guess they only needed what I could do for them. The few who are left are treasures. They support me and ask nothing of me. They want my wholeness and are willing to stand with me as I face my pain. I am graced to count them as my friends. I feel for Krista, who has no one. How much can she bear without any outside support? I couldn't do it, and yet she scares me. I am glad we can't have relationships outside the group. I feel as though she would swallow me up.

Our lives unfold more each week as we feel safer with each other. I am deeply grieved when I hear of the horrible things that have happened in each life. This one small room seems to contain a full spectrum of degradation, abuse, and neglect. Things you only hear about and shudder at, things that don't happen to anyone you know, let alone yourself.

I want to say, "Stop it," to myself. "Stop being out of control, stop controlling, stop overeating. Stop. Stop. Stop being me. Stop being wrong, bad, fat. Stop."

I think we all felt shocked that Tanya could have blocked out her sexual abuse with her dad at 19. That she could have done so as a young child was so much easier to understand. That she could be going to a psychiatrist and be engaged and be having a sexual relationship with her father and no one knowing, not even her, is so hard to take in.

Lisa shared tonight a little more about the demonic presence that constantly harasses her. An incubus, a sexual relationship with a demon that she can't break. It seems really bizarre, especially to those who haven't had an experience with or belief in the demonic. We all try to believe each other, no matter how weird. It is all we can truly give. Tonight it may be too much to give for some.

Dr. Ney says Virginia is having problems at home. The Social Services are considering taking her children. We all are hit hard with the impact of Virginia's grief as a mother and with concern for the children's safety, children like we were. We feel torn, feel the complication of a many-sided problem and pain for everyone, not just the "child." It seems too much to take in and process as yet.

❖   ❖   ❖

WEEK 7

In spite of a harrowing week, everybody was present and ready to get on with business. They were beginning to form strong identifications with each other. This was helpful in that it provided support and encouragement. On the other hand, they sometimes saw in each other similarities that really did not exist. I had to warn them once again that they must not talk to each other outside the group. This is a standard group therapy rule, and it is designed to prevent subgrouping and the tendency to work outside of the group where the work cannot be analyzed.

Tonight Virginia looked quite composed. She was able to tell us what had been going on for the past two weeks. She apologized to everyone for not being there, but said she felt she wasn't able to handle the stress of doing the group and contending with her home situation. She talked more about a friend of hers who was talking about killing herself than she did about herself. It was clear to everybody in the group that Virginia was indicating her own despair. I made a mental note and was determined to follow her up. Unfortunately, it was the last time Virginia attended the group.

It's difficult to decide exactly which patients will benefit most from these groups. They have to be in enough distress that they prefer the difficulties of the group to their inner turmoil. They have to be strong enough to carry on when things get rough. They can't have more turmoil in their lives and in their minds than their egos can stand under the tremendous pressure of this kind of group psychotherapy.

Virginia certainly had a lot of distress. She was tough. After all she had been through, she had to be tough. But remembering those terrible experiences, plus trying to understand the intricate complexity of motives and feelings, takes a special kind of toughness. I thought she had it; otherwise, I would not have invited her to join the group. But I could be wrong. I had been wrong before and carefully had to help put together the broken pieces. Maybe Virginia knew best what she could take. She had a great eagerness to change, but there were too many things happening in her life. She felt she did not have the energy or the determination to carry on with the group.

As soon as everybody had checked out on their present state of health, we proceeded with the group exercise. They were to say to each other, in pairs, and with increasing emphasis, "Stop it, please," then "I want you to stop it," then "I insist that you stop it right now."

Although it sounds simple, most of the people in the group found it almost impossible to assert themselves properly. They couldn't look into each other's eyes, and when they tried to be assertive, they invariably smiled, giggled, or in some other way discounted their communication. There was a common tendency to raise one's eyebrows, a nonverbal expression of pleading. I pointed out that when accosted by a possible perpetrator, there were always three alternative reactions: (1) to plead for mercy, but this might result in invoking an automatic response of sadism from the aggressor; (2) to attack first, but this was sure to produce both fear and anger in the would-be perpetrator; (3) to look directly into the person's eyes, make an assertive statement, and treat the person as humanely as possible. This last would prevent an automatic reaction, give the person the best opportunity to think about what he or she was doing, and to be rational rather than animal-like in his or her responses.

Eventually, the group members became increasingly able to assert themselves and were able to look each other directly in the eyes, and to make firm, unambiguous statements with appropriate affect and the right kind of nonverbal expression to match the verbal statements. I had pointed out that I had used this technique with abused and neglected children because, if nothing else, it helped them stop any ongoing abuse from either adults or other children.

Tables 1 and 2 are samples of the type of responses we practiced. Similar statements are made about verbal abuse, emotional neglect, and sexual abuse. These are statements directed to the perpetrator. We need also a series of similar statements directed to the observer (Table 3).

TABLE 1
PHYSICAL ABUSE

Victim	Perpetrator	Victim
Why did you hit me, Mommy?	You deserved it! You were bad!	No, I didn't! I was not bad!
It hurt!		
Please don't hit me.	Shut up! I'm your parent!	Parents are supposed to love and nurture their children, not hit them!
Please stop it! I can't take it!	No, I won't stop! If you're not careful, you'll get something worse!	That's all you do. I don't like it when you threaten me!
I won't let you hit me! You're not going to scare me any more!	You take this! And this and this! Now get out of here!	No. You won't do that to me and I won't get out!
You can't frighten me any more! Now STOP!	Okay, then it's good-bye...good-bye forever!	You can abandon me, but I will look after myself!
Okay, you asked for it. Now you are really going to get it, you bastard!	No! Please don't!	Now you're getting what you deserve!

TABLE 2
PHYSICAL NEGLECT

Victim	Perpetrator	Victim
Mommy, why don't you look after me?	Don't be silly! You can look after yourself. I'm just going out to have a drink with my friends.	Why can't you see how much I need to be looked after?
Please don't leave me!	Shut up and stop hanging onto me! I'm going!	I won't be able to survive without you. Please don't leave me!
I won't let you leave me!	You can't stop me, Silly! I'm bigger than you are.	You are always using your size to threaten me!
Stay right here or I will...(tell someone, go to a neighbor, etc.).	You be careful and don't forget that your mother needs her time away; it's good for you, too.	Don't kid yourself. You are doing this for yourself, not for me or anyone else!
I insist that you stay here! You can't threaten me any more! I won't let you!	You can't stop me. Good-bye. It's good-bye forever!	If it's good-bye, then that's how it must be. I can look after myself. I'm a big person!
You think you're leaving? Well, I'm going to leave before you and you will never see me again! NEVER!	No. Please don't do that to me!	It's what you deserve after all the times you neglected me!

TABLE 3

Victim	Observer	Victim
Why didn't you do something?	I didn't know. Honest! How could I have known?	You should have known because you are my mother.
Yes, I know you knew. I told you. Remember?	No, you never told me. You may think you did, but you didn't tell me. I didn't know.	What was I supposed to do? Stand in the middle of the room and scream it?
Stop pretending you didn't know! You make me so mad when you do that!	I didn't know, and besides, I couldn't have done anything anyhow!	You were afraid to do anything to help me.
Now this is what happened to me. Listen, I will tell you all about it.	I don't want to listen. Don't say any more.	You are going to hear all of it, whether you like it or not!
You must believe me! It's all true.	You are making it up. You're just trying to create trouble.	No! It really happened, and I have other people who can vouch for me.
You must do something to stop this.	I can't do anything. Your mother would leave me. or Your father is too big. or Something worse will happen.	If you don't do something, I will!
I insist that you do something, and since you won't, I will, and I'll do it right now!	Please don't tell anyone. You frighten me.	There isn't any other way. I must do it. So here goes.

Obviously, the statements directed to the observer can apply in all situations, so the exercise won't have to be done five times here.

After the group exercise, Anna, whose turn it was to begin first, looked uncomfortable, and she finally blurted out that she was not accepted by Dr. Green. She said she thought it had something to do with the bad relationship she had had with her mother. She remembered how her mother had banged her head against the wall. This reinforced in her the feeling that she was not wanted. Sometimes she would fight back a little, but she always lost, after which she would begin wishing that she were dead so that her mother would understand how she felt. It was an attempt to express anger and vengeance, even if it was at the cost of her own life. Anna then spoke more directly about her anger toward her husband and how she had prayed in her mind that he would get "chewed up in a machine." She said it was hard to get in touch with her anger, but she admitted that she certainly had it. It was so hard, in fact, that she had tried to avoid doing the homework.

Krista stated that hers was a red-hot anger. In fact, it wasn't anger; it was rage. "I am so angry. They have never cared about me. I had this fantasy that I could stand there and yell at my brother, but I knew that I couldn't do it. I also knew that someday I am going to kill him. They are not going to get away with it."

The difference between Anna's and Krista's feelings of anger stemmed from a child's difficulty in dealing with anger. Most children can't feel or express anger because (1) they are afraid to destroy the parent upon whom they depend; (2) they fear retaliation; and (3) whenever they do, they are discounted by the parent's quips or belittling comments: "Ha, that's not really angry."

In an effort to deal with their anger, adults who were abused as children tend to deny it and express it in themselves or toward others in other feelings, or they feel some anger, but it is isolated to certain situations and certain people. Or they scapegoat one or two individuals, projecting onto them the source of their own anger and wanting the persons punished, often in a totally inappropriate way.

Lisa stated that she felt much like Krista, who also had been adopted as an infant. She began recognizing there was a deep anger toward her adoptive mother. It is almost as if the adoptive mother had taken her away from her own mother, but she also knew that the deeper anger was toward the birth mother who would dare to give her up. She wished that her mother were dead, and when Lisa was involved in satanism, she put a curse on her.

Now that we were beginning to touch the extent of the anger, it was amazing to see how powerful and destructive it was. I pointed out that becoming aware of one's anger and owning it was the first step toward dealing with the anger in such ways that one wouldn't do self-destructive things.

Amy said that her parents were always fighting and she hated it. Sometimes she would watch them and spend that night restlessly in her bed, fantasizing yelling at her father. The problem was that she was always afraid of being angry in that house because there was so much anger already. She had a feeling that adding to it might make the whole fragile structure of the home fly apart. She mentioned that her two brothers were filled with black rage and felt that somebody had to pay. One had, either accidently or purposely, stabbed the mother with scissors. Even though the mother was an angry person herself, she never had expressed that anger because she didn't seem to know what to do with it. Amy, reflecting on that the anger and hostility and how it had destroyed her life, eventually stated, "I want my life back."

Tanya also said she felt a deep anger, but she added that she could never get angry at her father because he was so pitiful, and when he wasn't pitiful, he was too angry and she was afraid of him. She remembered just wanting him dead. That alternated with a feeling of wanting to be dead herself and in this way letting them know how angry she was. She recognized that when she was angry at her mother, she acted sexually with her father. It was as if the mother, abdicating her role as mother and wife, was so removed that Tanya was going to assume those functions of a regular mother and throw them in her mother's face. In speaking about the incestual relationship with her father, she stated, "I sexually abused me." She looked startled upon hearing herself saying that. I pointed out that it really wasn't a slip.

Linda stated that she tried very hard never to allow herself to get angry, but at times it just came out. She would lose control, sometimes hitting her children. When she was trying hard to control herself, she would smash her hand against a wall and had broken her finger on one occasion. More frequently, she struggled so much with her anger that she felt she was going crazy. She had a strong urge to kill herself and to do so violently. She spoke simultaneously of herself and her mother when she said, "I would like to throw her around the room."

Shawna, the last in the circle, portrayed the feelings of all in the group. "I want my revenge to be slow and painful. I want them to hurt as much as they have hurt me."

It had been a particularly exhausting night's work. After that, one would think people would want to get home and into bed, but it was a dismal, wet night and they were caught between wanting to hurry home and not wanting to leave the security of the group.

In an effort to help them deal with the anger, I asked them as homework to try to trace all the fears behind the expression of their anger. I also asked them to look at the self-destructive things that they did that were really intended for other people.

❖   ❖   ❖

Anna

I am the first to share this week, and that is good because I feel consumed with what I need to share and would probably be out of tune with everyone else until I did. My heart pounds. I can feel it in my throat. Disapproval of the group, Dr. Ney, and Dr. Green looms in the forefront of my fears.

A deep breath. Last week after the meeting, I got in touch with the fact that I had been feeling nonacceptance by Dr. Green, and not just at last week's session; there has been a vague sense for several weeks that I hadn't been able to define. I sort of decided she wouldn't like me, that I wasn't her type. I felt like "fluff," overemotional, too "made-up" for her. When we were paired up for role playing, I looked into her eyes and saw her. I really saw her. Acceptance and compassion and caring—they were all there. I realized that I had projected my fears of what women in authority think of me onto her.

"Dr. Green, I am sorry." She graciously responded, and I could tell she was surprised by my admission.

After assigning last week's homework, Dr. Ney wanted us to role play again, using the same partners to practice getting in touch with our anger. I just couldn't do it. Dr. Green grabbed me by the shoulders and shook me, saying, "Get mad at me. I won't break. Do this!" to demonstrate how I could touch my anger. I was instantly overwhelmed; flooded with feelings of worthlessness, I began to sob. Her actions had stimulated the memory of a time when my mother had shaken me by the shoulders, banging my head against the wall. I can remember going cold and saying, "Why don't you just kill me while you're at it?" She stopped instantly and fled from my room. Whenever she was angry at me, I felt worthless, that she hated me, that I was always a problem—bad, fat, whiny, in the way, or something. I just wanted her to love me, to love me like she loved my brother and sister. When I try to find my anger toward my mother, I can't. I just wanted her to love me. I was very rebellious and angry as a teen but just can't seen to connect with it. "Why can't I feel my anger toward her?" Dr. Ney responds that "anger can be hot or cold" and asks the group if I were angry at my mother or not. They agreed that I had been, and still am, angry at my mother.

I hated my life and my husband. As a result of having had abusive baby sitters, he always took his kids' word over mine and gave them such power.

If I complained enough about it or caught them setting me up in front of him, he would rough them up, yell uncontrollably, totally losing his temper, and then blame me for making him do it. I learned quickly that I couldn't go to him with any "kid" problems. I stuffed all my feelings and anger inside until once again I would try to explain my position and needs, thus repeating the cycle. There were many times when I didn't please or measure up in some mysterious way and I would become "invisible." He might not go to bed with me until he decided I had paid my dues. My anger then was expressed in total despair and revenge. I would dream about his going to work and being killed on the job so that I could get away from him in an acceptable way, as a widow. I couldn't even consider a divorce: three destroyed marriages made me out to be a loser. I couldn't handle that. After I became a Christian, I used to hope and pray that God would take him away for his sin toward the kids and me. As the girls got older, he began to pick on them continuously. He became so competitive with them, emotionally and sometimes physically abusive, yelling, shaking, threatening, playing mind games, and giving the silent treatment. I wished he would change, go away, die—anything—just as long as he would leave them alone. My anger festered in my gut like a boiling broth. I hated what he did to them, and I hated my helplessness to stop him. And God...where was he?

As a child, and in every serious relationship, I would sometimes think that I would show them, that I would kill myself and they would be sorry. Again Dr. Ney points out the cold anger in wishing I were dead to show them. He continues, explaining how we first touch our pain and then we can feel the anger. I have to own my pain and experience it and then I will know my anger. I am afraid of knowing my anger. I think it could be very destructive and out of control.

All of us seem to be having a hard time with the role playing tonight. Dr. Ney interrupts us with an appalling story of a three-year-old. He asks us what he should teach a child who has been "buggered" and who he knows will be sent back to the same home. Even the wording of the question shocks us and commands our serious attention. He explains that the child needs to learn to protect himself by making an assertive statement and appealing to the perpetrator's humanity. This he teaches the child by role playing. We return to the task at hand, sobered and determined to push through our personal barriers.

The anger expressed around the room tonight was very disturbing for me. There seemed to be such a need to strike out and hurt those who hurt us. Some seemed to be filled with it. Wanting to do awful things to your parents seems just too profane. We shouldn't be feeling or speaking this way. It was just too evil. Shawna wanting to get even in the slowest and most painful way, Krista wanting to kill her family, Linda wanting to beat her mother up, Lisa and Tanya wanting their parents dead: this made us just like our parents. I am so afraid and confused. I am not angry at them for how they feel. I just don't want us to feel this way. I felt that way about my husband. Is a death wish toward one's parents so very different, so heinous?

WEEK 8

By this time, the group members had taken up fairly static positions in the room and had chosen regular role-playing partners. Although there was some discussion about changing, there seemed to be a natural affinity, and so they decided to stay with the ones they had.

The group was devastated to hear my report that Virginia would not return. I pointed out that I would continue to see her individually and hoped that she would join the next round of groups. I would keep an eye on the family and, if necessary, help deal with the home situation. Unfortunately, Virginia didn't even come for her individual appointments. I was able to find out that she was being cared for. But we were all worried.

Shawna, who was last the time before, was the first in this group. She began by saying that in the last group she had learned the value of keeping her eyebrows down when making assertive statements. It had worked at her office. She then talked about the self-destructive way in which she smoked or ate too much. As a child, she was teased about her baby fat, but later she gained weight and recognized that this was for protection. She could use being slim or fat to control attention from males. She said, "There is such power when you walk into a room. You look very attractive. All the eyes go in your direction." She then talked about her struggle with believing in the times when she had become so depressed and hopeless about it that she thought of killing herself with a knife. It was almost as if sticking a knife into herself, cutting out the fat, would be the best and most destructive, painful way she could do it.

Her role-play partner, Linda, said that she always became depressed around Christmas time and she anticipated that this Christmas would be a particularly depressing one. Normally she could make the effort to ensure that Christmas would at least be good for her children. Now she began to realize that something was stopping her from helping them, and she wasn't even making a wholehearted effort to get well. She also recognized that there was sarcasm behind her humor that usually came through. She could see the self-destructiveness of the sarcasm because it could alienate people. She recognized that she had been deliberately cruel to her mother, and wondered if there were any point in continuing their relationship. Relationships, particularly with men, were always hard. She mentioned that she preferred real men.

Tanya stated that she hated Christmas. She also tended to gain weight, and used it for a variety of reasons. She knew there was a sense in which she was eating in response to a self-statement or a parent's statement, "Here, take that." "I always thought I was fat. I guess I am passive/aggressive. I did sexual things with my father because I loved him and would do anything to make him happy. I also felt very destructive toward him. We are tied together, he and I. I know I can't succeed because he didn't. Yet he was always a financial success."

Lisa was looking brighter and said that she had had a good week emotionally, but that her life was "hell." "I also realize overeating is self-destructive. I also sit in the darkness sometimes and pretend I don't exist. It is as if I had died. I feel I have died. I don't know why I couldn't just accept living." This was a clue to something very deep in Lisa that I didn't see at the time, but now, reflecting on it, I begin to understand that something had died and she was just beginning to realize that.

Krista stated that even when she was fat, she thought she was thin. She found that the most self-destructive thing she did was always to be doubting herself. She had enormous difficulty with making up her mind. Others in the group chimed in about their great difficulty in accepting or loving themselves, mainly because they seldom, if ever, heard it from their parents.

I pointed out that children tend to doubt themselves more often than they doubt their parents' love. To doubt their parents' love is much more terrifying than to doubt their own ability to receive love. It is better for them to think, "I am not worthy of love," than it is to think, "My parents are unable to love."

I introduced a group exercise at this point in which each person, in turn, would state with as much sincerity as she could, "I love you." The next person was to respond with whatever she felt. The majority responded, "I doubt that."

Amy said, "There are some strange things happening. Even at a party, I find myself worrying so much that I get sick. Recently I had a temper tantrum like I have not had for a long time. I can't stand to hear my mother say, 'I am worried about you.' I wish she would grow up. I feel so guilty about the feelings I have for her."

Anna said that she had worked hard all week, as Anna was always wont to do. She had gained some insights, although she had slept little and her mind was in chaos. Still, she didn't lose herself. She mentioned that reality was coming back to her. "I hate her [her mother]. She never loved me. Some of that hate went up in smoke. I used to smoke three packs of cigarettes a day. I used food to punish myself and my husband, who never liked me fat. Then I was anorexic. 'I'll show them.'" And she could take off weight very rapidly. "Somehow I knew I had a need to be abused. It was as if there were a neon light on my forehead. I had boyfriends who abused me. I became addicted. Still there are some shadows that I can't quite identify. If I knew who they were, I would deal with them." I mentioned that it may be possible to make shapes out of those shadows, of painting with her eyes closed. Anna was a very successful painter.

This is another group exercise. In pairs, they said to one another: "It is your fault." And, with increasingly strong emphasis, "It isn't my fault."

We were now moving into the third phase. Guilt was a function of the possibility, even through fantasy, of destroying the person upon whom their lives and their futures depended. I asked them in their homework to think of those things about which they felt guilty and how that guilt influenced their lives.

❖   ❖   ❖

Anna

I Hate Me → I Hate Him → I Hate Mom

I can see that "I hate me" is safer than I hate him or Mom. If I hated those who look after me, who would care for me, who would protect me, who would love me? So hating and hurting myself became a habitual pattern that has caused much sorrow and destruction in both my life and others' lives. I want to stop hating and to start loving me, but it is frightening because that means I have to pass through those feelings that have always been too overwhelming to face: anger, hate, rage.

Several weeks ago, when my sister, Helen, called to see how I was doing, she asked my permission to talk to Mom about my abuse. She already had obtained my brother's permission. During her recent visit with Helen, Mom had been quizzing her and had apparently, when the desired information was not being furnished, asked pointedly, "Just what is wrong with Anna?" My sister's cautious response had been, "She is having some bad flashbacks from her childhood." Finally, after much prodding by Mom, she had to confide that they were abuse memories and that I was very troubled by them. Immediately Mom retorted that she really doubted it, that there couldn't be any way that had happened. My sister eventually declared, "You'd better get used to it; it happened to Steve, too." She further explained briefly one of the three incidents of sexual abuse that had occurred early in his childhood. Mom broke down, deeply grieving that such horrible things could have happened to her son. Tearfully, she answered my sister's many questions about dates, places, and people that would directly relate to my lost time frame. Helen shared that the conversation had ended with Mom's statement, "I hope she doesn't want to talk about this all the time now." Helen was glad I hadn't talked to Mom myself. Her denial and harshness would have been devastating. She promised to stand by me and to "be on my side, believing me no matter what I told her." I felt loved and safe. It felt so good to be believed. She was angry and her anger made me feel so protected. Before we hung up, I asked her to find out if I'd ever been left alone, without the rest of the kids and Mom. My worst memories included a season of ongoing violence and oral sexual abuse where I was alone.

As I thought about the call, I realized Mom didn't believe my story until my sister or my brother, whom she always believed, had confirmed it. As the impact of that sank in, powerful emotions erupted. "I am angry. I hate her. All I want is for her to love me." Both voices were screaming inside at the same time. "She weeps over one shared incident of my brother's and I have had years of horrible, violent abuse and not a tear, not even acknowledgment that it ever happened. She doesn't want to talk to me about it; she won't even talk to me about it. I hate her. She must hate me."

Three days later, Helen phoned again. After quizzing Mom about a possible family separation, she found out that I had been put in a foster home, my brother had been sent to relatives, and she had gone with Mom. Apparently, Mom had only one room with board for some months until she could afford an apartment where we could all be together. I hate her. She always looked after them. She never loved me like she loved them. My "inner child" had told the truth; I wasn't lying. I had been alone. I believe me. I am going to fight my doubts with persistence. I can trust me.

Remembering Dr. Ney's saying that "destructive things are angry things" helps me to focus on this week's homework.

ABUSIVE THINGS I DID TO MYSELF

Smoking—more than three packs a day—I must have wanted to get caught: I threw the butts on the roof and out the window instead of flushing them down the toilet. I was trying to meet some elusive need that could never be "filled" by puffing on a cigarette.

Overeating: Driven by the need for comfort, love, touch, affirmation, I found solace in food, a friend who never seemed to fail me. Yet in reality, its abuse caused me some of the deepest hurts of my life. I think I must have been subconsciously punishing myself, my mom, and my husbands with the lack of consistent control over my weight. I don't know how to stop.

Undereating: Desperate to be acceptable, sexual, desirable, wanted, or just desperate and angry because of ridicule and rejection, I quit eating. Dependency on food, hunger, or loneliness would drive me back to eating, then I'd vomit from the guilt of failure and fear of becoming fat, which led to deep depression, making me vulnerable again to the comfort of my "friend." During the short spells of "seeming control," I felt powerful, beautiful and sexual.

Relationships: All of my long-term relationships have been abusive in one way or another. "My men" all had problems with alcohol, drugs, or violence, or had some form of sexual dysfunction. Each of them was emotionally unavailable and powerfully controlling, often in a subtle passive/aggressive way. I tolerated their abuse of me as long as I did in each relationship by reasoning that I just needed to change, improve, try harder. The final good-bye was always preceded by abuse toward one of the kids. I seemed to think I deserved it, but I knew that they didn't. This pattern continued until I became a Christian, and then I put up with abuse toward the kids as well, somehow thinking it a greater wrong to separate and break up a Christian family: surely I only need to pray harder, submit more, fast, love, or have more faith. When I learned of incest in our home, I sent our daughters away to protect them, kept the boys at home, insisted that my husband get counsel, hid the terrible secret, and worked to keep it all together. Doing the right thing; protecting my husband's reputation; sticking by him; putting him first; protecting our marriage, the church, God, our boys, while sacrificing my daughters and myself. Once again repeating the old pattern of abuse and abandonment. Now, as I look back, I see that I was driven to make it work, to fix it or cure it, or I was no good, a failure.

Once again, the old voice haunts me, "You're fat, you're ugly, you're no good." My weight is steadily climbing. I want to start another diet, yet I know from years of experience that weight loss through dieting is only temporary. All that hard work and then failure again. I think I get back at my mother, my men, and myself by punishing us with my fat, but I don't know how to stop. I have passed this compulsion on to my children. I feel so helpless.

Shawna is sharing about her weight problems and says that she feels powerful and in control when she is thin and doesn't have to be in control or sexual when she is fat. The lights go on! I know that there is truth here for me. I focus on her words, letting them break through my stubborn resistance: eating can suppress sexual feelings. I can eat to suppress my own sexual feelings. I can get fat to suppress "their" sexual feelings toward me. It is not safe sexually if you are not fat. Dr. Ney is telling some-one, "Your body can speak what your mouth won't say." Thin, I am sexual. Fat, I am not sexual. Again, Dr. Ney's voice breaks my introspection, "Who are you saying 'stuff it' to?"

Linda begins her list, and I notice from the nods of agreement that we all seem to have sarcasm on our lists, our own special weapon to prevent intimacy. Tonight is one of the few nights so far where Dr. Ney explains some of our peculiar behaviors. "Sarcasm is a blunted hostility that forces laughter. It is indirect anger expressed in a sociably acceptable fashion. The tongue finds words that in childhood were unavailable, but now uses them against those who often don't deserve them: your mate, your chil-dren." The impact of his words hits us all.

3

Guilt: Dealing with Their Responsibility and Mine

When people are painfully traumatized, they feel a combination of anger and fear. Whether they express more of one or the other depends on their relative size as compared with the perpetrator and the situation in which they find themselves. That is, if they are bigger, they tend to be angry, and if they are smaller, they tend to be frightened. Chapters 1 and 2 dealt with the pain and the expressions of fear and anger. One expression of anger is the tendency to fantasize revenge. Children who are abused often have elaborate fantasies of murdering their parents, or they wish that the parents would be killed in an accident. Thus out of pain grow anger and fear, and out of anger and fear grows guilt. In this phase of the treatment, it is vital that each patient face the guilt that she has experienced and then learns how to deal with it.

For the purposes of this book, guilt is defined as "the emotional and/or rational perception that you have broken some universal law and must now experience the consequences." Guilt in some respects is that uncomfortable brief feeling that would arise if you were to hurl yourself off of a high building. "I have just broken the law of gravity. What a foolish thing I did. I wish I could unmake that decision. I know that I will soon experience the painful, if not fatal, consequences of that decision."

Feelings cannot always accurately discern whether a person has a real or an artificial guilt. Some people feel guilty when they are not (a type of false guilt). Others are guilty when they feel that they shouldn't be or are not clearly aware of any law that they have broken. People who are more aware of reality are more realistic in their assessment of guilt.

Children tend to feel guilty for a variety of reasons:

1. They fantasize aggression or accidents involving the parents who have harmed them.
2. They feel that their needs are impossibly large and would overwhelm their parents.

3. They blame themselves for any fault or failing of their parents, or fighting between them. They do this mainly because of their attempt to ensure the survival of a family on which their future depends.
4. They must blame themselves because to blame the parent is to face the impossibly hard reality that the parents are incapable of looking after them. If that were so, there would be no possibility of surviving.
5. They exaggerate the importance of the harm they have done.
6. They have intentionally or accidently hurt someone.
7. Many experience an existential or survivor guilt. They feel that they are not supposed to be alive. This feeling might arise because their mother suffered the loss of a baby during pregnancy or a sibling died in an accident or as a result of an illness. If a sibling is beaten, some children feel that they should have taken the beating instead. Since they did not, they sense that it may be about to happen to them in the near future. People who have an existential guilt not only feel that they should not be alive, but also that there is a temporarily suspended sentence (often a death sentence) hanging over them that some fate has decreed will soon have to be carried out.
8. Older children may also feel ontological guilt. This arises because they feel that they have not developed their full potential. It also occurs because of their self-destructive tendencies.

It is vitally important, within the group, to differentiate among fault, blame, and responsibility. Fault and blame have the moral connotation that someone should be punished. Responsibility is used in a more scientific sense of contributing to an event. If there is a tragic triangle whose existence depends on the contributions of the perpetrator, the victim, and the observer, then each must bear a portion of the responsibility for tragedy. Young children have a very strong sense of right and wrong. This results in a feeling that somebody is altogether to blame and somebody else is not to blame at all. Movies that show villainous cowboys wearing black hats and the good cowboys in white hats appeal to people with a primitive morality. Unfortunately, this distinction is not supported by scientific evidence.

The harsh facts show that some victims contribute to their own victimization. This is not to make them punishable, but to recognize a deeper tragedy that results from mistreatment in children. Children may contribute to their own victimization because:

1. In their desperate need for attention, they become passive and do not properly protest assault or protect themselves.
2. After being traumatized in the first instance, or neglected, they try to work out the origin of the conflict. They do this by reenacting the

tragedy by inciting people. For example, the physically abused child (even when placed in the most loving foster home) can provoke violence against himself or herself by his or her continued irritating, obnoxious, or destructive behavior.

3. They can be seduced partly because they are curious and partly because they can be titillated. Seduction is a little like hypnosis. It can only work if there is a tacit agreement that allows the seducer to proceed.

In my attempts to explain how victims contribute to their own victimization, I often encounter a very hostile response that leaves me somewhat bewildered. When I provide clinical examples or scientific evidence, I only seem to evoke more vehemence. I suspect that some of this comes from a childlike determination not to give up a feeling of innocence. The admission by victims that they contribute to their own victimization means that they are partly responsible for it and so no longer are entirely innocent. It is tantamount to giving up their childhood, which can only mean that they cannot become themselves.

The angry protest against this view also stems from the current politics of victimization in which those who are power hungry use those who are deprived or victimized by provoking in them a great sense of injustice—an injustice that can only be rectified by the person who wants the power. "Oh, you poor things! Nobody cares for you, but I do. I will make it right. Just join my army. Once we have defeated the enemy and taken power, we will make things right for you and your children." The problem is that once the people who head this movement gain power, they become just as victimizing as anybody else was. Unhappily, those who must be "innocent victims" (i.e., innocence that they insist on) will tend to go on being victims.

During this group, it became increasingly apparent that people will gradually gain an awareness that they are partially responsible. This is helped by a role play in which four patients participate—a perpetrator, a victim, an observer and the judge. Hopefully, the judge can assign a reasonable portion of responsibility to each of the others. Thus, if there has to be a total of 100 percent responsibility for the abuse or neglect, then 10 percent goes to the victim, 50 percent to the perpetrator, and 40 percent to the observer. Obviously, no judge can rule in this way, but it helps the patients to realize just how tragedies have multiple contributors.

When a person doesn't have to be innocent, others don't have to be guilty. They can be treated more as individuals. One woman admitted that she set herself up for a rape by going to a party at a lake as the only woman among six men, and then staying around even after it was obvious what was going to happen. But it is as irresponsible to accept all the blame as it is to accept no blame.

It appears that most people who have been injured, abused, misused, or taken advantage of in any way, want their "day in court." They want to put forward their most persuasive arguments and have their innocence declared to the world. Often their arguments have been rehearsed for many years. This role play gives them the opportunity fully to justify their complaint.

It becomes easier for patients who were abused as children to recognize their partial responsibility when they realize that their parents were probably victims themselves. This does not mean that they should not be held accountable for what they did, but it does mean that there were mitigating circumstances. Many of their parents have, in fact, experienced greater abuse than have the patients described in this book.

Parents who were poorly nurtured as children tend to doubt their ability to control their own needs. As an expression of this, when they become parents, they tend to be excessively controlling of their child's desire to have his or her needs met. For example, "Don't eat so much, Jane, or you won't be hungry enough for supper," or "If you don't get up now, you'll go on sleeping for the rest of your life." Children who have these continual prohibitions placed on them cannot trust their own inner desires and doubt whether they could ever be satisfied. They feel guilty about these inner desires and try to keep them hidden. Adults who were deprived as children cannot ask for what they really need. They don't want to know the truth. "Either my parents are incapable of meeting my needs, or I am unworthy of their love." Both truths are devastating.

Those who do not clearly recognize their tendency to re-create their tragic history can reflect upon various patterns in their lives. Often, they repeatedly select the same work situation or partner. After a brief and intense relationship, they find that tragedy repeats itself. They break the relationship and mutter to themselves, "I can't believe I did this again." The fact that they repeat their own tragic history makes some people feel very guilty.

WEEK 9

In response to the question posed the week before, all had worked very hard but were ambivalent about sharing what they had learned. The idea behind the homework was that it used the time between sessions to good value. It directed their thoughts. Otherwise, they would be working in a random way, and although that could have been useful, it did not promote the direction of the treatment that I felt was absolutely essential. It might be debated that the random associations or thoughts coming out of the subconscious provide a more direct route to conflicts. However, it wasn't just uncovering the routes to conflicts or gaining new insights that was important, it also was learning new skills. It was making progress that was so essential to this therapy.

Shawna, feeling exhausted but determined to work hard on her treatment, had actually taken two weeks off from her job. During that time, she had allowed herself, and her husband had permitted her, to regress. Now she was feeling guilty for taking the time, but during that period, she had been able to think back about her incestuous relationship with her father. She felt that she had caused the abuse mainly because she didn't do anything to stop her father and because she hadn't done anything to stop him from abusing others. She wanted him to know, but had never said, that having sex with him and "I love you" were not the same thing. Yet there were times when she did enjoy it. "I am trying to be honest." By being honest she meant that she had to look at other guilts. The hardest, she stated, was that she had had an abortion while in her early 20s.

Anna stated that almost everything she did made her feel guilty. She felt that her guilt was partly a result of her mother's lack of guilt. Her mother claimed the real problem was that Anna was a very guilt-ridden person. Anna did not agree. I wondered if she wanted to fix her mother's guilt although, on the surface, she wanted to unload her anger. In doing so, she was afraid of what it might do to those around her. Somehow, in dealing with these feelings, particularly the anger and the guilt, she was beginning to realize that there was a limit to her capacity to enjoy life.

"I don't pray well, but I try," Tanya, who normally followed Anna, stated. "When I am guilty, I pray a lot. I am not sure what it does, but I think it helps. I realize that my guilt leads to getting other things all mixed up." In turning to Anna, she said, "It is amazing that you let me know you. I have so many secrets about myself. I can't let anybody know me, but you give me such a good example. I have had to pretend so many things that weren't there."

I pointed out that the shame from carrying secrets became, for many children, "I am ashamed of myself." Children carry secrets. They are not even aware of their potential destructiveness. Usually it far outweighs the reality. They think that they possess a much greater power than they really have.

"I didn't do my homework. I didn't have time to write down the homework." Everyone knew that Lisa was making excuses. Above all, she had terrible things to hide, and these she blamed on her inability to remember. It was interesting, however, that when she did begin to talk, she always stopped at a certain place, as if what was to follow could not be tolerated or, if tolerated, would result in her rejection by the group. "I allow abusers to put their guilt on me. I don't know why they abuse me because they are guilty, but they do, and I share their guilt. I frequently also feel guilty about feeling angry, and it is an enormous anger." She spoke about her difficulty in remembering, and then said, "I don't want to go into it any-more."

Children obviously are very curious about what goes on in their families. They want to know and they don't. They are afraid to find out in case that it might be such an overwhelming bit of information that they cannot deal with it. Therefore, they don't ask, but they listen and watch carefully, trying to put things together. It would be wonderful if children were always able to ask questions and receive direct and honest answers, but there are some things that parents shouldn't share with their children. My rule had always been: don't share with your children problems they cannot do anything to fix. These are usually marital and financial problems, but there are others.

The guilt with which most children have the greatest difficulty is the feeling that they do not deserve the good things their parents give them. Parents who were neglected make a big display of giving their children the things they themselves did not have as children. This only serves to make the children feel guilty. When they reject or rebel, the frequent intimation is, "You don't deserve all these good things." Why? "Because you are bad."

❖   ❖   ❖

Anna

I am exhausted all the time. My joints hurt. I feel and look lousy. This therapy consumes me; I think about it day and night. My life outside of "group" is almost nonexistent. The work is hard but it is the closest I've ever been to truth and I hunger after it. I am beginning to trust myself, to own my memories, and for the first time in my life, the seemingly unrelated pieces of my chaotic puzzle are fitting. Puzzle piece 1: Last night, as my husband undressed in our room, I hid my head as usual. I've never been able to look at him naked unless we are making love, and then I really enjoy his body. As I lay there with my head covered, I could feel deep shame rising. I let it consume me. With it came the memory of the man who had grabbed me toward his naked body, pushing my face into his limp penis, holding me hard against him until erection, and forcing oral sex to ejaculation. I understood. Sorrow swept over me like a flood. My embarrassment over my husband's unstimulated body was not just because I was prudish; I had been wounded. Now that I understood, I knew I could be free. Puzzle piece 2: Bathing had been a scene of distress since puberty. Skin irritation, including intense heat, itching, and redness, develops immediately after contact with water by bathing or showering, but not by swimming. We tried every imaginable suggestion—soap, no soap, hot water, cold water, shower only, bath only—resolving nothing. I settled for daily sponge washes. Now I am certain that the allergy must be connected with the near drowning death threats in that bathtub that were meant to silence me, especially since the water allergy parallels my sexual development. I am eager to discover the roots of my other phobias, fears, allergies, and sicknesses, and become free.

Mom phoned again. "I've been talking to Helen. She told me that you were sexually abused. Dad always says I am naive. I guess I am. When I see and hear things about sexual abuse to others, I feel so bad. I can't believe it happened to my little girl." Beginning to cry, she continued, "I don't sleep very well as you know, and now I lay there thinking about it—trying to figure how it happened. I don't know how it could have happened with me not having seen something. Especially when I bathed you. There were never any marks. I can't believe it." Sobering, she said, "I believe you, but it's so hard to believe it happened. I'll try to remember what I can to help you." She seemed really upset, sad, helpless. I could feel her pain, but I never fixed it. I never absolved her by saying she couldn't have helped it. I just listened. I didn't feel so angry at her any more. I believed that she didn't know of my abuse and I believed that she was suffering. I felt so sad—not mad anymore, just so sad. I could still get in touch with my anger when I thought about my teen years, when she had to be in control of everything and didn't let me be a separate person, a separate thinking being. As for blaming her, I guess I have blamed her for all my troubles in some way. Now I want to know who the shadows were who abused me, faces and names with the bodies. I want to deal with them, not with my mother. As I thought about Mom's call, I realized that I could have said, "That's okay, Mom," but I didn't. I didn't, and that is what is so strange. Make her happy, make her not sad, make her not angry. That is what I've always done before. This time I just let it be there.

This depression won't lift. I feel wasted. I didn't know how she would feel so I justified my anger toward her. I have such grandiose ideas of myself. I can make everyone happy. I am responsible for making everyone happy. My being good or bad depends on "if they are happy or angry." I wish I hadn't heard her sadness, then I could blame her and be angry at her. She's feeling guilty. She's not a mean, ugly person. I want to blame someone. I want to be angry at someone. I want the world to say, "Poor you."

The group is slow at getting started. They are fooling around. It makes me irritable. We are wasting time. I am here to work. Fooling around is childish, foreign, and not okay. It is uncomfortable. As I share my discomfort with the group, I tell them that I don't play well and would like to learn. Some of them respond as though I had scolded them, others understood that I saw my need to relax and to change, and one argued that I played well already. We were in good form tonight. My turn to share my homework.

I feel guilty when and *What did I do about it?*
- I felt guilty when I overate so I'd throw up and then feel guilty for throwing up so I quit eating and became anorexic.
- I felt guilty when I stole food because of the driving hunger so I quit dieting or starving and ate.
- I felt guilty when I was fat, expressing it by beating myself with an angry hateful attitude toward my body. Once, as a young teenager, I acted out the hate by literally beating my own body with my clenched fists.
- Today when my weight is too high, my guilt takes the form of depression. I want to stay home and hide my body.
- I feel guilty when I eat chocolate bars, rich desserts, or too much bread; drink milk; or have seconds or more than one alcoholic beverage. I find that I usually avoid these foods altogether or have them with "safe" people.
- I feel tremendous guilt if my parents, husband, children, friends, or anyone (even the telephone operator) is angry at me or is hurt by what I have said or done. I have to fix the anger, chaos, or upset *now* or elaborately defend myself.
- I have deep feelings of guilt connected with masturbation. I learned to control or stuff my feelings and rarely relieved sexual feelings or frustrations in this way because of the intensity of the guilt.
- Sexual thoughts or feelings aroused toward anyone except my husband cause me shame. As soon as I recognize their presence, I shut them down, while denying they even existed.
- I often feel guilty for my husband's, children's, or church's problems. I try to fix them all.
- I feel guilty when I win a game played by myself, thinking I must have cheated, even though I know I haven't.
- I can see that to resolve my guilt, I swing from fixing, rescuing, and controlling to denial.

Dr. Ney says that because of the guilt I feel when I am angry at my mom, I switch the anger to myself. That makes sense. It is much safer to get angry at myself than at my parent. He says, "A deep sense of self-doubt on the part of children can come from knowing that a parent doesn't love them, but because that is too hard to accept, they doubt the truth of their own feelings." They would rather believe that they are wrong, that their feelings are wrong, than to believe that their parent doesn't love them. I can be angry that I was abused. This anger is not directed at anyone, just at what happened.

I realize that I am afraid to confront my stepdad (and other men) because I fear his rejection, anger, and eventual abandonment. This is in contrast to the apprehension I feel about confronting Mom (and other women), which is concerned more with offending, hurting, or causing irreversible pain for her.

Several weeks ago, I went to Tasha after the group and shared my frustrations about Amy's rescuing. Tonight, when she started again, Dr. Ney stopped her and reminded her that she had admitted to a problem with fixing others and that he and Dr. Green were here to help her get over this difficulty by pointing it out whenever it came up. She was terribly embarrassed, as any of us would have been. Being corrected, and in front of the group, is really hard to take. I guess it's that overwhelming need that all of us in this group seem to have to "defend our innocence."

❖   ❖   ❖

WEEK 10

As this session got under way, it was obvious that people were having difficulties. Only five group members were there; Amy and Linda were missing. Dr. Green also was absent.

Humankind has never been particularly good at dealing with guilt and responsibility. The vast majority of people prefer to put the onus on somebody else. Scapegoating seems to be, and to have been, universal throughout time and in all societies. I had noted that children sacrifice themselves in an attempt to preserve the group. It appears that the young virgins who once were chosen to be thrown into a semiactive volcano in Mexico never tried to escape. They did not have to be imprisoned. It seemed they considered it an honor to die in that way, for the preservation of the group, which sacrificed children to appease the gods, who would then send rain and great fertility.

Tanya stated that she didn't have a good sense of her family, just of her father and herself. Her mother was a hazy image in the background. She was preoccupied with her father. "His lack of stability and his unpredictability affected the whole family. My mother was sad, but she always tried to make my father happy. To keep herself from going under, she spent hours and hours talking to me and I had to listen. I ended up feeling guilty and responsible for the whole mess."

Lisa looked a little embarrassed, admitting that this time she had written down the homework, but that nothing would come except some sense that she had died. I asked whether it was possible that she had been so close to death that she did die, and that she had died for her family. Upon my having said this, she looked very startled. Something was beginning to focus in her memory.

I no sooner had mentioned this when Anna, out of turn, broke in, "I feel like I was floating in a bathtub and I was drowning." Lisa said, "I don't know what tears at me, but I know that somehow I helped what happened. I can remember being taken away and asking, 'Mommy, where are you?' Not only did she reject me, but I know I rejected her at a very early age."

Krista stated that she had been adopted at two weeks of age, which she could remember. "Somehow I feel that my mother didn't want to give me up. Even before I was told, I knew my adopting family wasn't part of me."

Usually I waited for everybody to report on their homework, but sometimes it seemed better to interrupt with a group exercise. In this instance, I asked each in turn to say to her partner, "Please listen to me." The partner was to return with, "No, I won't. You are not worth listening to. I don't want to hear what you have to say." Then, with greater emphasis, the initiator would plead that she had to be heard. There was something she had to say. Having finished, we then went on to talk about the wounds that parents felt their children had inflicted on them. The parent was given the opportunity to say, "You hurt/confused/wounded me." The group member was encouraged to say, "Yes, I hurt you, but I was hurt so much more."

Krista stated, "My father never talked to me. I was trained to socialize, to put on a performance and I always did a good job at it, but it wasn't me. There were two sides of me. I have had such enormous difficulty putting them together. I hid my feelings and went along with theirs but it gave me such a sense of unreality. It is almost as if I were saying, 'Okay, I am bad, so I will show you I can be a nice person.' I have gone through tons of abusive friendships, but the worst is my parents. They joked that they would sell me because I was such a bad child. No one comforted me. Somehow I feel they would have killed me. Ever since, I have lost a lot of enjoyment getting to know who I really was."

Anna, who had been very upset by Krista and her emotive outburst, said, "The only screaming I can tolerate is my own. I have gained some insights. I begin to realize how much I am afraid to be cut off. My mother didn't protect me from anything. I hope I am a better mother than my mother was. I need to write to my children so that they can be free. Their freedom will cost me a great deal. I feel so ripped off and incredibly sad. I was never able to be a child. Even if I wanted to be, I was told, 'Don't be such a baby.' They never allowed me to be a child, and they were always asking me to do and be something that children would never do or be."

Shawna was looking intently at Anna. "I don't know what you mean by that, but somehow it is important to me. I was there to protect my parents, who were always fighting. They always fought more intensely at Christmas time. I felt like a crisis worker, always having to intervene. I still look after them. I never get to have fun because I am burdened with such enormous responsibility. I have a feeling that there is an enormous burden on my back and I can't get rid of it. It makes me even older." And indeed, Shawna tended to hunch over and deform her otherwise beautiful posture.

Another hard, long night. This one, in particular, was difficult for me because I could feel the hostility between Anna and Krista, and much of it may have been stirred up by me. It wasn't easy for them to talk about guilt and family. As homework, I asked them to think about scapegoating and to identify the person who was most likely to blame for the difficulties in their life if they didn't take the blame themselves. I wanted them to think a little more clearly about who was responsible for the enormous difficulties that they still got into.

At this point, I felt it was important to discuss with the group the concept of shared responsibility: the model of the perpetrator, victim, and observer.

❖   ❖   ❖

Anna

This is the format for the pre-Christmas week's homework.

Think about your family and its structure:
- What did I do to make it stable?
- What would have happened if I didn't do it?
- What did it cost me (in childhood)?

In describing the homework, Dr. Ney often gave us a word picture to help us get in touch with forgotten childhood feelings. For this particular assignment, he had us picture an argument between our parents and then think about our reaction. He told us, after we had been given reasonable time to identify our own responses, that children usually get in between and stop the fight, often by transferring the blame to themselves. I couldn't remember one fight of my parents, stepparents, or foster parents, but could identify with my own children's response. That was hard, to recognize your own children behaving in such a self-destructive manner.

FAMILY STRUCTURE, ONE TO SIX YEARS OLD (PRIMARILY AS TOLD TO ME)

1. Mentally ill, largely absent father, abusive toward me.
2. Codependant mother, mainly absent due to illness and employment.
3. Older and "much loved" brother and sister (favored by parents and grandparents).

I tried to make my world stable by clinging to my mother, wimpy, whiny, and fearful. I thought "they" would all go away if I didn't watch and hang on. This behavior cost me freedom, laughter, play, delight, innocence, and trust.

FAMILY STRUCTURE, SIX TO 12 YEARS OLD (PARTIALLY AS TOLD TO ME AND PARTIALLY MY MEMORIES)

1. Compulsive/addictive stepfather.
2. Codependant mother.

Both were extremely controlling—he silently and subtly, she overtly. Manipulation, guilt, and fear were the tools of obedience.

3. My sister was the family hero, claiming approval and appreciation for her very presence. My brother was the surrogate mate from his first years through preadolescence. I had the lost child role: food addict, bookworm, academic achiever, lonely and unimportant.

I did as I was told to maintain family stability. I didn't rock the boat, ate in my loneliness, masturbated for affection, lived in my room or at a neighbor's. I was afraid that if I did upset the status quo, I would incur their anger and be sent away.

This avoidance of interaction with the rest of my family and the lack of truth and expression of feelings cost me the fun and friendships of childhood. Play without worry, self-acceptance, development of my creative bent, and expression of my growing intellect were lost to me. Habits that were developed to fill the place of love, acceptance and encouragement still haunt me today.

FAMILY STRUCTURE, 12 TO 18 YEARS OLD

1. Same parental patterns.
2. My sister stayed the hero, my brother became the family mascot, and I switched to scapegoat. Rebellion against the harsh control over my mind and the subtle abuse of my body caused such con-

flict and confusion that I defied every authority, at home and at school.

If I hadn't been the difficulty, their marriage would have had problems. This was put to the test when we all left home in the same year. The marriage conflicts came out of hiding and have continually intensified over the years. All that remains of the marriage is a cold war.

Being the scapegoat cost me "loving me" and, as it goes, others' loving and accepting me. It cost me the exploration of my creative, intuitive being, as well as the beauty of youth and innocence. I never tasted the joy and anticipation of being all I could be as a young, healthy woman leaving home to embrace her future. I feel ripped off! I was angry and incredibly sad.

My parents don't know who I am. They never took the time to know their child. Now, today, my husband doesn't know me. I can talk to him for the longest time, trying to communicate my feelings or explain my problems, yet never seem to really get to the point. I have hidden my true feelings for so long that I can't find them even when I try so hard and so much depends upon it.

The mental recording of Mom's last phone call has tugged at my mind constantly. The questions, "Who is she really feeling for? Is she hurting for me or herself?" keep plaguing me like an old familiar tune that rehearses unbeckoned. I realize that her own pain is quite likely all she can feel at this point. I have concluded that to be liberated to deal with her, I must write to my own children and free myself of guilt and accept my responsibilities as a mother. I think this will allow me to be more honest with myself and not to mix up my mothering with hers.

We all seemed to be anything but enthusiastic regarding the Christmas holidays. However, when we were told there would be no break and that homework and showing up on the 27th were expected, a round of groans clearly expressed our disapproval. Dr. Ney said we were at a very difficult stage of our therapy and continuity was essential. Settling back down, some of us shared our fears or apathy about the holiday season. I shared that I had been particularly down about Christmas this year, the first I can remember where I wasn't anticipating the fun. I dreaded upcoming family get-togethers. I felt lonely, afraid, unable and unwilling to play the role expected of me. As I sat one morning in quiet meditation before the Lord, I sensed a child sitting under a beautiful tree decorated with green tinsel and red balls. She was sitting all alone, watching another child dancing, laughing, making people happy. As she watched, she understood that the child wasn't genuine, but phony and hollow. Just to stay quiet under the tree in her loneliness was difficult but real. As the image faded, understanding rose. I am sitting, a lost, lonely, sad child. The "other" one gets up and "dances life's game," but I am still sitting. No more will that other one get to pretend that she is me; she is dying. (Little did I know at the time how prophetic those words were to be.) I will stay here with the lost, lonely, sad child until she is ready and we'll get up and live life together. Death to the phony, people-pleasing self wouldn't be easy, but would be lonely, hard work. But it would be okay—more than okay, it was right, it was truth and the way to life. Peace was mine as I realized that this Christmas I could be myself, no pretense, just me. Dr. Green seemed really to connect with my "sightless vision," affirming me and my interpretation.

As our meeting was closing and the homework assigned, Dr. Ney explained the unending triangle of perpetrator Ö victim Ö observer.

There was much upset in the room. People were arguing with him about the impossibility of a child's being responsible for anything. There was no way that a child or a baby could do anything to encourage or deserve sexual abuse, violence, or abandonment. Sexual abuse seemed to bring the loudest and most repetitious complaints. I didn't get into the debate. I couldn't think past my exploding emotions. As we were dismissed, I fled to the bathroom.

❖   ❖   ❖

WEEK 11

In response to the homework and as a consequence of the struggles the group had been going through the last week, everybody looked wan, almost holding their breaths in anticipation of what might happen next. Tanya talked of the difficult relationship she had with her son, Paul, and how it was straining her time and energy. Krista discussed being so stressed that she thought that maybe this might be the time to turn the other cheek and avoid any further confrontations with her family. Linda had been greatly churned up by the previous week's discussion of her abortion and she was beginning to lose a lot of sleep. Still she hung in, with three jobs and a little family to look after. Anna talked of her struggles with one of her children, her weight, and her husband. Lisa looked phlegmatic, but obviously there was a great deal more going on than met the eye. Shawna didn't have much to report concerning her week, but, as she often did, with a bit of encouragement and plenty of time, she tended to become less laconic.

This evening, Krista began, and it wasn't long before her eyes were filled with tears. Always with the tears came anger, as if she were angry at the fact that she was crying or needed to cry in order to deal with the issues or had been made to cry as a child. She was struggling with the whole business of responsibility. She couldn't believe that somehow she was responsible, though intellectually she knew it was true that she was angry at her parents for letting her brother abuse her so frequently, so obviously, so harshly. "I don't want to believe you. Aren't all adults responsible for their own actions? Can't a 60-year-old man stop himself? On the other hand, I feel emotionally that it is all my fault. How am I ever going to get this together? My mind says that, as a child, I wasn't at fault. The adults were. My emotions tell me it was all my fault. You are trying to tell me it is partly my fault."

I tried to point out that the core person in an adult abused as a child knows that it wasn't right, but that the outside person, if such a distinction can be made, has to accommodate to the situation, and will begin to accept gradually, and then almost completely, that he or she was the reason for being abused. In actual fact, the model we use provided the necessity for the perpetrator, victim, and observer all to recognize their contributions to the initiation and continuation of abuse. How much was whose responsibility, God only knows. But it was much more important that they accepted their responsibilities because until they did so, they would all go on just being victims. Victims are helpless. Victims don't take charge of their lives. Victims continually complain to other people so that friends and relatives eventually are driven away. Yet the world would much prefer to have a simple paradigm in which the victims and the observers were innocent and only the perpetrators had fault. If this could be proved, then nobody else would have to feel guilty. The guilt would lessen to the extent that they could scapegoat the perpetrator.

Anna not only was angry, but she was direct. "I am angry with you, Dr. Ney, as I have been at no other time in my life. I am so angry that it feels like some kind of electric shock across my chest. I am angry and hurt and I feel betrayed. All my life, I have wanted to be able to blame somebody really badly. I have begun to understand how people have hurt me. I felt enormous relief in being able to blame somebody, and now you are taking that away. I was beginning to blame my mother because I knew that if she only had recognized what was going on, she could have taken me out of it. Now I am beginning to realize that I have kept bad people around me so that I could always be the innocent one. I could forgive my mother if only she would take her share of the responsibility. It hurts so much when other people deny their part."

Anna was an artist, and in many ways a poet. When she became excited, she was quite eloquent. "Blame is dead. Who is really responsible? Is it my parents or their parents or the parents before them? Or God? I feel

I was marked from the womb and had this awful need to be loved. It shows in my body language."

I was almost overwhelmed by the intensity of the emotion in the group. I was finding it difficult to help them gain an insight. It was awful having to give children the heavy responsibility of defending themselves against abuse and neglect. Children should have the opportunity to be free and almost irresponsible. They should be innocent so that they can investigate the world, yet much of my time in dealing with children who were abused is spent teaching them to assume responsibility and defend themselves. It is never just what happens to children. There should be somebody always rushing to their defense. But they can't just defend children; they have to defend the parents too. In all this confusion, it was difficult for the group to see the answers, and it was because of this that they were beginning to despair.

Children need to believe that their parents are responsible. The world would be much too frightening a place if they were irresponsible. Children need to believe that their parents are responsible, and that if they are guilty of being irresponsible, they can be punished, and that if they are punished, they might change and behave in a much more responsible way for the children. But children are wise enough to understand that society's usual way of trying to correct the parents (that is, by sending them to jail) does little more than alienate the parents in time, place, and emotion. There is hope in blame. If someone can be blamed, he or she can be punished, and if the person can be punished, he or she might change. It's no wonder that people want to blame someone. In a childlike way, they feel that this would correct the problems they experienced as children.

Shawna was as agitated as I ever had seen her. "I blame pretty much everybody. I blame the doctors a lot. I blame my brother a lot. I can always make it his fault. Now I am beginning to see it was partly my fault. Why didn't I say something? Why didn't I stop him?"

Linda had a similar theme. "I used to blame everybody except myself. I do take full responsibility for what I do to my children, and it is pretty horrible. It's not fair. Inside I know I am a good person, but I lose control. I never blamed my father before, but I am beginning to blame him."

Amy's pregnancy was beginning to show more and more and there were dark circles under her eyes, more from loss of sleep and of reasonable nutrition than from the pregnancy per se. "It's very stressful now that Sam is home. I keep trying hard to trust him with the baby, but I am afraid he is going to hurt it. There is something missing. My stupid parents ruined my small life. I feel so empty and weird. It's not right what happened to me. I wanted to hit her. Is it normal? No, it's not normal. I didn't want a weak mom. Now I know the truth. She is a weak mom. Mom, why were you so weak? Why didn't you do something for me?"

At this point, it seemed appropriate to deal with that very theme, so we engaged in an exercise of question and answer, each taking a turn with the other. The question was, "What could I have done with my life if I had had a reasonable childhood?"

This was two days after Christmas. None of the group had had an enjoyable Christmas. Tanya stated, "I came back from a visit early because the group was so important and I was not enjoying myself. I believe God is responsible. I spent so much of my life trying to figure out my parents. I assumed it was all my fault. I don't think my father could admit it was his fault. Why was he so weak? Who made you not my daddy? Why can't I fix you? I felt God deserted me. It was always too late to tell my mom. I should have done it earlier. Maybe she knew. It is so important to know. Why didn't she know? I began to think that maybe I was crazy. I guess I always thought I was crazy."

The tension was getting to Lisa, who was not her usual, rather immobile self. "I know who was responsible. I don't want to be the victim or the perpetrator. The whole cycle is becoming clear to me. I can now understand perpetrators. I can see why they are perpetrators. I think my mother tried to kill me. That is what it seems to be. I keep getting involved with really evil people, but I can't go on fighting it. Why am I drawn to them? I hate it and I am fascinated. I am a good person and I love God. It is not who I am."

The grief, anger, and relief that were expressed were difficult to listen to. No one wanted to brave the cold, bitter night, but before I was able to wind up the group, Tanya, Shawna, and Linda found reasons to leave early. They left looking so hopeless that I almost wanted to chase after them to check out whether they were going to be all right. The time between the group sessions might be hard work for them, but it was a time of great worry for me.

❖   ❖   ❖

Anna

It wasn't my turn to share first tonight, but I informed the group that I had to clear up something before we started. Last week, when Dr. Ney described the homework, using the perpetually alternating perpetrator—victim—observer triangle, I felt intense emotions. I couldn't isolate any one emotion specifically; it was a turbulent mixture of anger, hurt, frustration, and rage. A deep inner turmoil boiling to the surface. At dismissal, when I dashed to the bathroom, I choked out sobs that caused an electric shock type of pain across my chest and shoulders and down my arms. It scared me. I hung on to the sink scarcely breathing, fearing that any movement might make it worse. I had no idea what was happening. I wondered momentarily if I were having a heart attack. It lasted several minutes, briefly starting again twice more when I tried to move. After about five or six minutes, I was able to compose myself and prepare to leave. As I left, both Tanya and Shelly saw my upset and tried to console me by sharing that they didn't think babies could be responsible for any part of their own abuse. I barely acknowledged them while fleeing for the safety of my car.

Anger and hurt consumed me as I drove home, and for a long time after. Shaken and still a little frightened, I lay in bed for some time before I was able to calm down enough to examine the night's confusion. As I reflected, I discovered several things. First, I was furious at Dr. Ney for even suggesting that I was in any way responsible for the abuse I had endured. I felt betrayed by him. Finally, I was beginning to understand myself. I was coming out of denial. The blackness over my memories was lifting and my life was making sense for the very first time. The incredible weight of "guilt" that I'd never recognized or understood was leaving. I was beginning to trust him, Dr. Green, the group, my "inner child," my memories, myself, and in only a few seconds, he had destroyed my hope and budding trust. The whole thing came crashing down on me. I hated him. I wasn't coming back! I had no one to blame. I want to blame someone so badly! He's taking it all away. Let me blame someone!

Even though I never remembered the abuse until a few months ago, I guess I always wanted to blame someone. Deep inside I wanted to blame, my mother mostly. If only she hadn't

If only she had…
If only she…
If only….

I don't think she ever could have done anything "right enough" to heal my hurts then. Even if she had been a loving, comforting mom, I'd have had to find someone else to be the bad guy. I am innocent and I'll prove it! I kept having "bad guys" around me, all my life. I could be the good, innocent one. I even thought that I could forgive Mom. Is she, too, responsible for her part in my abuse as I was with my abused girls? Now I see that this also was a way to keep "me," the child, innocent. My husband and myself, as adults, are guilty of my daughters' abuse or he alone is fully guilty, but whichever way, she, the child, is fully innocent. Thus I am, as the child, fully innocent. Oh God, how I do not want to be the bad guy. I have always believed inside that I was the bad guy. I escaped being the bad guy to myself and to others by making those around me bad or by choosing bad guys. Oh, I feel like you've ripped me from my mother's womb before time. Like my mother took away my right to be angry with her phone call. How could you make me face all this so soon? How could you, Dr. Ney?

As I read this to the group, Dr. Ney apologized for the pain he had caused me and affirmed that maybe it was too fast. He looked truly grieved over my anguish. I forgave him and the questions started around the room. He stopped them, saying that if it was okay, he didn't want the usual feedback, because what I had discovered was best learned individually through each one's own processing.

Everyone had had a hard time over Christmas. Dr. Ney was right about not taking the week off. I doubt any of us would have managed very well. We all seemed extremely agitated and angry. It was really uncomfortable several times. Keeping eye contact and really listening as each of us took her turn seemed especially difficult tonight. I always found Krista's anger particularly distressing. She is so aggressive, leaning forward and commanding audience. She reminds me of my father. I usually avoid people who prompt this response in me. Here, however, I have determined to handle, not avoid, any situation that arises. This I know would be a valuable tool in the outside world.

Shawna was having a bad night. We seemed to take turns having emotional baths. Tonight was Shawna's turn. Owning her part in the sexual abuse as a teenager tore her apart. We all wanted to help her, take part of her pain. All we could do was listen intently, pass tissues, and let her hurt.

Tanya shared about God's deserting her. Her anger toward God seemed so violent, even more than that toward her mother or father. I wonder if I am mad at God. Is it right to be mad at God? Finally, we'd been around the room and it was my turn to share homework. I felt wrung out before I even started because of the heightened stress in the room tonight and the anxiety I'd carried all week about confronting Dr. Ney with my anger.

Last week's questions:

1. What happened to me?
   I was sexually and physically abused. I was emotionally starved and abandoned.
2. Who was at fault?
   It was no one's fault; no one to blame. Blame is dead.
3. Who was responsible?

   The abusers: They are responsible for their actions, though they, too, were probably abused and thus programmed to abuse; they were destined for abuse through family heritage, sin passed to the third and fourth generations. We are each responsible for our sins before God and we can, in Him, stop our compulsive, addictive, abusive behaviors.

Mom: Though she never saw or participated in the sexual abuse, she was, as my mother, accountable for my protection, especially as a baby and young child. She was responsible for caring for and nurturing me emotionally, physically, spiritually, and mentally. Even though she, too, was programmed through generational sin to be codependent, the opportunity for help to quit abusing or denying abuse or find safety is and was available.

God: I am his child and he is responsible for protecting his little ones. He says he will never forsake us. I can see that even through this abuse he did what he said. He is still here with me. I can actually see how his love guided me more and more as the darkness lifts in this valley of pain and death.

Me: I am responsible for seeing the truth, for discerning that:
a. I was "marked" to be abused from before the womb. Family heritage and familiar spirits set me up for abuse.
b. Once I had been abused, I was doubly marked. My body language; my desperate need for love, touch, and affection; and the familiar spirits all cultivated me for continued abuse. Unless I fight to stop this abuse now, in this generation, my children and grandchildren and great grandchildren will carry the "family mark."
c. I am also responsible for seeing that I have set myself and my children up for abuse by choosing abusive relationships. I maintained my "innocence" at the cost of ongoing abuse of me and my girls.
d. I must discontinue abusing myself with or without food, no longer punishing myself or others with my fat.

Ultimately, I am responsible for protecting myself and my children, for not setting myself or my children up for abuse. I cannot blame anyone for my life, my choices. I no longer can make "them" wrong. Dr. Ney, I am still upset with you.

❖   ❖   ❖

4

Despair: Saying Good-bye to What Might Have Been or Could Be

Our patients have now dealt with their pain, their fear, their anger, and their guilt, and naturally they will feel that this is a wonderful time to experience new growth and healing. Another part of them recognizes the difficult truth that they have missed out on what they should have had as children. They were robbed of a reasonable childhood. Much of their lives has been spent in trying to re-create that childhood and meet the needs that should have been met when they were young. It is not hard for them to realize through role play, observations, interpretations and discussions just how much they missed as children. No one and no situation can re-create that childhood because each building block is age and stage specific.

Patients soon realize that they cannot repair the damage that has been done to them. They will always have disabilities. They cannot recapture their childhood. Their needs will never be met. Their present relationships can never satisfy them. They can never become what they were designed to become. The demanding little children inside them can never be satisfied. No amount of nurturing of the "inner child" can make one an adult.

Children who grow up without enough food do not get sufficient protein to develop their brains. No matter how much protein they get as adults, they cannot repair that damage. They will go through life with an intuitive awareness of what they could have been had they been properly nurtured, but they cannot be as intelligent as they were genetically meant to be. The discrepancy between what they are and what they could have been produces an enormous incipient rage. It only takes the manipulation of some flamboyant leader to stir that rage into action in the form of guerrilla activity or all-out war.

Since children have an intuitive awareness of what they could become, they know what they need as individuals. A child who grows up in starvation conditions never gets used to being hungry. A child who is starved of affection can never accept the fact that there is not enough affection available. You never get used to feelings of being neglected. To get the nurture you needed as a child, you have to continue being a child. Therefore, your children are shortchanged. They need their parent to be adult.

The realization that one has been robbed of a reasonable childhood, and that it can never be recaptured, can produce despair. People fear that despair—they have looked at it often—and wonder if they can possibly proceed through it. They feel that there can be no hope on the other end. My practice, over many years, has confirmed my impression that people who are able to go through the despair find a resurgence of strength and hope. This occurs because the organism must survive. Hope will be reborn from the ashes. The deeper into the despair that one allows oneself to go, the more realistic and strong is one's hope.

When children are neglected, they fear that they will lose all contact with reality and become psychotic. When their needs are not met, they cannot develop properly, but they must keep trying. Thus out of necessity and fear they develop two false images. The Dancer, always trying to please, hopes that somebody will recognize that he or she is good company and, with a bit of nurturing, can develop fully. The Urchin, cringing in the corner, can be miserable or demanding, wishing that someone would see through the facade, see the potential, and meet his or her needs. The Pilgrim is the central, organizing part of the personality who tries to keep the individual intact and to control the demanding or aggressive Dancer and Urchin. The expectations of children's false images may have been realistic for them but the Pilgrim is now too old to benefit from those expectations and should let these two childlike false images go.

The story of Cinderella expresses this phenomenon well. The Urchin sat among the ashes waiting for the fairy godmother (somebody who would come along and give her exactly what she needed). She suddenly becomes a princess, but being a princess is always self-limiting. Thus, what she gets is not what she needs. Without the intervention of the wonderful prince, she cannot go past midnight without returning to her state as an Urchin. The prince is possibly a psychotherapist who intervenes and makes her realize that she doesn't have to be an Urchin or a princess, but can be a real person. The Pilgrim is unstated, but is obviously the person telling the story. In real life, people often describe the Urchin and the Dancer inside them, but without getting very much recognition. Children, because of their vulnerability, develop defenses that include these false split images. These serve both to detract the aggressor and to provide additional appeals to would-be nurturers. Some people put up their "shit detectors," which generally malfunction because they end up suspecting that everything coming their way is worthless. At the same time, they deeply need to be looked after. They often go through the garbage they get looking for tidbits of something nice. The Dancer always has to be socially acceptable. In men, this is often, "You've got to be able to hold your head up."

All wars are debilitating for both sides. When people war within themselves, they are bound to feel tired. These are often wars between the little false images who are demanding that their needs be met. When these needs are not met by people outside themselves, they become demanding of each other.

The Dancer and the Urchin cannot be nurtured back into wholesome life. They want to stop existing and should be allowed to fade away or die. To do this, we have used the guided imagery of each of the patients holding a badly injured child in her arms. She is encouraged to make every effort to keep the child alive. Eventually, the cold body is put on the table and covered with a sheet. There is a strong built-in aversion to death and dead bodies, and so the false images have to be relinquished.

Out of fear, some people become angry at having to let go of the Dancer and the Urchin. They perceive that we are trying to make them give up or kill their "inner children." This is not the case. The "inner children" are false images and cannot continue to live. In some respects, they are already dead. Once they are allowed to pass on, the Pilgrim can emerge and assert himself or herself. The degree to which a person does not want to do the guided imagery of letting the false-image children go is proportional to the need to do it. After the "children" have gone, some people want to change their first names, and should be encouraged to do so.

One patient stated that she was wrestling with letting the false images die. She was afraid that if she took it seriously, it would be the last of her. "It is a little bit like having all my clothes off. One side of me is amicable, a shadow of other people's expectations. The other is a bumbling idiot. One is idealistic, always giving a very good first impression. Unless they protect me, I wouldn't know how to relate to people without them." Another patient reported that after burying the little false images, "the person walking toward me didn't have a face, but I know it was me." Still another stated, "I really felt that they [the two false images] needed to be buried together. I don't know why. Now I feel disconnected. Most of me is dead."

Neglect due to poverty is always devastating, but it can be just as hard to mature in a wealthy home. It is hard to assert one's identity. Many fear that they will lose the material things that wealthy children learn to expect. Whenever they get something new, their unhappy mood is momentarily lightened. It becomes an operant conditioning that induces deep-seated materialism.

Most people never seem to lose the awareness of what they could have been. It is as if they were built according to a Blueprint that they continually consult to see how well they are developing. Generally, they perceive a large discrepancy between the Blueprint and what they have become, and this irreconcilable difference results in a deep bitterness. The Blueprint is often expressed in the childhood daydreams of what they wanted to do with their lives.

Many people, rationalizing why they never became what they were designed to be, state, "I didn't really try. I guess I really didn't want to. But if I really had wanted to, I'm sure I could have succeeded." The myth that you can be anything you want to be is encouraged by the media. The consumer-products industry is continually maintaining, "You can be anything you want to be, if you only try." The unspoken message is that they want you to work harder because then you will have more money and will spend more money on their products. When people do spend money, there is a temporary analgesia—a good feeling that comes from opening a new package. Unfortunately, this action produces a vicious circle of spending. The euphoria soon fades and is replaced by more unhappiness, which they then try to relieve by more buying.

Once people are able to let go of their false images, they begin to look at a very different world. Those false images were expecting things that should have been granted to them when they were children. Since they never received them, they were always disappointed in their situations and relationships.

WEEK 12

It was just after New Year's Day. It didn't look as though the group had done much celebrating. In fact, they weren't thinking very much about the new year. They were grim-faced and determined to get on with the work at hand.

Anna began with, "Good news, everybody. My husband and daughter were arguing and I didn't have to fix it and I didn't feel helpless; I felt powerful. But I am very concerned. My son somehow knows that my two daughters were sexually abused and he is acting it out. I didn't know he knew. I certainly never told him, nor did my daughters."

Anna continued on the theme that she had been thinking about, dealing with it more courageously than anybody else I have known. "Because I had to be innocent, he had to be guilty. Finally, I talked to my husband about it, and he is now beginning to admit his guilt, but I feel terribly guilty about willing the death of the real Anna when she was just two and a half. Ever since, I have been a shell, but now and again I have glimpses of the real me inside. She had great potential. She could have been a great artist. The shell has an endless desire to control. I mourn for your loss and mine. She could have enriched your lives." We all murmured about the loss of the Anna who wasn't given a chance. Anna is a good artist and she admitted that she wonders what she could have been had she been given a decent childhood.

Linda was still quite tense but certainly more forthcoming. "I still don't know what I could have been or have done with my life. I'd like to go to college, but I have always been discouraged by my parents. I am working in an office and making excuses for myself as to why I don't go back to school. I have had the same job for 18 years. What I have always wanted is just to be happy, loved, and protected. Maybe someday it will come. The child inside of me is Veronica. Maybe Veronica would like to be a psychiatrist, a funny psychiatrist."

Amy was almost tearful before she began. "I refused to let go of that person, my real person. I know I definitely would have been different. My parents didn't know me. They should have explored me. They should have wanted to get to know me. It was stupid of them to ignore what I could have been. I was never given a chance at education. I wanted to be so proud of myself. It's really depressing thinking of all this stuff."

In dealing with young people and adults abused as young children, it became apparent to me that children are born with potential and a blueprint for that potential. This makes them acutely aware of when they are not obtaining the necessary building materials for their development. Even though the beautiful person they might have become never properly develops, the Blueprint never quite fades, and they spend much of their adult life looking at it and bemoaning what could have been. Many popular courses and self-help books are based on the idea that given the right guidance, the right technique, and the effort, one can be anything—a movie star, a president—and this is not true. But still people cling to that illusion, becoming increasingly embittered because they feel that circumstances and other people are preventing them from realizing their potential. They spend much of their lives angry at those who disappoint them. If only they could let go of the illusion. If they were able to mourn the Person they could have been, then they would find a great deal more joy and satisfaction in their present lives and relationships. But that mourning is incredibly difficult. The group was just beginning to realize this.

To emphasize some of the problems inherent in the process of mourning that they were just beginning, I asked each of the group members to tell her buddy about her personal disabilities. This would heighten the differences between what she should have been and what she became. I asked them to describe the home from which they came and how they contrasted it with those homes in which they wished they had been raised. I pointed out that it was their fear of failure and of taking risks that was the real disability. That fear had been deeply engendered early in their lives. After all, how can children take risks in a situation in which their parents either will treat them harshly or abandon them if they do?

Tanya was an artist with words, and with words she painted a series of pictures that she helped to illustrate with photographs from her childhood. One was of a huge crabapple tree in bloom. Then she described how, while the tree was still in bloom, it snowed, and the snow clung to the blossoms, the branches broke and were twisted, and the tree split apart. "That tree is me," she said. "There was enormous potential in that child, as in the tree, but it kept on snowing. Now that tree is only half of what it was. Some of it I can't get back and I know some of it can never grow. I cried with the teacher who was scapegoated because I didn't achieve that potential. It wasn't her. It was me. But I began to feel that God loved me again. At one point, I registered in premedicine. I wanted to be a psychiatrist. If nothing else, I wanted to cure my father. You see, there are two "inner children." One died between the ages of eight and 12. The other died much earlier. I could let the older one die, but not the young one."

I pointed out that as hard as it might have appeared to her, until both little Tanyas died, their characteristics could never be integrated into the adult she had become. In this process, roses grow out of ashes, but until the ashes were there, where was the soil? Nothing grows on rock.

Amy had to butt in. "It is the little person inside of me who continually gets me into trouble."

Lisa was tired. "I have not had enough support. People use me for a sounding board when I so desperately need others to lean on. I definitely don't feel like doing this. No one was ever there for me. I know that I would be married and have a family now if I had had a decent childhood. I kept pushing special people away. They were never good enough, and I didn't realize that what I was really looking for was something only my parents could have given. I have a panic rising inside of me. I want to be an artist. I want to cling to that. I want to write books, but I know it cannot be."

I pointed out that until the Person they could have been died, the "child" would keep on demanding, and as a demanding child, it kept getting in the way of any attempt to be a real parent. Until the "child" could be an adult, she could never be a parent.

Krista was obviously in great distress. "All this stuff is overwhelming. I am not finding it at all easy. I wanted four kids. I dreamed of helping people, but at the age of 15, I ran away from home with my boyfriend. I have always been the black sheep, but success is always less important than just being loved. I want a family most, but I know they didn't want me. My birth mother didn't want me, even to be alive. I am really sad. I wasn't supposed to be. I hate myself."

The group was in the midst of defining, owning, and then letting go of the Person they could have been. It was an incredibly sad process because no sooner could they visualize those Persons they should have been than they were confronted with the necessity of recognizing that it didn't happen. That Person, in fact, had died. In order to prepare them for this, I asked them to draw two pictures, one of themselves as they were and one of themselves as they could have been. I noted that this would not be easy, that it would bring them close to despair, but I suggested that they let themselves become as sad as they wished to be.

In a world that is struggling to be calm and happy, it certainly is not considered therapeutic to encourage people to be sad. Yet because they are so often trying to avoid the sadness that is necessary, people become depressed. Here was one occasion on which I wanted the people in this group to be as sad as they needed to be. I knew that would be very sad. I had to be careful that they weren't overwhelmed by grief, and so we checked everybody out very carefully before they left that evening.

❖   ❖   ❖

Anna

Rereading some of Dr. Ney's comments from last week: "Children always want one person they can think of as good, innocent as well as themselves, and one to blame." "It is hard to discover that no one is all good or all innocent." "It is not right what happens to kids!" "Be angry about it, yell about it, there is power in your anger." "Shout! You may be amazed at what you say." I feel foolish, awkward, and embarrassed even to think of shouting out my anger in front of anyone. I can't imagine how I will ever be able to yell out at the group in role play. "I don't want to" isn't strong enough to describe the apprehension I feel when I think about being asked to yell. I haven't resisted anything he has requested of me, but this small thing seems to be a real stumbling block. I just don't know how I'll make myself do it.

We were asked to construct the Person in our mind's eye that we would have been, to put our hopes and dreams on the line. What we could have done with our lives and why we didn't do it. "Be brave!" he encouraged. Well, letting myself visualize long forgotten dreams was difficult.

I don't know the real Anna. She died. I willed her death, at two and a half, in that bathtub. The false me, an empty shell that anyone promising love could program, played my part in life. Shell wanted to be a nun after watching *The Nun's Story*. Daddy was Catholic, after all. Then Shell wanted to be a missionary and saved all her money for her own Bible because a Sunday school teacher took an interest in her. Then Shell wanted to be a teacher; teachers approved of you, if you tried hard enough. And just look at the potential for family favor if you succeeded. Shell, however, became a florist so she could leave home and marry her drug-abusing boyfriend. House rules: You have to have some kind of education before you can get married. Flower arranging was quick. Occasionally, over the years, I had glimpses of Anna. So though I willed her dead, she really didn't die. She's immortal. She really didn't live either.

Anna had great potential. She tried to tell Shell several times over the years, but Shell simply covered her ears.

Anna showed herself again in the eighth grade when she painted excellent watercolors far beyond Shell's abilities. Shell didn't let Anna paint again until she had an emotional breakdown at age 26. Then she painted for several months as therapy. No lessons, just painted, and sold every one. They came up from inside. Shell couldn't visualize. She hadn't ever seen anything in her mind's eye except blackness, and she was unable to control what Anna painted.

After Shell's first body memory, six months ago now, she painted the best painting of her life. It is mystical, free, and deep, and seems to speak boldly yet also whispers. Shell could never command Anna to paint, nor could she control her. The painting happened or it didn't. Long periods, even years, could pass between the urgent painting episodes.

I now believe Anna could have been a great artist if she had been free to explore and develop the gifts entrusted to her, to abandon herself to the beauty and power of creation. The sexual and emotional abuse she endured destroyed her ability to trust, the basis of all growth and true freedom. The cement of rigidity became Shell's security. Seldom did Anna peek through the cracks.

Anna surfaced again through spurts of creative thought, uncontrollable by Shell. These thoughts took the form of stories or poetry and often baffled teachers as they sparkled on an otherwise dull horizon. Fleeting glimpses of fresh, intuitive insight. Where did it come from?

Once again I realize that her talent could have been encouraged and developed. Instead, her intellectual abilities were quenched in a vise of overpowering parental control, while, at the same time, being stunted by Shell's endless drive to conform and acquire the treasured acceptance, approval, and love that she lacked. Anna was never able to explore her creative and intellectual self as Shell continually thrust her back into compulsive conformity, with the fear of abandonment hot on her heels.

It is apparent that Anna could have excelled in the artistic or literary world. She would not have been drawn like a magnet to abusive relationships, but would have attracted healthy, affirming ones. She would not have been driven by compulsive addictive behaviors that burned up her energy and destroyed the very essence of her being. She would have had the opportunity to enjoy a healthy whole balance in every area of life—body, soul, and spirit.

We have lost a great deal—lost one life forever as God meant it to be. I mourn for your loss and mine.

As I read, the silence was heavy in the group. I knew they felt the loss of what I could have been as deeply as I did. Several shared that I expressed for them what they couldn't put into words. They all thanked me for sharing. Our deepening intimacy was evident. The people in this room knew me as truly as I knew myself.

Linda's turn: "Do I have to follow that?" Laughter. She always broke the tension, made us laugh.

Tonight Tanya brought out a picture of the most magnificent crabapple tree in full bloom. She explained her losses by telling us the story of the tree. She was so sad. We could feel her pain through the tree.

Dr. Ney told us that unless the Person we could have been as seen by a child dies, her characteristics and qualities cannot be integrated into the adult. The hopeful little child will keep getting the adult into trouble. This child also gets in the way of parenting. Wow, there was a lot of reaction to this. So many quick minds and answers (Tanya, Krista, Shawna, Lisa), all reciprocated immediately. I am going to have to think this one through.

❖   ❖   ❖

WEEK 13

Everybody had come with pictures, but not everyone was eager to show them. Some of the group members were obviously excellent artists. The others could produce nothing much more than a stick figure, but they still wanted to use the opportunity to depict for themselves and for others the growing recognition and reality of what had happened to them. The group was anxious to bring me, Dr. Green, Tasha, and Shelly up to date on what was happening in their lives. Tanya found that her son reminded her of her father, and, for the first time in many nights, having realized this, she was now interacting differently with him and he didn't wake up in the middle of the night. Lisa spoke of the memories of her mother's abusing her. She said it was good to face them.

We began a discussion about dreams, and they became interested in each other's dreams, both daydreams and night dreams. I pointed out that people daydream because it creates a hope, and even if it is a false hope, it serves the purpose of allowing them to survive. The man who lives in the desert and dreams of lakes gets up the next day to try again to find water. The sad thing is that dreams can create a false hope, and the dreams that these people hung on to made them wander across deserts to find lakes, water that never existed.

Linda said she felt like an orangutan and her home was a blank piece of paper.

Amy drew a beautiful picture in which all the hearts were full and connected. She depicted a scale on which the hearts were balanced. She was obviously referring to the situation between her and her husband. She noted that not everyone was being nurtured.

Tanya said she found it very difficult to face what could have been. She felt she was living behind a veil with her husband and three kids. She brought pictures of her mother, who looked beautiful, yet somewhat elusive. Her hope had been to be a Dancer and travel the world.

As we went from one member to the next, they became increasingly sad, but there was a wholeness in the sadness. They struggled to deal with their desperation and disappointment. What to do? They knew they couldn't have their dreams, so they asked each other, "Can I have your dream?" As a group exercise, I asked them to chat with each other about what it would take to make their dreams come true and who would be the person who would do it. Tanya, in describing her teen years, stated that she felt indescribably bad. She could just see her mother, over and over again, dressed as a sexy stenographer.

Lisa began showing the pictures of her dream house. It was lovely. It had all the things that anyone would ever want. Her real situation was very different. Lisa's picture, which was very well drawn, showed Lisa and a husband with an infant sitting in a beautiful garden, just the family, with the grandfather hovering in the background, being very protective. The picture of herself, as she was, was of an adult with a child's face with a hand firmly over the mouth, stopping her from screaming.

Krista laughed sardonically. "Mine is a generic house in the woods with a fireplace, except that there is no fire. There is a fat cat and there is a fat me. I am alone in the house with the world going by, and sometimes it is really sad."

Anna depicted herself as she could have been—part of a family certainly, but there wasn't any house. There was wholeness, healthiness, and comfort. However, in her situation as it really was, she saw herself with rigid lines, unbalanced, no dreams, lots of anger. Even looking at it made her angry. She suddenly realized how angry she was at God, the observer with all the power who could have set things straight.

Shawna's picture was of herself resting against a tree, but she was alone. There was a wall around the tree and herself, protecting her. She drew the picture of herself as she felt she was—very small, very alone, with the world bearing down on her. Having gone through the pictures, and although it was very late, I asked each of them to follow a bit of guided imagery, and this is how it went.

> "I want you to imagine yourself with a child in your arms, the child you would have been at any age that you think is appropriate. I want you to see that child with longing in its eyes. You must recognize that the child has some type of terminal illness and is dying. No matter what you do, how much you hold the child, cuddle it, caress it, and pray for it, the child is dying. There is nothing you can do to stop this child from dying. Weep for the child as it weeps for you. This child is dying, and when it breathes its last, you hold onto it even more firmly. You cuddle it, hoping it can stir again. Eventually it becomes cold, and so you put it down on a table with a white tablecloth or sheet. You begin to walk away from the child, yet you feel you must pick it up again to cuddle it, hold it, and cry over it some more. Eventually, you put it back and you place a sheet over it, but even then you are not convinced. Look at that child, take away the sheet, hold the child again, and do that as many times as you need to. When that is done, they will bring you a box. Put the child in the box. Tell them where they should take it. You follow them to the woods or to a garden or to the sea, and you are going to bury that child. The child is you. When the child is buried and the earth is placed upon it, you turn away from the grave, and as you walk away, you see in the distance somebody who looks like somebody you know. As you come closer, you recognize that person. I want you to tell me who that person is."

In 90% of the instances I have done this, the person they see is themselves, as they really are. They see themselves in a fresh light, and always they welcome and enfold their newfound self.

Having gone through the imagery, I let them sit quietly while the tears trickled from their eyes. I asked them to go home and do it once again, this time not only imagining it, but doing it symbolically. Some type of burial somewhere alone, quietly, where they felt the child could be at rest. For those who believed in God, I wanted them to commit that child to God and to ask for God's care and protection forever.

❖   ❖   ❖

Anna

Slowly, as the days passed, I began to become aware of a deep resentment and bitterness toward God. When Tanya had shared her anger against

God, it concerned and frightened me a little, and yet, at the same time, I wondered if I, too, might be angry at him. Being angry at God seems sacri-legious, disrespectful, impious, sinful, and altogether frightening. Because of these feelings, when anger first started to manifest itself toward God, I shoved it away. Now, however, it demanded my full attention. I allowed myself to think, really think, about what had happened to me and God's unlimited power and predestined plan for my life. The answers others had given me, which I had believed, seemed so hollow now. I asked him, "Are you, oh God, impotent? How could you, an all-powerful, all-loving, all-knowing God, let a child, barely one year old, be used as an object for someone's twisted pleasure? My father was the perpetrator and I was the victim. You, oh God, were you the Great Observer in the Sky? Why didn't you stop it? Why did you let him do those horrible things to me? Why didn't you do something? Where were you? They were sick, or weak, or demonized. What were you? You were the only one who could have stopped it, and you did nothing. Nothing! A great big God who is help-less? You let him hurt me and the others who followed. You just let them all hurt me. You say you love me? You say you love me. Oh God, why, why? Why did it happen to me?" My "inner child" seems to appear now and then during this conversation from here on.

"You are not safe. You let me get hurt. Why did you let me get hurt again? No, I can't trust you. Why were they bad to me?" (Child)
"They were very, very sick. Sick with sin." (God)
"Why did you allow this evil in my life?" (Anna)
"Because I have given humans a will to choose good or evil. These chose to follow evil. This grieved me very much. Know that I never left you for one moment and know that my favor never left you even when you chose sin for yourself. I never turned away from you. If you let me nurture you and love you and lead you through this, I will turn it all to good. I love you and will protect you from evil." (God)
"But you never protected me from evil before!" (Anna)
"I will be with you all the days of your life. I will go through all your pain, sorrow, trouble, and, yes, even the evil of others toward you. I will be there to teach you and lead you, and if you will obey me, do as I say to you, you will not fall into evil again." (God)
"But you never protected me from evil before." (Anna)
"People will always be able to choose evil on this earth and hurt the inno-cent by their choices. You can choose good and thereby hold back evil." (God)
"I don't understand." (Anna)
"Good begets good." (God)
"But I wasn't bad." (Child? Anna)
"Sin was passed on to you and evil befell you. But I knew you and I al-

lowed you to live through this because I have plans for you. I want you for my purposes. This is the greater good. I have suffered all with you, my child." (God)

"You trusted me with this experience?" (Anna)

"Yes. I knew you and loved you before time. You are chosen. I have called you and kept you from Death, who would have stolen you away. I would not let you go. You are mine." (God)

"Like Job? He was tested. Satan was not allowed to kill him but could do everything else." (Anna)

"Yes. You are mine. You have not failed. You have worked hard and now you can rest and trust in me. 'I AM' the Lord your God, who has brought you through the darkest hour and will lead you into joy, peace, victory, and blessing. Behold your God who has loved you with an everlasting love and behold Him who will bring all things to pass just as He has promised." (God)

"Thank you, Lord. I am beginning to understand. Please write understanding and wisdom on my heart as well as on my mind so that I can perceive you and your love deep within. Then I will be able to share it with my "inner child" and she will be able to trust and not be afraid." (Anna)

"I have written truth on your heart. I will bring it all to pass in my time." (God)

"Are you still sitting there?" (Anna)

Before the conversation began, I had asked God to help me in prayer. I had a sense of the "inner child," separate and sitting beside me on steps leading up to the throne of God. Father God had come down and sat near us. The dialogue led from there.

"Yes, I am here. Always here." (God)

I sense the child crawl over and He reaches down and picks her up and cuddles her. I am watching. He invites me to come, too. I must integrate with her to come. I am afraid. He just holds out one hand. The child beckons, "It's okay, come. I like it here. It's safe." Hesitantly I come to him and we blend her in me and me in her.

Later, as I ponder this most remarkable prayer time, I am overwhelmed with the love and goodness of God, my Father. He, a God who cannot look upon sin, never turned away from me in my sin because of his great compassion toward me, the abused child. I feel so loved and so special, so blessed. How can that be? Only God can change the heart so. My heart is full of worship for the first time in months.

I am reflecting on my notes from the group to prepare myself for this week's homework. "You cannot integrate the Person You Could Have Been unless she dies." What happened with God in prayer? We blended. Wasn't that integration? No, I guess it was more of an acceptance of her reality. Her fears, her life are not a separate story, but they are my story. My notes summarize Dr. Ney's comment, "Look at your disappointments because they create bitterness, which destroys." As I look at my husband, I try to see that my dreams and my hopes for the father I wanted I endeavored to create in the men I chose. He can never be the father I didn't get. I have to let that "father" go or I will destroy what little we have left.

Continuing, Dr. Ney explains, "Disappointment is still there as long as the 'child' still pleads, 'Can't you be my mommy? Can't you be my daddy? Can't you fix my childhood?'" I can't hear those childhood pleas, but I can hear these: "Don't leave me. Please love me. I'll be good. Please. Please." I grieve deeply as I meditate on the losses and the sorrows of my lost childhood. I wonder if this pain will ever leave. It is so hard to concentrate. I drag my mind back to my notes. "Some ingredients were not there which the child needed to mature, much like a protein deficiency in a starving child. It cannot be added later. Love, nurture, touch, and encouragement cannot be added later to 'fix' the childhood. These unfulfilled childhood needs are diverted." I must have substituted sex for my need for touch and love, and food for my need for nurture and comfort. Continuing, he says, "Every child, even those who have incurable deficiencies, are driven to follow their inner Blueprints. What was your Blueprint? What could you have been? Who are you now? Put in the context of your environment, is your dream from childhood coming in the way of happiness today?"

I drew two large pictures of me in my circumstances, the first one as they are and the second as they should have been.

I depicted myself as overweight, afraid, stiff, addicted, and obsessive. My family was bent with burdens too great to carry. The church was imposingly stretched out of shape. God's light and power were barely visible around the circumference. Weights and fetters from the past surrounded all of us. There was so little hope. The only flickers of promise that dared to break the darkness and the chains are God's path directly to me, a few friends whose hands still reach out and this group where I have met unconditional acceptance.

In the second picture, I drew the same family. However, I was full of life, my body was lithe, and my step light. My family, protected; all was illuminated within and without by his presence. The chains, fetters, and darkness were there, but they couldn't touch us. There was a sense of purity, wholeness, and balance. Peace prevailed.

All of the group's "as it is" pictures portrayed the incredible destruction in our lives so well. The loneliness, despair, anguish, and losses were painfully evident. We are all so different in the ways we expressed our past, but the results are the same: grief and loss. Our "as it should have been" pictures were, however, not so accurate. They all seemed to have a fairy-princess feeling. Not very realistic, and yet we all seemed to cling tenaciously to them. As we close tonight, Dr. Ney says he is going to lead us in some guided imagery. He talks softly, describing us as holding the child in our arms and gradually surrendering her to death. I am horrified. Agony rips through my soul. "I will not let you die! I just found you. I just accepted you. Why? I don't want to let you die." I brim with anger. I don't want to bury her. She has been buried in me for so long. I sit as the class is dismissed. Head bent over my knees, sobs taking my body. Dr. Green sits close and someone else comes to comfort. I cannot be comforted. Rage rises up and I scream out my fury. Totally oblivious of my need to be in control, ladylike, or any other such thing, I abandon myself to my anger. When I am spent, Lisa and Dr. Green hug me, their eyes speaking compassion. As I left, Dr. Ney assured me that I could call him if I were in trouble. On the way home, I remember wondering earlier that day, as I passed the place where Grandma's ashes are buried, if I'd rather be buried or cremated.

WEEK 14

Everyone was present and, in spite of the fact that they had had a terrible week dealing with the loss, the death, and the mourning of the children they could have been, they were ready for work.

Amy began: "I am trying to teach Sheila obedience. I find that the little Amy in me is still trying to make Sam into a father, so she and Sheila compete for the father who isn't there. I feel like saying to her, 'I can't look after you any longer. Your father died before you could spit on him. I couldn't let her go. The more I let her go, the more I came to be in touch with my own feelings. I now realize what it is like. I felt a little different after writing this. I felt more like a mom. I felt a little older. I was able to say good-bye, but I can't bury her."

Tanya began somberly. Then, with the disheveled look that she sometimes had, she threw back her hair as her eyes became widely dilated. "I didn't know the little Tanya. I called out to little Tanya. I was prepared to let her go, but I didn't want to lose the feelings that were attached to little Tanya. I still want to get to know her. I don't want her to go before I get to know her. I began to wonder what would have happened to her if only I could have known what life would have been for little Tanya. I have been drawing myself dancing. She did her best. I'm proud of her. I'm unable to dance for the world in the way I was meant to dance. I put little Tanya in a box and I buried her in the ground and I sang a hymn and felt I was going out of my mind."

Lisa was more animated. "I couldn't," she looked at me balefully. "I didn't want to, yet somehow I feel very different because of what I did do. I feel separated from the baby Lisa. There is a real me who is growing now. I feel real peace. I feel really good. I feel there is a person in me, a premonition, a promise."

I pointed out that the person inside who is deprived of the nurture that she could only have as an infant feels resentful when the adult grows from the nurture the child is receiving, and so tends to undermine it and to express resentment because it is not what a little child wants and needs. They acknowledged this, noticing how often they felt resentful when looking at a baby who was being properly nurtured. Linda, in fact, began to notice in herself strong feelings of wanting her son to comfort her.

Krista said: "The baby is dying. It was rejected on its first day of life. I died as an infant when my mother gave me away. Then I had a second death with my adopted family. The baby was hoping for someone to love it. God wanted to bless it. He wanted it accepted but the family thought its demands were insatiable. They kept saying that it was a bad baby. Now I must let that baby die because it controls me. I can't sustain it any longer. My hunger for love has been my undoing. Now I don't have to nurture the baby. I feel that I have been released."

Anna spoke boldly: "I am afraid of my anger. It was hell for me, but it was very helpful. My husband built a little wooden coffin, and while he was building it, he wept. It is one of the few times I have seen him weep. I saw myself skipping and running away free after the box was put into the ground. It's hard to bury forever. One keeps wanting something to come back. I can remember my miscarriage and my daughter's miscarriage, but somehow I wasn't afraid to feel. I looked at how ugly that little infant was before I put her in the box, how scarred, thin, angry, and sad she looked. I must say that I am glad she is in the earth and now she is being comforted by God."

Shawna was much more alert. "I went straight to the office and wrote down everything I was feeling. I couldn't finish because of the war and worrying about my husband in the forces. You know, he is going to have to go out there. I remember hearing the mare scream when her foal died. The little thing struggled so hard, but it didn't have a chance. I kept feeling someone was behind me when I was typing, but I kept on going. Yet I wasn't ready. I wanted to give the little person inside me a few moments, see, so I haven't buried the child yet."

Lisa had fire in her eyes. "I've done my homework. I have been doing it all week. I'm glad to say that my mother is going into therapy. I felt both sad and happy. She now accepts a lot of the responsibility, but I feel sadder than I have ever felt before. I had a picture of myself taken when I was just a child. I burned that child. The picture had always been a comfort to me, but the child had to go. I can remember the eyes, the eyes that shone, only the eyes."

Much of the time, adults who were abused as children maintain a facade of two false faces. Others help them to maintain it. The facade is: "I can give you something that you need if you will give me something that I need." They were beginning to see the real person in each other and they didn't have to have false faces; they didn't have to be polite because they wanted to be treated politely in order not to hurt the Person they could have been.

It was late, but it was apparent that some were still struggling with the death of the Person they could have been and the need to bury her. Shawna had talked of the need for burial at sea, so it was quite spontaneously suggested by Anna that we should drive to a nearby beach and, with Shawna, bury the little one. We all got into a car and through a misty night went down to a beach shrouded in fog. The tide was out and little wavelets lapped on the sand while the sea birds, with soft cries, flew in and out of the small area of visibility and back into the fog. After saying a prayer, as we stood together on the wet sand, Shawna placed the little image of herself in a wooden box and pushed it into the water. We all watched it float away. In the quiet eeriness of that night, deep emotions were felt by everyone. Only once would they speak of the burial, but it had an impact that would last a lifetime.

Now that some of them had let go of the child who was so demanding, trying to get for itself the nurture that a child should have, they were able to face themselves and their real needs. In this way, they could look at the real possibilities of having those needs met by other people. They could have real expectations for both themselves and other people. As homework, I asked them to start evaluating all of their relationships in terms of realistic expectations.

❖ ❖ ❖

Anna

"Bury the Person You Could Have Been, in the form of a child, in practice. When it's done, walk away from the grave and look to see who's coming toward you." Simple words; unbelievable task.

I began to realize that my little child was very angry and that she didn't want to die last week when Dr. Ney guided us through the burial imagery. Me, a 45-year-old woman, afraid of "a child's rage." I couldn't touch her, let alone pick her up. I was so afraid. I'd promised her, a few months ago, when I first got in touch with her, that I would never abandon her again as I did when I left her in the bathtub. Now I was going to let her die? How could I abandon her more than to plan her death, the very thing she didn't want, the thing she fought against so hard, for so long? The pain was unbearable. I was being asked to "kill" her.

By morning, I was in a state of total confusion. I didn't know what to do, I was so filled with fear. Unable to keep going with my daily commitments, I pulled off the highway searching for the nearest telephone booth. For the first time, I phoned Dr. Ney. His secretary said he was busy with a patient. I told her that he had promised me that I could call if I needed him. She asked me to hold and in seconds he was there. I slid down the wall of the booth, curled up and crying in fear. He talked to me soothingly until I was able to tell him what was happening; between sobs I explained that I had been trying to pick her up, and that every time I tried, it was always the same. She would be crouched behind the bathroom door, a poor little frightened child of two and a half, curled up in the corner, wounded and terrified. My heart would almost break as I reached for her. Then she would fight, kicking, screaming, and biting me in her fury. Repeatedly I backed away in horror. "I can't do it. She is just too angry. She doesn't want to die," I sobbed. Gently and slowly, he convinced me that my battle was real, that he believed me, he believed my child. He said how strong she was and how hard she hung on and how she was a survivor. He heard me. His love, protection, and comfort passed through those telephone lines and wrapped themselves around me like a warm blanket. Gradually I was able to stand up and my moaning subsided. As our conversation ended, he confirmed my thoughts that I should keep trying to talk to my little child. I grieved my way home, intermittently crying and trying to resolve what I had to do.

THE PROCESS—FRIDAY

Sitting in God's presence, determined to stay until I had accomplished my goal, I looked once again behind the bathroom door. There she was, curled up tightly against the wall. I slowly approached her, reaching out, speaking softly; she lifted her head. Her face was contorted with rage and bitterness. She was grotesque. I was shocked and, even more, frightened, if that were possible. She screamed that she would not die, that she hates me, and will continue to punish me, and that I could never be punished enough to fill her need. She struck out kicking, hitting, spitting, and scratching. I remember a cute little kitten tangled in the garden net that I'd had to use a broom to hold down while I cut it free. She was the same. There had been no love and tenderness to shape her. It was then that I knew I wouldn't be abandoning her by continuing to reach out until she let me hold her and holding her until she quit fighting and died. I would only be abandoning her if I ran away from her anger and ugliness. Jesus touched the lepers. I would touch her and accept her in all her ugliness. No one had ever done that before. I continued with her, and finally she let me hold her. I acknowledged all her deformities. Holding her, telling her I loved her anyway, I assured her I would not leave her. As she grew quiet, I looked down into her face. It was not twisted anymore.

We had talked about her anger, hatred, bitterness, vengeance, shame, fears, control, fat, sexual confusion, and self-pity, and had seen how she had become all these in defense because of what had happened to her. There was no way back. To die would be her only rest. I promised to hold her until we were both ready to give her life up to Jesus with all of her dreams and hopes, fears and pain. I promised also that when she died, I would take her body and lovingly prepare and bury it, grieving the loss of her life and remembering her always in my heart.

THE PROCESS CONTINUED—MONDAY

My husband was incredibly supportive when I shared both my fears and needs on Friday. Over the weekend, he built a small wooden coffin. Together, we picked a beautiful spot where he prepared the ground. On Monday, I went over the whole process to make sure I was truly reconciled with every aspect of her death. For the first time, I let my mind follow past her death in my arms, through the burial, and looked up to see who would be coming toward me. "I am not sure...it might be me. Maybe after the physical acting out, I will see more clearly."

One more time...wondering if I'd be able to follow through. This time as I looked up I sensed "me" skipping, laughing, free and childlike. A fleeting glimpse, not a specific age, more like an essence...I knew she had been perpetually crouching in the dark prison of her rage and bitterness. Now she is free. I am free, leaving behind us the insurmountable burden, forever. Yes, it was terrible what happened to her, but I am leaving that burden behind. Now I have the hope I need to go on with the funeral.

Later it was still very difficult to say a final good-bye at the graveside and to bury forever the poor little abused child who was once a very big part of my life. I planted bulbs on the top and in the spring I hope to see new life in the place of death. I felt empty. I could not see anyone coming. The rest of the day and most of Tuesday I was extremely tired and slept a lot. Maybe soon I'll know for sure whom I was supposed to see.

Tonight we all looked wasted. Last week was the hardest so far. Not everyone had been able to finish the burial work. It seems that those who didn't have any outside support had the greatest difficulty. After all of us who had been able to complete it had shared, we agreed to go with the others to a nearby beach and witness their good-byes.

The night was dreamlike. A soft covering of fog settled around us as we crossed the sandy beach to the shore of the open ocean. Waves gently curled around our feet. Gulls whispered their lonely cries in the distance. Eternity enveloped us. Truly God was here to receive our gifts. This was the first time we had ever prayed together. Tonight God's existence was not challenged, for had we not responded, the rocks themselves would have cried out his praise.

It is important to state that Dr. Ney's response to me, while in the phone booth, was a major turning point in my recovery. I don't know what would have happened if he had been "just too busy" to talk to me. That final abandonment may have set me back permanently. His love, patience, and acceptance and conviction of "my truth" secured in me the courage to embrace death. When I was the most vulnerable, he proved his trustworthiness. He didn't use me, hurt me, or let me down.

5

Relationships: Determining What Expectations Are Realistic

Because our patients were abused and neglected as children, they did not develop fully and tend to have needs that cannot be satisfied. These are often expressed as demands by the false images. The deeper demands are usually kept hidden, except under special circumstances, which generally arise after the person is in some kind of relationship. While courting a friend or business partner or potential mate, these deprived people tend to show, by words and behavior, that they have much to give. Later their needs show. Their needs are so large they cannot be kept hidden.

Wounded people tend to attract other wounded people, but none of them know that because they all keep up the false images so well. The implied message is, "Look how beautiful and/or handsome I am. Love me and you will find that I am a princess." The unspoken message is, "I am really an Urchin. I am afraid that you will discover that, but I must have my needs met. Once you are committed to loving me, I'll show you who I really am."

After they have been in a relationship for some time, they begin to allow the demanding part of their nature to show. There is usually panic on the part of the partner, who begins to realize that he or she was not picked as an adult partner, but as a potential parent. When this happens, one partner tends to withdraw, which makes the other desperate. The desperateness then becomes a pleading, and he or she quickly reverts to the role of the Urchin. Within a short time, both discover that they are Urchins, and that they really have very little to offer each other. This results in a mutual dissatisfaction and disappointment that fractures the relationship. Following that is a period of isolation and partial recovery. If they are not too wounded, they try again, only to find that history repeats itself.

Sometimes partners in relationships try to reshape each other to become the kind of parent they wish they had had. The mutual pushing and shoving to change each other are deeply resented. They are fragile enough not to want to have anybody try to change or remake them. The person who desperately wants something, either for himself or herself or for the good of others, is always in a one-down position that others can use to their advantage.

In the work situation, this may start off with the Dancer saying, "Oh, what a wonderful boss I have." The beginning of the relationship may be based on flirtation. If the boss responds with an interest in sex, the other is totally disgusted, blows a whistle on sexual harassment, either is fired or quits, and looks for another boss who will be much more of a parent.

Now that one is getting rid of the false images, one can see how detrimental they were. Still it is hard for the wishes of those "inner children" not to express themselves in terms of unrealistic expectations. One cannot not communicate an expectation.

To have realistic relationships requires mutual realistic expectations of oneself and others. For the patient, this means:

1. Letting go of the two false images, Dancer and Urchin.
2. Allowing their Pilgrim to be seen. They have now recognized that they will be scarred and/or partially disabled for the rest of their lives. To recognize their limitations and their emotional triggers keeps them from falling into the frequent pitfalls. To say honestly, "I cannot do it," is both sad and freeing. It is letting go of the Dancer. It is recognizing one's strengths and consequent responsibility to relinquish the Urchin. At the same time that people accept their disabilities, they must also recognize their abilities. To accept a talent or a strength is to accept additional responsibility. People may fear the additional burden, and, therefore, may deny their strengths.
3. To bury and mourn the person they could have been.
4. Once the false images are dispensed with, the limitations and strengths are accepted, people can dust off their Blueprints and start making plans for their present and future. Now they can engage with other people in mutually renegotiating expectations and plans until they become realistic. Expectations that are too high are always self-defeating.

Group therapists are not immune to the unrealistic expectations of patients. I have found it rather difficult when the patients, feeling that they have been badly misunderstood, begin to demand more attention from me or from each other. If I point out that there is a residual part of them that is still trying to have their child needs met, they sometimes become angry. Those who stay with the process and work it through come to a much deeper realization of how often they have foisted their unrealistic expectations onto other people.

In the group, the patients also tend to have unrealistic expectations of each other. "I thought you were a real friend. Now I have found out that you are wounded just like me. How can I count on you?" Some of the personal interactions become tense at this point in the group process. Frequently, there is a particularly hostile interaction between two of the members. If this can be resolved, it is healing for all in the group.

Negotiating realistic expectations cannot be accomplished theoretically. It has to be done face-to-face. This will be the first face-to-face encounter during the group process, and it is usually painful. If expectations can be negotiated, a ripple effect moves throughout the family. Initially a partner becomes angry, then feels relieved that the expectations of him or her do not have to be so extensive either. Together, a couple can grow much more comfortable with each other.

People are often led to believe that they can be anything at any time if only they try. This not only increases the tendency to materialism, but also increases the chance that one will want to change one relationship for another. It is in the interest of the merchandising media to promote dissatisfaction, with both oneself and one's partner. Every time two people begin a new relationship, they engage in a type of bartering whereby gifts are given and credits stored for later demands for affection, consideration, etc. The media promote dissatisfaction with one's partner by depicting happy situations involving people who are usually young, virile, and single. It is helpful to our patients to recognize how, individually, they are vulnerable to media suggestion.

Parents often use their children to help re-create their own unrealistic future by placing unrealistic expectations on the children. When they gain realistic expectations of themselves, they are not as likely to subject their children to unrealistic expectations. Much of the anger parents feel arises when they become disappointed in their child's attitudes and/or performance. That disappointment grows out of a disappointment with themselves. They hope that the child can make his or her life more successful, and thus that the adult can gain, vicariously, some of the joys he or she had anticipated would come with the success that was never achieved. When the adults become more realistic about themselves, they are less likely to be disappointed in their children. When their expectations are lowered, they are more likely to be pleased with their children, and thus the children gain encouraging plaudits rather than the discouraging disapprovals that harm their self-image. A good self-image helps them to try harder, and to keep trying when the going gets tough.

WEEK 15

Tonight everybody was present but they looked very tired and anxious. They evinced mixed feelings of rage and sorrow. Although we were hoping to move on to the issue of realistic and unrealistic expectations, most were still struggling with the little persons inside them who needed to be put to rest to prevent them from continuing to tear them apart with their insatiable demands. In her pregroup report, Linda said that her high level of anxiety was related to the little person inside her with whom she must deal because it controlled her emotions.

The struggle inside them was a war to end all the wars that they had been fighting within themselves for so long. Unfortunately, like all wars to end all wars, individual and international, people were loath to engage in them lest they were committing themselves to something that they could not complete and that it would not be the end of the wars. I tried to point out that it wouldn't end all the wars, but it would give them a good idea of how to go about fighting any future ones. I noted that this war, like all the others, was internal, and that internal wars are always harder to fight than external ones. Most nations, like people, prefer to fight an external war rather than fight among themselves. I pointed out further that it was now time to open their eyes. With the child put to rest, they no longer had to respond to its demands, expecting impossible nurture and guidance from other people who just wanted to be their friends and trying to set up a reciprocal situation in which they created an illusion that they had a great deal to offer when, underneath, they knew that they were very empty.

Tanya stated that she keeps trying to present a facade that fools other people into thinking she is normal, but is tortured by watching her false image dancing when she wasn't allowed to continue dancing herself. She can remember her confirmation classes, and she remembers acutely the lack of fulfillment from each of these end points that were supposed to launch her into something better. She stated that she had given up dancing and God in preference to having sex with her father. She said she hadn't known what to expect of her father, and she was not sure what she could expect of her husband. At this point, she was just waiting, but her eyes were beginning to see what people really were like and how much she could expect from them.

Lisa was certainly more alert and there was animation on her face that hadn't been there before. "I have always expected people to abuse me. I'm beginning to see that this is unrealistic. I can see that some people will love me even when others abuse me, but not everybody is going to abuse me. I'm beginning to realize that even some good people will hurt me, some unintentionally, and I am struggling to relate this to my mother. I can't see anything of any value in her. I have no expectations of her, yet she is incredibly disappointing to me. After searching for so long and finding her, I thought she would be my mother. All she did was attack me."

After so many weeks of intense group therapy, some of the relationships were beginning to sour. Krista stated that she was preoccupied with a remark made by Amy to the effect that Krista didn't have any relationships. "I'd written off all my friends. Maybe it is true, but I sure didn't want to hear it."

Anna looked particularly unhappy tonight. "This is all really gross. I want everybody I know to like me. Why don't they? I try so hard to please them. I now see that all my expectations were unreal. There were far too many, but I don't know that if I were to set them aside I would have anything with which to replace them."

Shawna had a tendency to lean forward at the waist and to stare across the room very intently, and although there was no particular hostility in her look, some of the group members thought that she was angry with them. "I expect people to read my mind and see what I can give them, but I know I set up a facade that makes them think I've got more to give than I really have. I guess we're not good at this. We'll need some practice." I pointed out that very early in their development, children who are neglected and abused start forming unrealistic expectations and hopes in a vain effort to survive in an otherwise overwhelmingly disappointing situation. Children can't live with disappointment. They can survive only with hope, and if they have to create unrealistic expectations in order to evoke their own hopes, they will do so. However, the extensive fantasy creates even worse situations in which they are even more frequently disappointed, and thus the cycle continues. I suppose the group was beginning to realize that as parents they had to be realistic with their children and to be frank when they had to disappoint them.

Amy looked healthy, partly because of the wonderful health-sustaining hormones generated by her pregnancy, but the lines in her face indicated the depth of her sadness. I wondered if all of this trouble that she was going through would affect the baby's development. There is increasing evidence that psychological states create hormonal changes that have an effect on the fetus. One of the more alarming findings from animal studies indicates that females stressed during their pregnancy produce higher levels of estrogen, which tend to feminize the offspring. Amy was not going to back away from this, even though she was very protective of her children. "This is very pertinent to Sam and me. I begin to realize that my expectations of Sam came from my disappointment with my father. I'm trying to make Sam into a father and he has had an even more deprived background than I had. I begin to realize that the more I push, the more he runs, and the more he runs, the more I am disappointed, and the more I am disappointed, the more I begin to push. It's all very stupid. I wish we could stop this."

As a group exercise, I asked them to pair up, with one saying, "I expect you can do anything you want," and the other responding with, "No; in fact, there are things I could never do and don't expect that I can do because I will disappoint you even when I don't want to." The exercise was a struggle. The facades that they had maintained over so many years were well entrenched and it was hard to remove the masks even though they wanted the freedom of being honest with each other.

As homework, I suggested that they think about the yearnings of a child and the things that children really need and whether they could provide those things to their own children. I asked them to talk to one important person, to ask the person what they could realistically expect from him or her, and then to apologize for expecting too much. There were murmurs of protest, but they understood very quickly and they all went off determined to deal with these situations.

WEEK 16

This cold January evening everybody was present and very determined to get on with the difficult tasks they knew were waiting for them. Lisa, with her dark hair, dark clothes, and hunched shoulders, stared intently at nothing in front of her. She was preoccupied with an intense struggle to break the bonds to her satanic abusers. "I feel so bonded to those who abused me. It's amazing how I should find somebody as a teenager to continue abusing me as I was abused as a child. I am determined to break this cycle and I am beginning to see how it happens. I had to recreate those awful scenes that I can barely remember as an infant. Something in my mind made me find the right people to make it happen all over again. I am so afraid of triggering some subconscious mechanism and making it happen again. I find as I write my homework I gain a lot of insight, but there are some blank spaces yet."

When Krista was frightened, she was defensive and sometimes provocative. "I don't feel loved as an adult. I certainly never was as a child. I eventually phoned my friend, Tim, but it took a lot of guts. I was so surprised he didn't push me away. I expected him to. Everybody else has. When we talked about my expectations, he admitted that I make very heavy demands for support. I suppose I expect him to deal with a big chunk of my life, but whom do I turn to? I feel like a real jerk. Nobody listened to me as a child. My mother particularly always turned a deaf ear. Now I'm not too sure whom I should turn to, but I know I want to be comforted when I am lonely and sad. Why was it that I was never comforted as a child? Now I just grab onto people and they run away from me. I am beginning to see how the expectations in my adult life were those of my childhood that were never filled."

In the midst of everybody else's pain and grief, Anna looked radiant. "I can't feel awful. I realize how I was trying to make myself perfect in an effort to recreate a childhood I could never have. Maybe if I was perfect I would be loved perfectly. With this knowledge I now have a wonderful sense of freedom and aliveness. I did my list with my husband and he had reasonable answers, but it was a real struggle. I am so glad to give up the anger of the person who couldn't be." I pointed out that everybody needs to be able to express that deep disappointment and rage. Maybe everyone needs to be able to record that protest and mark it on a gravestone or in a biography.

Shawna looked grim. "I let my husband down. He could see the logic of negotiating realistic expectations but he couldn't do it. I got increasingly mad, and when he started expressing his expectations I responded with 'How dare you expect all of this from me.' I began to see we have been supporting each other's unrealistic expectations and continually getting disappointed in each other."

Linda was pleased and quite prepared to let everybody know. "I presented the expectations to the man in my life, and when we began to talk about our disappointments it led to spilling my guts. I spent three hours at it. He's a very sexual man and can be very supportive, but I must say I get absolutely nothing in return for all that I give." I pointed out that she could never find a man in her life who would replace the brothers and father that she didn't have.

Amy looked haggard and people were beginning to become very concerned about her and what the stress might do to her pregnancy. It later turned out that her beautiful baby had quite well adapted to coming to group. "I didn't do my work with my husband. We've been fighting all week. It's been getting harder and harder. I must admit, I'd rather expect nothing than deal with disappointments, but still my expectations are there. I can see that I'm trying to make my husband into the father I didn't have. He continually disappoints me just like my father did."

Tanya had taken a different tack. She often did. Her thinking was often tangential, but when she got around to expressing what was going on inside her mind there were some deep insights. "It seems to me God likes a bit of a fight just like my father. I've had many intellectual and emotional expectations of God. Many of these are projections of my father. My little Dancer and Urchin wanted perfect parents. I knew I had lots of potential. I tried to talk to God about this and I expressed my anger. Having done that, I must say I feel much better. Maybe God and I can get along better now."

The homework was to continue negotiating for realistic expectations. This time it was their turn to indicate what a significant other could expect of them. They had to be clear about what they could or could not do for anybody. Now that they had laid to rest the person that could not be, it was much easier for them to be realistic with other people. Now that they didn't have to be perfect trying to recreate a perfect childhood, they didn't have to form unrealistic expectations of themselves in the minds of other people.

❖   ❖   ❖

Anna

After a day of constant conflict and confrontation with my teenagers, I escaped to the car. Running. I am not sure whether it was for their sakes or mine, maybe a little of both. I drove down the road in a knot of frustration. By the time I'd driven to the corner, I was screaming in rage. At the stop sign, I pushed the brake and the gas hard to the floor, roaring the engine until I thought it would blow. Shame for my uncontrolled behavior flickered briefly as I drove on. I tried desperately to snuff out my raging emotions. As I drove, I couldn't seem to make sense of my intense reaction, nor was I having any success in subduing it. I ended up at a friend's, one with whom trust and intimacy had long been cultivated. I was unable to go inside, and she suggested that we go for a drive. I had barely backed out of her driveway, searching for an answer to her question, "What's wrong?", when I exploded. I pounded on the steering wheel, crying, cursing, and screaming with fury until my rage was spent. She just sat there, supporting me, saying nothing, not shocked, and making no effort to stop me. She just witnessed my rage. After it was over, she affirmed her love for me, saying also that she was glad that I was finally able to release my anger because I'd needed to do that for a very long time. Hugging me, she left to walk back up her driveway. By the time I arrived home, I felt numb. I couldn't believe what I'd just done. Although it was only 8:30 PM, I went to bed and right to sleep. The next day, when I sat down for morning devotions, I felt as though the eyes of my spirit were downcast. I was so mortified by my previous night's behavior that I couldn't look into God's face in prayer. Consumed with shame and remorse, I wept before him in silence. I wrestled with the growing notion that what had happened was not only okay, but necessary. Overriding this quiet assurance were confusion and questions. "Please help me. I thought the ugly, angry bitterness died with the child. What was that? Is there more? What do I do? I feel so guilty." Unable to reconcile myself before God, I left him, feeling an agony of defeat.

Afterward I confessed to my husband what I'd done and the shame I felt regarding it. He was pleased that I'd been able to get the anger out and was not at all concerned that I'd sinned. As a matter of fact, he was genuinely surprised at my reaction, stating that he'd have no such guilt. While we were finishing the conversation, a neighbor appeared at the door. Looking in, she said, "Oops, bad timing." She thought my tears meant that we'd been arguing. Remembering that she had recently been through a court case, which resulted in the sentencing of her husband for the sexual abuse of their daughter, I shared briefly that I was in therapy for sexual abuse and that we had just been discussing it. She hugged me tightly and then pushed me back to arm's length and asked, "Have you raged yet?" There couldn't have been a more timely word. I knew that God had sent her to me, to reassure me of his love and to absolve me of the shame and guilt. The afternoon found me full of praise to my God, rejoicing in the beauty of creation around me. A deep sense of well-being once again rose up within me. Life was good.

Once again, Dr. Ney had given us a lot to chew on: "War is you have to change! Peace is I am going to change. Now you will have to respond to my change." This made sense to me. I've truly proved that I can't change anyone by desire, power, manipulation, or good behavior. The source of this drive to change someone seems to be found in the unmet needs of the child. The child wants something, say, love or attention. The parent responds, "No, I can't give it to you." (In reality, this means the child can never get the need met, leaving no room for change.) The child reasons, "I am unworthy of love." (This is easier to accept because the child can always do something: improve, change, try harder, misbehave, control, or do whatever is necessary to get the need met.)

Are expectations damaging? Yes. "They set you up for disappointment or they set up others for criticism." With this in mind, Dr. Ney asked us to consider the real and unrealistic expectations that we have of those closest to us.

Regarding my husband:
1. He will be the sexual initiator.
2. He will support me in my acquiring further education.
3. He will meet my sexual, emotional, and physical needs.
4. He will understand me and love me.
5. He will accept me as I am, not comparing me with other women.
6. He will make plans for our future instead of just letting it happen.
7. He will be the spiritual leader.
8. He will cultivate a relationship with all of our children and grandchildren.
9. He will take responsibility for the sexual abuse of our daughters.
10. He will be positive in his views of others and will quit criticizing.
11. He will express his needs and wants in an open, loving way.
12. He will control his anger.

13. He will pick up after himself and keep the bathroom clean.
14. He will work through his past, recognizing his fears and working through them.
15. He will be excited about our being on our own in a few years instead of seeing it as the end of life.

This is sickening. I realize that I want everything my way. The right way! Think like me. Be like me.

Regarding my children:
1. They will be there when I am in the mood for them and disappear when I am not in the mood.
2. They will act and speak properly, especially in public.
3. They will respect me.
4. They will keep their rooms and themselves tidy.
5. They will do homework and chores independently.
6. They will develop a relationship with God.
7. They will handle their anger so that it doesn't touch me.
8. They will not control or smother me.

In other words, be perfect! Don't be needy.

Regarding my mother:
1. She will stop nagging, controlling, manipulating, and correcting me, my children, and my stepfather.
2. She will believe and respect me.
3. She will let me be an adult.
4. She will value me and my differences.
5. She will love me and accept me as I am, whether I am fat or thin, whether I think her way or not.
6. She will learn to apologize.
7. She will take responsibility for her mistakes, past and present.

Let me think! Let me be my own person.

Regarding my dad:
1. He will deal with his addictions and compulsions.
2. He will stop mauling me.
3. He will love and respect me.

Think and behave like a father should.

Regarding God:
1. He will keep me from all evil.

2. He will never leave me.
3. He will never let me get hurt.
4. He will never let anyone abuse me.

If I am good, he should keep me safe.

Regarding the church family:
1. They will be there for me.
2. They will love and accept me just as I am.
3. They will see and meet my needs.
4. They will not always have needs.
5. They will value my time, space, and property.
6. They will be vulnerable.
7. They will let me be human and make mistakes.
8. They will let women be whole, functioning church members.

Rules order my life. I want to break free from all the regulations. I am trapped in my past, trapped in my relationships, my home, and the church. Rigid rules and form provided a false safety. I am really trapped. Examining myself and the environment that I have created is heartbreaking. Grieving and introspection are hard work. Exhaustion, bouts of rage, and breakthroughs of astonishing peace keep me in a whirlpool of emotions. "War repeats itself, passing from one generation to the next, until the conflict inside is resolved."

WEEK 16

Anna

To be able to analyze an expectation for its validity, we were told to look at the track record of the person of whom we had the expectation. We must go by whatever the track record says....Now we can decide if it is realistic to expect whatever from the person. The object is to be able to say to adults, "I want you to know my needs so that you won't have to guess."

As well, we would be able to discern and deliver appropriate expectations to our children. We were assured that not only would it be easier to live with clear expectations, but it would also prevent disappointment.

Asking us to relate today's unrealistic expectations to the desperately hungry, demanding little child seemed as probable as finding a needle in a haystack. We were all exhausted these days and forgetting beckoned; probing deeper seemed an insurmountable task.

The drive that demands my perfection and pushes me to harangue everyone around me must have its roots deep within the hurt little child's need to be good enough to have Mommy love her and the abusers stop punishing her. The fantasy that I would live "happily ever after" if I only tried harder; was a better Christian, a more submissive wife, a patient mother; worked more, prayed longer, did anything better or differently—this fantasy must surely have its source in the child's never-satisfied love hunger. My expectations reveal the delusion. "Everyone, myself included, would be healthy and happy if only we would 'fix' anything that wasn't perfect." This must be an extension of the child's need to make the ugliness go away forever. The incredible number of my buried expectations demonstrates the demanding little child's desperate need to control everything, to coerce the future and maybe thereby somehow conquer the past. I can hear the child's voice repeatedly as I reread my lists. She silently screams, demanding her way, so needy and desperate. With my own children, however, I am more often haunted by the dreaded echo of my mother's voice. This child seems forever compelled to fix, control, punish, or copy those she both loves and hates.

Working through these past days since the burial was not as I had anticipated. I have been surprised by feelings of joy and well-being, temporary seasons of light, as one by one these unrealistic expectations exposed themselves, withered, and dropped off. The power that fed them is dead. She no longer makes the choices in my life. A wonderful sense of freedom fills the void, making it easier to look within, behind, and ahead. I think that this incredible aliveness is steadily growing. While I still have doubts, I am becoming more and more convinced that this is the way we were designed to respond to life.

I chose my husband as the person with whom to share my list of expectations because I figured that this relationship was not only the most pertinent, but also the most dysfunctional. Making it as honest and complete as possible, I covered 30 separate points with him. We agreed that many of them were unrealistic. A few we even laughed over. Others we discussed, making reasonable changes that would help meet the needs of both of us. Some he thought were unreasonable, such as my desire for further schooling. He determined that unless there would be significant financial gain, schooling would be out. This angered me. I felt controlled, misunderstood, and, yes, even victimized. My "pleasure" needs did not have enough value to warrant the minimal expenditure. Internally, I resolved that I would not let him make the decisions for me in this area of my life anymore. I knew that his limited education colored his view, but I could no longer "protect" him. He became angry and defensive with the points that touched his relationship with the children and grandchildren, as well as those related to improving himself educationally. The only topics on my list that he refused to discuss were those regarding the future. He said that "these would cause too much trouble between us," and he wasn't willing to rock the boat anymore. I left the subject, feeling very unsettled. In the past, I would have pressed him on every issue until there was agreement. We would never have covered the whole list. He would have retreated in anger and then silence. I would have responded to the anger with anger or martyrdom and then later "fix" the problem in any way possible, usually by taking full responsibility, selling myself for peace.

Through this therapy, my increasing weight has eroded my security and self-esteem. I feel so fat and ugly. I am undesirable. I want to be wanted but I can't be trusted when I am not fat. I am either bad or fat. I am sexual, desirable, and filled with confidence but not trustworthy, or I am fat, nonsexual, depressed, with low self-esteem, but reliable and safe. I was fat as a child and teenager; my stepfather despises fat. I married men who despise fat. When I was single and thin, I was promiscuous. Please unloose the mysterious chains and set me free.

How can I separate my sexuality from my weight?

In the group, we hear that a child with deep unmet needs can be easily exploited. I understand more easily how the same children are abused or raped repeatedly. I can also see how people in authority, such as clergy, doctors, and teachers, hold such a precarious position. We as abused or neglected children long for our needs to be met and can substitute anything for temporary relief. Dr. Ney says this is the basis for all addictions. How I long to be free from addiction and compulsion, as well as to become strong to fight against victimization.

Listening to Dr. Ney: "Inside you say, prove that you love me. Prove it over and over. Now think. Do you say you love me more than I can hear, more than I want to hear, or more than I know how to hear?" My husband doesn't say he loves me. It hurts me so much. I cry inside to hear that he is happy with me, wants me, and loves me. Can it be that I can't hear him, or is it possible that he is unable to love no matter what I do?

During the break, Krista invited me to her house before next session to cut her hair. "Finances are low," she shared. I hesitated, feeling threatened, not wanting to get too involved. Forgetting the rules of no outside friendships, I contrived a cover by saying that I had too many commitments but would meet her early and do it here at the office. We agree on a time. I retreat for an unwanted drink of water, wondering how I got myself into this.

While I was sharing my homework, Dr. Green's frank comments on my sexual needs hurt me so much that I fled from the room. I was leaving the building when she caught up with me. She talked, but the words bounced off the walls of my anger and hurt. I defended my position and declared my pain over her sharp words. She apologized for any hurt she'd caused me and confided that sometimes things come out sharper than she intended. Eventually we returned and rejoined the group, seeming to have reconciled. I didn't really participate much the rest of the evening.

WEEK 17

All the group members were here this evening but the two facilitators weren't. I can't quite remember what kept them away. I'm sure it was legitimate, but I really missed them, and so did the group. It turned out that Tasha was attending her daughter's school play and Shelly had to work or would lose her job. In fact, both were very persistent group members. These facilitators continued to play a quiet role in the background, which included nodding in agreement, handing tissues out when people cried, and speaking from their own experience when others were becoming depressed and discouraged. There was no question but that without them it would not have been the same kind of group. On the other hand, the group served a very important function for them. It helped them to see their problems from another perspective. Group psychotherapy tends to make people introspective, and, as they become more interested and concerned with themselves, psychosomatic symptoms tend to increase. There is no question but that self-centeredness is bad for one's health. This was one way of helping them overcome it. They both reported great changes in their lives, not only as a result of their own therapy, but also from vicariously participating in the therapy of others.

This evening, Linda looked very anxious. "One of my brothers attempted suicide and the other one is thinking about it. I seem to have stirred up an awful lot of turmoil in the family, but I'm not sorry." Linda reported a lot of memories coming up in her mind. Tanya said she began to realize that many of the unrealistic expectations with which she had been struggling within herself concerned her mother.

Krista began the group tonight by indicating that she was still struggling with her boyfriend. "I told him that my expectations of him were unreal and that he probably had unrealistic expectations of me. I insisted on talking with him, and as I did so, I began to realize that he controlled our friendship and that he doesn't want to change. He asked, 'Why do you keep coming back?' I began to realize that nothing was going to change because he wouldn't let it, so I said good-bye. People tend to have unrealistic expectations of me, but I know I let them do so. I've now begun to look at my own choices."

It appeared that Krista, with the other members of the group, had switched from creating unrealistic expectations in the minds of people to dumping them all and insisting that no one have any expectations at all. I pointed out that realistic expectations meant that people could count on them for some things that realistically they were able to provide. The expectations that they had previously created would mean that they would have to be submissive to fulfil them. Now that they were beginning to assert themselves, it wasn't reasonable to dump their expectations altogether.

Anna and Dr. Green had been involved in an intense struggle for some weeks because Dr. Green was clearly a transference object. Anna was placing on her all sorts of characteristics that weren't there but that belonged to her mother. For Dr. Green, this posed a great difficulty because she was not used to not being treated as she really was. This was one of the most intense psychotherapy experiences in which she had been involved, and she said that she appreciated any guidance I could give her. Anna said, "Dr. Green, you pushed a lot of buttons in me. I hadn't really gotten in touch with these feelings before. Now that I have, I find they are so intense that I'm not sure I can deal with them." Having dealt with some of those feelings, Anna now turned to the other big cause for turmoil in her life, namely, her husband. "I couldn't separate his physical drive from his love for me. I couldn't trust myself with him. Now I feel freer to enjoy him. I had enormous difficulty in letting go of the baby whom Daddy abused. It was like an enormous pain in my stomach. I placed the baby in the arms of Jesus and now I feel peace." It appeared that Anna had great difficulty in giving up her painful existence partly because it was familiar to her. "I created false expectations in others. I read them all to my husband, and he said he felt I was putting an awful lot of pressure on him. He's afraid I'm going to leave him now. I would like him to change but I feel so powerless to do that."

I reminded her that one cannot change other people. The more you try, the more they resist. That resistance is an instinctual mechanism in children. If you try to feed them or change them, they immediately become suspicious. There is a natural tendency to resist being forced to do something because you begin to think that the person is doing so for his or her own benefit, not for yours. However, you can change people by changing yourself. It is a great power. To begin with, just changing creates a mystery in the other person, a curiosity. It also creates a disequilibrium, and in that disequilibrium, the person searches for other ways of responding. People tend to give away their power by giving away intimate knowledge about themselves, but it makes the other person much more comfortable, and in that comfort, the person can change more readily. With an honest and intimate knowledge of one's spouse, one can feel secure and can change in one's own direction rather than having to change in the direction that the spouse would have one change.

Linda looked perplexed. "I don't know what realistic expectations of myself are. There are many parts of my life I've never challenged. I have a feeling that there are things I could do if I only try." As soon as that came up, the group reminded her that such feelings often came from the child striving in her, the child kept alive in order to help her survive and whose unrealistic expectations were maintained partly by the North American ethic that one can do anything one wants to if one really tries.

Amy was well along in her pregnancy now, and although she looked healthy, she said she didn't feel that way. "I'm not feeling very well. I did show Sam my list. There was no reaction. I'm not sure if it made it easy for him. I feel really blocked. I don't know myself. I don't have anybody with whom I can be honest. I'm afraid that if I'm more honest with Sam, he will give me less of what I need and that disappointment will drive me to leave him. I keep fighting to change things and I know it won't work, but I'm not sure I can trust this other way. I need to be committed, but the more I look for that, the more Sam doesn't want to get married. We now have two children and still he is afraid. I don't know what it is going to take."

By this time, Anna and many of the others were beginning to make insightful comments to their colleagues, and this was one of those occasions. "You are your husband's relationship with your little girl. You can't force him into relating to her. I can see that when he doesn't, you feel as hurt as if you were the one who was being neglected."

Tanya had a habit of looking confused and distraught. She would throw back her hair and lean forward with a wild-eyed look. "I didn't do my homework right. I didn't realize that I can have expectations and that people can have expectations of me. My husband thinks that I am strong: I can make curtains, work, and do everything, and he is just waiting for the time when I'll be free of this problem so he can put those expectations into operation. I get depressed just at the thought of it."

Lisa continued to look better. She was less depressed. Instead of her usual black, she was wearing some color. "I set myself up for disappointments. My adoptive parents should have seen from the beginning that I had problems, but they never got any help for me. I am beginning to learn to accept myself, and that makes it easier for other people to accept me. I still feel a deep resentment over the fact that my life was taken from me, but now that the child has been set to rest, I feel that a lot of the pressure has been taken off me and I can accept myself better. I still struggle with memories and I get angry with myself because I can't put them away." Lisa was reassured that as time went on, terrifying memories would still come to the surface. This was so partly because she was getting stronger and her memories were able to surface to a greater extent.

As a group exercise this evening, we engaged in a discussion of what children can realistically expect of childhood and their parents. I asked them as homework to do an amorphous blob. This is a technique that I have used with children for many years. They start with a vague outline of their egos, putting inside the outline characteristics that they know are true and outside the outline characteristics that are attributed to them or believed of them but that are not true. Arrows going from the outside to the inside, or vice versa, would indicate characteristics that they would like to change. In addition, as time was moving on, I asked them to consider with whom they needed to be reconciled. Who would be the hardest to reconcile with and who would be the easiest?

❖   ❖   ❖

Anna

Before we started our homework this week, I needed to share the insights I had gleaned during the week regarding my conflict and following flight from the room. I explained to the group:

"Last Thursday, I had tremendous anger toward Dr. Green. Her comment that I 'couldn't feel wanted unless my husband chased me around the bed' was degrading to me. I was overwhelmed with shame. I couldn't bear to look at any of you, so I ran from the room. I felt that my expectations of my husband's and my sex life not only were private, but were realistic. Her words told me that I was cheap. I argued that I only wanted someone to love me, to make love to me, holding me gently, cherishing and valuing me as a woman and wife. I reasoned that two or three times a month, just so long as he wanted me, was okay. It would fill my need. I wrestled with myself for many hours before I was able to allow the truth that she'd wanted to convey slowly to seep into my conscious mind.

"If he wanted me sexually, he loved me. If not, I was unlovable, ugly, too fat, no good, totally rejected. I could function best if my sexual expectations were low because I didn't have to deal with rejection very often. I had confused my physical drive and my emotional needs. I realized that I didn't know how to separate his lack of physical attraction and drive from his love for me.

"Sometimes I would become so frustrated that I'd say inside, 'I know I am desirable. I'll show him.' My Christian principles always caught me up short and prevented me from infidelity. I realize now that I also stayed fat so that I could blame his rejection on my fat and not because I was undesirable. When I was thin a few years ago, I was so unsafe. I didn't trust myself to be faithful. I looked up an old boyfriend with the intention of setting us both free from a past relationship that I'd tucked deep in the recesses of my heart. Now I know that I was compelled by several motives. Yes—to release us both from sexual and emotional ties, but also to prove I was still valuable. He still wanted me. I got fat very quickly after that. I couldn't trust myself to continue in a relationship in which I was not wanted if there were options. I erased the options, never perceiving that my husband could love me in ways I could not hear. I had this enormous need. He was so threatened by it that he pulled away from me, knowing he could never satisfy it. I shared with him what I'd discovered. He affirmed its truth, saying, 'Yes, it is just like that, but I haven't noticed it so much in the past few weeks.' It is so amazing. I see him so differently. He is just the same, but I feel freer to enjoy him. We have laughed and played more in the past few days than I can ever remember. My sexuality is separating from his love for me, and somehow even the natural desire I have for him doesn't seem to be attached to who I am.

"The deep searching required for this sexual understanding led me to a new place—a place of profound pain—located in the pit of my stomach. I embraced it. I didn't want to give it up. It had been there so long. I had the overwhelming sense that if I let it go, there would be nothing left of me. I had buried the two-and-one-half-year-old that the foster parent had abused but this was the baby—the baby whose daddy had defiled, violated her. She had somehow bonded to the darkness and pain. She had previously let go of the darkness, but she wouldn't let go of the pain. It was hers. Evil and darkness had bonded to me, but I bonded to the pain, which was my choice. It proved our innocence and our neediness. Our right to demand justice. How could we give up an old companion, even though so 'ugly' a one, we had protected and embraced for years? We covered the pain with fat. Whenever I got thin, the pain was always more exposed and I was always more vulnerable. After the mighty struggle to surrender the pain to Jesus was complete, a knowing of my preciousness and value to him bathed me. The process had begun and I trusted that I could continue to give him any new 'pains' that came up, knowing that peace and gentleness would replace them, becoming my new companions."

At break, Shawna asked if she could copy from my notebook. "No problem," I responded. A few minutes later, Tanya asked the same thing within earshot of Dr. Ney, who said, "No one copies directly from someone else. Put it in your own words. You will learn it best that way." I felt rebuked by his tone. Leaving to get a drink, I overheard him in the hall explaining to Tanya that he didn't want to stir up competition with our homework. Wow! I thought I'd felt rebuked earlier. Now I felt ashamed as well. Dr. Green piped up: "I'd like to have her whole notebook, not just the one passage." I was redeemed slightly. They continued down the hall for their debriefing.

Before beginning my homework, I reflected on some of Dr. Ney's one-liners that he dropped intermittently throughout each session. I found that this helped immensely in gathering and organizing my thoughts. As well, it became a reliable tool in focusing on the subject for the week. Scattered thoughts and turbulent emotions could otherwise rob me of valuable time. "When really needy children are looking for a parent, they give the impression that they'll do anything if you just love them. This creates false expectations. Creating false expectations is an illusion to make them love you."

My husband thought that he could parent me, that he could be in control, could do almost anything he wanted to me without consequence. I created this. I created the false expectation that I'd be a doormat through submissiveness all bent out of shape. I have to find a way to rectify this.

False expectations that I created in others:
1. I would always have an answer—the right answer.
2. I would always be available, especially for those in chaos.
3. I had unlimited time and energy.
4. I would keep my word regardless of the consequences.
5. I would be trustworthy.
6. I would be on time.
7. I would be able to lose weight or would try to do so.
8. I would succeed. I would do a great job at everything.
9. I would be in control, organized, efficient, reliable.
10. I would be emotionally strong.
11. This was the most important: I would obey all the rules, both spoken and unspoken, as well as those imagined.

At first glance, most of these seem like great attributes; however, they demanded perfection from me. I would carry them out legalistically, rigidly conforming, and expecting exactly the same from others.

What others can realistically expect of me:
1. I will have fewer answers, as I am increasingly aware of how little I really know.

2. I will be there for others after my needs and my family's needs are appropriately met. Temporarily, my wholeness needs are paramount.
3. Those relationships whose needs are especially demanding or threatening, aside from those of my immediate family, are temporarily on hold.
4. As abusive relationships are recognized, they will be confronted and/or weeded out.
5. I am learning to accept my body weight and condition just as they are and to accept responsibility for them. My evaluation is the voice to which I am determined to listen.
6. I am continuing to give myself permission to be human, to fail, to be less than perfect. This means I might be late, not go to a meeting, or even miss church; play, rest, do nothing instead of produce, sleep in or stay up late; be real, honest, silly, spontaneous, flexible; let my emotions show. I give those in my world permission to be human also.

Family expectations:
1. I will not always have meals ready at the stroke of the clock.
2. I will not do laundry on demand.
3. I will not always have the house in perfect order.
4. I will not always rescue those in trouble, even if asked or if I seem to be the only one able.
5. I will not "own" responsibility just for the sake of peace.
6. I will not always be practical and available.
7. I will work to express my anger appropriately.
8. I will tell you my needs.
9. I will take time out just for me.
10. I will try to be honest and open rather than protect you.
11. I will invite you to play with me, and I will play even if you don't.
12. I will work on my personal growth to free myself and, in turn, to free you.
13. I will continue to love you in as healthy a way as I know.

In going over these, my husband and I could see the tremendous pressure in the false expectations to perform and the promise of fun and freedom in the new expectations. I also noticed that he seemed even more insecure than normal. Also, a whole new development has occurred. He asked me if I wanted to leave him, and if my problems are his fault. In the past, I've always hung on, wondering whether he might kick me out, grow tired of me, or just find someone else. Never has he acknowledged any fear of my leaving him. At this point, Dr. Ney interrupts me, saying, "When you change, you have tremendous power. Share with others your new position so they can be secure. Don't hold this new mysterious power over them. Make him secure so he doesn't have to change." Well, it does feel good to be in the driver's seat for a change. I am not sure just how soon I want to give this up. It's exhilarating. Lots of laughter and suggestions on how to misuse this power follow. Then, in seriousness, I conclude that I will surrender this newly found power by reassuring my husband that I will not leave him, that unless he abuses me or someone else, commits adultery or is violent, he should not have any fear of our breaking up.

6

Reconciliation: Direct Negotiations for Compensation and Forgiveness

Up until this point, the group has been working together and in private, but there has been no contact with the perpetrator and observers. They now must engage in the work of reconciliation. What they have learned during earlier phases must be put into practice. Their new skills at assertion, expressing their feelings, negotiating, and being realistic are all going to be put to good use. Group members, having been told of the whole process, have been looking forward to this time with considerable trepidation. Some are sufficiently anxious that they engage in regression or denial or the projection of anger. Others grit their teeth and indicate that they are determined to finish at any price.

If reconciliation is not achieved, history must repeat itself. History repeats itself because people have not learned how to resolve the core conflicts. When a person does not learn from history, the original conflicts that are engendered from mistreatment continue and affect much of his or her life in such a way as to make the use of energy inefficient. The body and mind are so designed that they must be using energy efficiently. Therefore, they must resolve conflicts. In order to do this, the conflicts are usually reenacted. At this point in therapy, the reenactment is about to happen, only this time it will be controlled, supervised, and used for the purposes of providing insight and inducing new behavior.

Even though our group members basically understood it, they had to be reminded that hate is mutually destructive. Hate is a destructive anger plus a determination not to proceed with any type of reconciliation. It results in bitterness, which produces depression. Depression appears to interfere with the immune system and thus increases the likelihood of infections and cancer.

For a child, hate may have had some value. It provides the youngster with protection. Children avoid the persons they hate, and that is of con-

129

siderable value. But when they become adults, hate does as much harm to them as they might think it does to those who harmed them. Hate can be used as a drive to "self-actualization," but it does not produce any real progress in fulfilling the Blueprint. It is always destructive. Some people use hate to punish the perpetrator and/or observer over and over again in their imaginations. They also keep those who have harmed them in a prison of guilt and uncertainty. The perpetrator and observer never know when they may be confronted with their misdeeds, publicly shamed, and possibly imprisoned.

Everyone seems to want "a day in court." Since childhood, they have had a sense of "when there is an injustice, there is a just judge somewhere who will eventually sort it all out and declare, 'You're right.'" Unfortunately, this is very unlikely to happen.

The object of reconciliation is not to create an ongoing friendship, although that may happen. It is to enable our patients to become as adult as possible, to look directly into the eyes of the persons they fear the most, and to deal directly with some of their deepest wounds. The reconciliation is effective when the person no longer is persistently angry at those who hurt him or her, and can wish the best for them.

To enable people to engage in reconciliation they must first develop confidence and skill through a number of important role plays. The role plays are designed to develop new approaches and to desensitize them to the possible bad responses.

Our patients must face a number of fears when dealing with their perpetrators. These are that:

1. They will be attacked and harmed again because they brought up this painful subject. This feeling stems from their childhood perceptions of the perpetrators, who now are usually not nearly as big, powerful, or threatening as they remember them.
2. The perpetrator will tell everybody about what he or she is being confronted with in order to embarrass the patient. At the same time, the perpetrators will deny any responsibility for what he or she did.
3. The confrontatiotn will "kill" the perpetrator or observer. "I am sure she couldn't stand it. I know she has a bad heart."
4. The perpetrator or observer will permanently reject, disown, or disinherit the patient, or never speak to the patient again.
5. They will upset the tenuous balances in the family, something that most of them have striven to maintain for much of their lives.

We role-played the response of the perpetrator in four possible ways:

1. "Yes, of course, I understand why you are writing. I don't want to remember this, but I know I must."

2. "It didn't happen, and besides, it was all your fault."
3. "Don't say that. You'll kill me. You know my heart isn't strong."
4. "All right. If that is the way you feel, it's good-bye. You'll never see me again."

Experience has shown that the perpetrators are often easier to deal with than are the observers or victims. This is so partly because they knew that it was going to happen eventually, and they are very relieved that it is not going to result in their being imprisoned, punished, or embarrassed.

One woman reported that, after writing a letter, she was able to talk to the brother who had abused her. "I thought one day this would happen. He said, 'I'm sorry. I know I have caused you a lot of pain.' He didn't make excuses. I felt a great sense of relief. It opened up communication. Now it's out, I can't wait to see him. Initially, I was very nervous. Now I have a great sense of peace. I can forgive him, and there is so much less anger."

People who have been badly hurt find it difficult to forgive. They tend to do so with an offhand blanket statement that effects nothing at all. Forgiveness is a process. This period of reconciliation is to teach them how that process works. I am not surprised at the vehemence with which my patients say, "I will never forgive him. He ruined my life. I never want to talk to him again." It takes a lot of patience to remind them that what they are saying to their perpetrator is something that they are essentially saying to themselves. When they cannot forgive others, they are not able to forgive themselves because often they are partly responsible. If forgiveness is not achieved, it is very likely that the same cycle of tragedy will be foisted on their children.

Some have complained about the enormous feeling of loneliness as they go through the phase of reconciliation. They are bound to feel alone because they are putting a number of familiar people, with whom they interact daily through convoluted conversations in their mind, at a distance. It is almost as if they were feeling bereft of people with whom they have lived in a busy hotel and whom they asked to leave. While living in this hotel, a person could knock on any door and have a conversation, even though it wasn't a pleasant one and produced a lot of emotion.

Another woman, having written a letter to which she had had no response, said, "I'd rather be punched in the face than ignored." But she felt a release at writing the letter. There is a type of validation of one's perceptions and experience that comes from seeing something in writing or in print. How much better it is when both the letter and its contents are accepted.

The process of reconciliation centers on sending a letter. Because this letter has medical/legal implications, it has to be very carefully worded. Our patients are sent home to write draft letters, which then are carefully gone over in the group for corrections and clarifications. Even after the letters have been carefully rewritten, our patients sometimes experience great difficulty in sending them. It takes a lot of group support and encouragement from us to ensure that the letters are actually sent.

The letter to the perpetrator can include an invitation to initiate a written dialogue and respond within a limited number of weeks. The perpetrators must be assured that the issue is to remain confidential, that this is a better way of dealing with the trauma and disability than through legal channels. An abused child's secret is always a potential bomb. When a person deals with it in this way, it is like defusing the bomb. This results in the loss of a good deal of power for the person who maintained the secret. The letter should be addressed in such a way that it is an invitation to a process of reconciliation and healing.

The hope of forgiveness and a pathway to achieve forgiveness are the best gifts that anybody can give someone imprisoned with guilt. When the letters are sent, there is a lag period during which patients figuratively hold their breaths, waiting for some terrible outcome. My experience is that the patients are surprised at just how readily many perpetrators agree to engage in the process of reconciliation. The perpetrators are first invited to write back, and then to engage in face-to-face negotiations.

The negotiations include settling on some kind of compensation. I recognize that there is no way in which children can be properly compensated for the damage that they have sustained. However, the compensation also has to be more than symbolic. Sometimes victims will refuse any compensation for themselves, but will accept something that could be done for their children, perhaps in the form of money for education or, with grandparents, time spent playing with the grandchildren. But, until reconciliation has been achieved, most patients do not want the perpetrators to come near their children. They suspect that they have not changed and will harm the children, just as the patients themselves had been harmed.

The perpetrators have to engage in the process of reconciliation in a direct manner. Without the direct encounter, they will not experience what it feels like to be forgiven. Once the perpetrators have been forgiven, there are often major changes in their lives—not only in their attitudes toward themselves, but toward the world in general as well.

The inability of some patients to forgive may stem from a difficulty in giving up the anger that has driven them until now. This anger eventually will destroy them. It results in bitterness, which can interfere with the body's immune systems and thus increase the likelihood of illness. Without forgiveness for the perpetrator, they will be unable to forgive themselves or to have a forgiving attitude toward their own children.

The patients have to forgive themselves. They have to forgive themselves for harming themselves, making poor choices, missing opportunities, and sometimes for harboring hate for such a long time. Sometimes this is best achieved by writing a letter to themselves.

It is hardest to achieve reconciliation with the observers. The observers tend to have "watertight alibis." "It didn't happen," or "I didn't know about it. Besides, I couldn't have done anything about it anyway." To achieve reconciliation, it is often necessary to obtain the cooperation of the perpetrator in confronting the observers about their knowledge and lack of protective action.

Since there are no innocent bystanders, therapists should recognize and admit that they also have contributed in small but significant ways to the mistreatment of children. The patients will protest, stating, "No, you're not like all the other doctors/nurses/pastors, etc., we have known who didn't recognize what was happening to us. We don't think that you need to be forgiven." The therapist must insist that they do. After all, if we are not actively stopping the problem, we are contributing to it (especially in issues of child abuse or life and death). Generally, we also apologize on behalf of our professions, some members of which have made serious errors in diagnosis and treatment.

Reconciliation with children is always anticipated as being much more difficult than it really is. Unfortunately, children tend to forgive their parents all too readily and too nonspecifically. They must be encouraged to talk about each and every hurt that their parents inflicted on them. Adults find it hard really to listen to children. Children have so many hurts and these remind them of their own childhoods. Too often, it ends up with crying, and who wants to cry?

There also must be reconciliation with God. After all, harm to children is harm to their Maker. Many people have misconceptions about God. This is a time when all of their worries and fears and misconceptions can be discussed.

The perpetrators and observers also have emotions that need to be understood in order to communicate with them:

1. *Fear.* "I am afraid to respond to this letter because I think the writer just wants to humiliate me or put me in jail."
2. *Relief.* "I'm so glad that this is happening. I couldn't go on suffering guilt like I have. It is ruining my health and I couldn't enjoy my life."
3. *Suicide.* "I can't believe that I did this. I must have forgotten all about it. I would rather kill myself than face this. It is just too awful."
4. *Denial.* "It didn't really happen—besides, I couldn't help it."
5. *Self-pity.* "I don't know why they are going after me. After all, I'm just a poor old man/woman now, and besides, I was treated much worse when I was a child."

This is a very stressful time for the patients and they look for excuses to avoid coming to group. They need to be well supported. The help of the facilitator is vital at this point. Before they go home at the end of each group session, I am careful to take a reading on how they are faring. If there is any real concern about how well they are handling the stress, I notify their spouses or friends, or ask the facilitator to accompany them home.

WEEK 18

Mid-February and it was miserably cold and wet outside, but everybody but Lisa was there. Lisa had taken a short trip to California and everybody was happy that she could go, although they missed her, especially at this juncture of the group. I was always amazed at the commitment and tenacity with which people attended the group. Anna had a five-hour trip, but she was always on time.

Tonight, we began with the group exercise. I wanted each of the people to consider what their disabilities were. I pointed out that when children are involved in accidents, they are left with broken limbs or damaged brains, and everybody recognizes those disabilities; no less so, the disabilities resulting from their mistreated childhood were things that they had to accept and others had to accept in them. They were then asked to tell the group what their disabilities were and the group was either to confirm, deny, or add to that list of disabilities. In most instances, the group members were well aware of their continuing difficulties, including not being able to trust people, not having utilized their potential intellectually, having minds crowded with painful memories, and experiencing great difficulty in bringing up their children in an evenhanded way. Having done the exercise, we returned to the homework wherein each group member was to give a list of her ego characteristics, indicating what was true and what was not true of herself. Anna led off with a long list, and everybody tended to agree. Shawna began to realize that she hadn't done the homework well because it was hard for her to get a balanced view of herself. Linda found that defining her ego was easy enough, but said she didn't like what she saw. Amy concentrated on her mothering ability, and this left very few good characteristics among those that she owned as part of her ego. It was easy to see from her outline and the characteristics that she had a fragile ego. Tanya recognized that among her disabilities and part of her ego was her inability to trust her perceptions and her fear of not being loved. She seemed to be hypersensitive to confusing messages. Krista began clearly to recognize her passivity, her passive aggressiveness, and her tendency to domineer through pleading and tenacity.

We had gone through the group exercise and the homework relatively quickly tonight because we were about to tackle one of the other large hurdles of the process; that is, writing a reconciling letter to one of the perpetrators. Before they were sent home with that homework, I described what the letter should contain. I told them that it should read something like this:

> Dear _____:
> I am writing this letter to you because there is a continuing problem that I must deal with and I would like you to help me. There are many problems in my life, but the scars and disabilities left from my early encounter with you continue to plague me. In group psychotherapy, I am dealing with lots of these, but some won't go away until we both work on them. I hope in the future to be able to talk with you in an adult way, but right now I am writing to make it very clear. I realized I had to do this for many years and now I am doing it with a lot of trepidation, and I hope you will take it in the right way. Please be assured that this does not mean that I think you should be punished. The police and Social Services will not be involved. This is strictly between the two of us and it will be confidential.
> I want to forgive you, but it is hard. In order to make it easier for me, I would like you to (1) listen to me as I tell you that you have hurt me, (2) recognize all the hurts and wounds you have created and apologize for each one separately, (3) promise never to do anything like that to me or anyone else again, (4) show me some evidence that you have changed so that I can trust your promise not to repeat any of this, and (5) help me overcome some of my disabilities with some type of help or compensation.
> Here is a list of the ways in which you have hurt me and how they still affect my life....
> I would appreciate your writing back to me. If necessary, we can discuss this, but I would prefer that to be in Dr. Ney's office so that we can have an arbitrator.

After I outlined this letter, I saw expressions of dismay and horror on almost every face. I knew this would happen, and together with the facilitators, sought to reassure them. All of them were afraid that if this letter were to be sent, the person who received it either would attack them, die, or ignore them. All of these projected reactions were an indication of how they had experienced their childhood and people like that. The facilitators reassured them that they themselves had felt much of the same distress initially upon being asked to write such letters, but had persevered and found that none of their fantasized reactions of the perpetrators ever came true. In most instances, the perpetrators were glad to engage in the process even if it was painful. They generally felt relieved, having been released from their many years of self-imprisonment. They were glad to be able to compensate the person, and often they felt that what had been requested of them was less than what they felt they should give.

If the people in the group couldn't see the assignment in any other way, they could see it in terms of their being perpetrators in relation to their own children and of what their children might someday ask of them. Knowing how they harmed their children, they felt that if their children ever asked anything of them as they were asking of their parents, it would be minimal compensation. They also knew that they would feel relieved, and they knew that they would not die. However, the fears persisted, and because of that, and because I wanted to see what they wrote, I asked them to write the letter but not to mail it. We would go over each letter and make sure the wording was as effective as possible. I would make sure that there was the best chance for the perpetrator to respond in a reasonable, adult fashion. In this way, they would hold a door open as wide as possible for the perpetrator to exit, but they could not be guaranteed that the perpetrator would take the opportunity to do so. Still, even if the perpetrator did not take advantage of that opportunity, I was convinced by previous experience that their having engaged in this exercise would benefit them greatly.

With considerable trepidation, they left the group to go out into a cold, windy night. There was a lot of blowing snow and there were fears that their cars might not start. I noticed as they left that they looked after each other very well. I had indicated at the beginning that they must not spend time talking about the group in pairs, but there was a natural inclination to do so.

❖   ❖   ❖

Anna

We had been asked to draw some nondescript shape and to fill the inside of it with true characteristics of ourselves and to write untrue ones around the outside. Afterwards we were to draw arrows, going into our shape for the characteristics we wanted to incorporate and going out for those we wanted to get rid of. Well, we sure had a variety of shapes. As we commented on this, Dr. Ney asked us to examine our shapes and see how they paralleled how we felt we look physically. Groan...mine was a fat oval. Not far from the mark.

It was my turn to go first. I had printed "46" in the center. I wish that were not true. Inside the circle, I had written "defensive, people pleaser, addict, fat, fearful, demanding, rigid, controlling, codependant, impatient, perfectionist." I am encouraged that some of these negative traits are in transition and on their way out of the inner circle of my self. Thirty more words described the characteristics that I am glad I have: trustworthy, diligent, analytical, forgiving, a leader, creative, intuitive, and punctual being a few. Of the qualities that I don't possess but would like to, the most significant are being carefree, peaceful, interdependent, musical, content, and playful. Those negative traits that I affirm are untrue about me are unlovable, spiteful, helpless, frivolous, ugly, an airhead, messy, or obnoxious.

Krista was next. She commented that I was playful already and maybe just didn't recognize it in myself.

As we all shared our "shapes," I couldn't help noticing that Amy seemed to be preoccupied. She seemed detached lately, almost uninterested unless it was her turn, yawning and fidgeting a lot. I felt Shawna's and Linda's growing irritation with her.

When we finished, Dr. Ney explained ego definition. People with fragile egos do not know who they are. The degree of definite understanding of who we are is a good measure of the stability of our egos, who we really are.

He went on to explain how we in society have a hard time dealing with our disabilities, giving as an example the degree of difficulty we have in really looking at a person in a wheelchair. He stated that most of us never get to know who such a person really is. With that insightful bit of information, he suggested that we haven't acknowledged each other's disabilities in this group and that we were now going to do just that. Yuk. Only Krista seemed pleased with this announcement. Eagerly she announced that she wants to know what we think so that she can do something about it.

First, me? My stomach was tight, I felt so awkward. The silence was loud. I wondered if anyone could hear my heart beating. I determined to "hear" what was said. Dr. Green spoke first. "Anna, you have a judgmental problem; you presuppose what others think of you." She gave the example from the beginning of therapy when I had reasoned that she didn't like me. Shawna was next. She declared that my "body view was distorted." After some discussion, Dr. Ney interjected, "If you don't like your body, it shows up in ill health." Dr. Ney closed my turn on the hot seat with, "You are not hopeful." The first two suggestions were correct; however, I felt his evaluation was wrong. I explained that it was hope that had kept me alive and hope that enabled me to fight against all odds in this last marriage. He listened, acknowledging my reasoning with "I stand corrected."

Linda was next. She looked as uncomfortable as I felt. Noticing my increasing discomfort, I recalled the anxiety I usually feel for others when they are confronted, especially with their shortcomings. I let my emotions surface so that I could examine them. I felt tense, fearful, afraid of their hurt. I wanted to take their place. I wanted to stop them from falling apart, stop them from getting hurt beyond repair. What if they got hurt and it couldn't be fixed?

Dr. Green shared with Shawna that she hadn't applied herself to her healing as much as she could have, not writing out the homework or sharing unless prodded. Shawna looked hurt, rebuked, and then angry, really angry.

When we got to Amy, several people shared about her need to rescue and her seeming lack of interest. She was also offended. So far I hadn't been able to conquer my fear of hurting them. They all seemed so fragile, especially Amy.

Tanya's turn. She was strong. I felt safe with her. I know that we have developed a measure of trust. Carefully, I submitted that she had a problem with male authority, challenging and confronting boldly on even minor points. Confirming its truth, she allowed others to point out her weaknesses.

Lisa also seemed too frail for me to confront on any issue. Finally, only Krista was left. I mustered up my courage and plunged in. "You were a good part of my homework when you asked me to come to your home and cut your hair. Afraid to say No and not wanting to say Yes, I felt trapped. You have a very strong personality and I've often backed away inside, especially during role plays. I know that I fear manipulation and tend to run from people who trigger helplessness in me." Krista retorted: "Then you have the problem, don't you?" As tactfully as possible, I replied, "I think we both have something to work on." She was not impressed. I felt desperate to fix, undo, erase what I'd said, even though in all honesty I believed it to be true. Great...the thing that I feared had come upon me!

"A brief summary to date is in order," Dr. Ney began. "Original hunger and deprivation lead to pain, which makes one vulnerable to insult. Pain leads to fixed conflicts. Pain/conflict leads to fear. (Mobilize the fear. Please don't leave me.) Fear leads to anger. (I am mad at you!) Anger leads to revenge and/or guilt (real and unreal). Guilt leads to responsibility (either 100 percent or none at all). Responsibility leads to looking at the situation realistically. (Who has to change?) Cheated of the original plan means a lost childhood, lost adulthood. The death of the child releases the demanding child. A realistic appraisal of who you are and are not will affect your ego. Set aside unrealistic expectations of yourself and others that are fantasy. We will proceed to the next step of reconciliation, meaning that you will work out the problem, the problem being that thing that maintains the hostilities, bitterness, and revenge. This step is good for the mind and brings peace and health to the body." He mentioned back pain, cancer, and ulcers specifically. Bedlam broke out about this point.

"No way! You've got to be kidding! I'm not going to! I told you at the beginning I wouldn't do this!" Adamant responses to the assignment of writing a letter to one of the perpetrators erupted. I was afraid, particularly of writing to Mom, but willing. Taking some time to calm and reassure us, he then had us copy a brief outline of the letter he wanted. He has a way of getting his way.

> To _____:
> I am writing to you because we must deal with this problem. [*Describe the problem.*] I have been hurt. [*List the hurts.*] I have disabilities. [*List the disabilities.*]
> This is not going to be easy for you. [*This will let the recipient out of his or her self-imposed prison of guilt.*] There were a lot of factors responsible for what happened. [*List them. Remember to see from the other's perspective.*]
> I want to be able to forgive and forget, to put this away. So I will detail all the hurts, how and when they happened, and the damage they caused. I want your sincere "Sorry" for each one. [*The perpetrator must promise never to do this again to you or anyone else.*]
> I would like compensation.

Again, anger and confusion mounted in the group. "No way do I want him to pay me for what he did," generally summed up what most felt. I guess others may have had the same conflict as I did, that forgiveness is a free gift not to be bought, but no one said it. There wasn't much comradeship after the group tonight.

❖   ❖   ❖

WEEK 19

My staunch facilitator Shelly was away again and we missed her. She was taking some very stiff exams and nobody blamed her for not being there, but still we had to wonder if there were anything that could be more important than what was happening now.

Shawna stated there had been a problem at her job. Her boss had insulted her, and when she discussed this with coworkers, they encouraged her, and eventually she wrote a letter and received an apology. She was so pleased to find that the technique that we were learning for use in dealing with the perpetrators in childhood actually worked with others as well.

Lisa stated that she was trying so hard to get the satanist abuser out of her life. Brian picked her up when she was a rebellious teenager. She had lived with him and he had introduced her to various satanic practices. She couldn't remember all of it, but knew that there was a close connection between what she had experienced as an infant and what she experienced as a teenager. The horror of it all and the fact that she had willingly reexposed herself brought back many fears and many questions about her own sanity. Now that she was dealing with this, she had a much clearer idea of what she had to do, but it was very difficult. "I'm trying to get Brian out of my life but it is getting messy. Somehow I feel the old attraction—I don't know why. How could anybody be attracted back to a satanic life of abuse, degradation, and humiliation? Now I feel I've got to end everything. I hope this is going to work."

Amy said, "It was a good session last time. Thank you all for your honesty with me. I was able to stand back and look at myself. Now I'm going to apply this at home."

Shawna indicated that she had written a letter to her father, whom she now called Alan. She was very frightened that if she were to send it, he would die, he would be so upset. He would lose his job. Her mother would never know what to do. She had always been a sick woman, and if she had to face this, there was no way she could stand it.

Krista wrote to Ian very clearly: "Ian, this is what you did to me," and there followed a long outline of the hurts that she had received from her brother. She didn't know how he would receive it, but at this point she didn't really care. She was primarily angry. There was little desire on her part for forgiveness.

Amy had written, "Dear Mom, I need to deal with this problem." Even though Amy was very determined, she couldn't bring herself to send the letter. Even in later sessions when other group members noted how much they had benefited from doing so, she still couldn't do it. She wrote one to her father, but he was dead. That letter was easy to deal with. She was afraid to send the letter to her mother because of the possible consequences. After all, her mother supported her in her difficulties and babysat with her daughter to give Amy the freedom to do such things as go dancing, which she felt she had to do.

Tanya wrote: "Dear Mom: I wanted to tell you this for a long time. I'm angry at you because you didn't see my hurt." She then went on to relate in detail how her mother seemed to be totally oblivious to the pathological incestuous relationship that she had had with her father for so many years. It was, like Lisa's letter, full of determination. "I must let you know that I'm not interested in seeing you anymore."

Anna wrote a poignant letter. She was an excellent writer, and when stirred up, she could express herself exquisitely. "You made it difficult for me to face men, all of them, and yet I needed them. We must deal with this. I want to be free of this whole thing."

In the group exercise, various group members read their letters aloud, with the listeners pointing out inconsistencies that they had gleaned from other conversations in the group and adding things that the writer seemed to have forgotten. Then in pairs each read her letter to her partner, who acted out the role of the perpetrator. The perpetrator was first asked to be very resistant. "I don't want to read this. I'm not interested. Take it away. This has nothing to do with me. It didn't happen. Besides, I couldn't help it." Then the partner was asked to play the role of a perpetrator who might respond with panic: "This is terrible. I can't face this. I'm going to kill myself. Oh, my heart! You're going to kill me. If we have to go through this, I will die." Then the perpetrator was asked to play the role of somebody who was more receptive: "Well, I hated to read this letter. It brought back so many terrible things. I know you have to deal with this and so do I. I only hope I have the strength. May God help us."

There was a discussion about how they should address the perpetrator. I suggested that they use the perpetrator's first name because this would provide a certain anonymity that the perpetrator might need. It also indicated a change in the relationship. It was no longer "Dear Dad," but "Dear Alan," indicating that the writer wanted to deal with it as an adult. There was considerable resistance. After all, they still yearned to have that parent even though the child inside who had been so demanding had been put to rest. The adult part of them wanted to maintain a childlike relationship. They began to realize, however, that there was nothing that they could obtain from such a relationship. It would be better to be adults.

In the conversation, the issue of secrecy came up. They had been carrying secrets for most of their lives and the secrets had been very damaging. I told them that, first, to dispel the secrets would result in a wide variety of benefits. The secrets they had kept as children had restrained them from exploring the real world. After all, how could one explore if one were afraid of finding something that then had to be carried as a burden? Second, secrets meant that one had to pretend—pretend that things were better, pretend that things were going to improve. Secrets created a sense of unreality that produced a sense of dissociation from the real world. Third, children's conversations had to be truncated. They were always afraid of broaching a subject that the adult might deem prohibited. Therefore, they had to be careful of what they said. Their inabilities to explore had limited the development of their intelligence. The reticence to speak freely had interfered with the development of their speech and vocabulary. Fourth, when children were afraid to explore, they were afraid of seeing themselves. Now that they could deal with the secrets, their eyes were open to all kinds of reality.

As homework, I asked them to revise the letter in the light of the discussion and to send it, and then to write a letter to the observers involved.

❖   ❖   ❖

Anna

Tonight we were going to have a different format. Rather than sharing our homework and then role-playing at the end, we were going directly to the role play. Reading our letters to our partners and following with feedback on the contents, as well as responding in "role-play fashion" as the perpetrators would, was the plan. Getting in touch with feelings seemed very easy with these letters in hand. Denying your partner's truth and pushing against her triggered lots of anxiety. Analyzing the contents was tricky business.

I was paired with Krista again tonight. I read first. She pushed me to the limit, questioning and challenging nearly every point. At first, I lost control, was stumbling and weak in my resolve, but gradually I was able to read with clarity and determination. She was diligent in preparing me to face my perpetrators. When we got to the content, she said it was fine. Her comment gave me no comfort; I still felt uncertain. As she read, I tried to confront her as I thought her father would have done—denying the neglect and physical violence, as well as making a special point of proclaiming her brother's innocence. She outshouted me. Anger and power dictated the conversation. Caution and discretion laced my analysis of her letter. I feared giving her my opinion, thinking I would have to walk on eggs so that I wouldn't trigger her disapproval. This was a frustrating but familiar situation for me. It was as with my mother, my marriages, and even with some of my friends.

"Krista, I noticed a lot of anger in your letter."
"Well, I should be angry, shouldn't I?"
"Yes, but isn't this letter all about reconciliation?"
"I am angry and he is going to hear it! We are supposed to be angry."
"I noticed that you never said anything about the sexual abuse."
"The sexual abuse was a relief. Life was better after it started. He was nicer to me. It wasn't really a problem."

Her words stung me. It was as though the sexual abuse I'd survived was nothing compared with her past. I was lost for words, then saved by the bell. We were told to share with the group how we felt about each other's letters. When it came to my turn, I remarked on the excessive anger I'd noticed in Krista's letter.

When sharing our letters with our parents, we were asked to consider calling them by their first names. This was an indication of a change in the relationship, to signify that we had grown up.

Just before we closed, I asked Dr. Ney privately if he could go over my letter, reminding him that I would be missing next week's group because I was going to see my mother and deliver the letter personally. I continued by sharing my overwhelming fear of her and what she would do, imploring him to give me feedback, to make sure I'd covered everything, to make sure it was all right. Dr. Ney turned it over to the group and they assented. I was embarrassed.

Mom,

I realize that this letter is going to cause you a lot of pain; however, we both need to be free—you from my anger and bitterness and me from the confusion, hurt, and disabilities resulting from abuse. If we deal with the dark secrets of the past through forgiveness and reconciliation, we will truly be able to leave the past behind and press on in the fullness of life. The women of our heritage have a pattern of hardness, bitterness, and unforgiveness that destroys them and those they love. That is our destiny unless we break the generational bonds that trap us. I, for one, determine to do just that. I offer to you this opportunity as well.

There were many reasons, factors, circumstances that set me up for abuse. *Blame* has not been my motive for exploring these. After 10 months of intense pain in my joints and an emotional despairing that led me to think I was losing my mind, I began to have body memories. I sought a psychiatrist. I am now in group therapy. Months of hard work, rage, fear, and facing the terror of the past have brought me thus far. There are days in this dark journey that have joy and peace I never knew possible. Body memories, so you know, are memories brought up to the conscious level, from the womb right through the childhood trauma. Mine last two to three hours each. You become the memory in every way. Reliving: the body, mind, and emotions all feel, hear, see, and taste the experience as though it is just now happening. These episodes leave me numb and shocked for several days.

I discovered a little child deep within myself who had never grown up. She controlled my life though I was not aware of her. I had to let all her pain, sadness, terror, anger, rage, and bitterness come up, and then I had to let her die. This was the hardest thing that I've ever done in my life but it was necessary for me to be finally free. Remember, I am not placing blame on anyone. Responsibility, however, is mandatory to healing the past and the present. You, my father, the foster parent, the old man at the farm, the shadows without faces, my stepfather, and myself all share in that responsibility. We will focus on your responsibility and my responsibility, bringing up the others only as necessary for clarity. I purpose to deal with the others personally, just as we are now.

When you were married to my father, I can only imagine the nightmare it must have been for you, as you have been so silent about your pain. I know you were taught that silence was the right way; however, facts tell us that stuffed memories rot and fester, secretly destroying from the inside out!

I will share with you my heartbreaking story as I remember it through both the regression and conscious memories, exposing it and thus defusing its power to destroy my life.

My past abuse and neglect led me into a desperate and sometimes promiscuous lifestyle. Searching for love and acceptance and some reassurance of worth, I gave myself to abusive people because I thought I owed them.

I have severe disabilities because of this emotional neglect and the physical and sexual abuse. To protect myself, I covered my body with fat. To comfort myself in loneliness, I found food a faithful companion. I am emotionally addicted to food and have been anorexic, bulimic, and obese. I am trapped in the never-ending diet cycle and despair to be free. I hate my body. I have beaten it with my own fists. You also hate it, which you have exhibited in the years of displeasure and discomfort with my overweight. We have punished it endlessly and we don't have any skills to love and accept it. We are ashamed. I want to integrate my body and my being and I don't know how.

I am addicted to control—everything and everybody to keep my world safe. However, I keep getting into abusive relationships where I seem to have dominance, but, in reality, I am subjected to a toxic, codependant compulsion to choose and "fix" people like those who hurt me in the past. Driven as though I can somehow fix today and thereby erase yesterday.

I judge others, reasoning that they will always think the worst of me. My judgment of character is warped. I see only what I want and need to see to survive. I push myself to be all things to all people to make them love me, respect me, or at least like me. I can't bear any kind of rejection and will defend myself, apologize, take full responsibility, do or say almost anything to get "them" to say I am okay. I cannot tolerate anger. I fix it at any cost to myself or others. I am extremely oversensitive, taking any rebuke deep within myself.

The abilities to play, think clearly, relax, create, excel, and be healthy are all severely marked. I have shut down my mind and emotions in years of denial and thus have been blind to the evil of my past, but also unable to perceive its good. Seeing a distorted present, I have not protected myself or my children. Rigid rules secured to protect me make me hard to live with or work with. Because of the lie that I must perform to be loved, I became an overachiever, workaholic, and pleaser, and thus not true to myself or others.

Mom, I ask you to consider your role in my abuse and neglect. I need you to ask my forgiveness for each incident. I realize you didn't sexually abuse me or neglect me emotionally on purpose, but these things did happen and you didn't protect me. I want to be able to forgive you; I wait to forgive you. After you own your part and seek forgiveness, I would like you to compensate for the pain and losses in my life and subsequently my family's life. One way you could do this is to spend time and cultivate a relationship with each of your grandchildren, impartially. In doing this, you will have conquered the family trait of favoritism, modeling love and acceptance, and thus passing down a heritage of hope and healing.

I do love you, Mom.

Anna

Time was given for only one brief comment from Krista. She said she wondered if my mother would understand all of the words I'd used. It was late and we were quickly dismissed. I left feeling ashamed for having asked to read my letter and worried about the destruction it could cause with my folks.

WEEK 20

This evening only three group members, one facilitator, and Dr. Green were present. I was disappointed but not surprised. Anna had asked permission to miss the session in order to deliver her letter to her mother in person. Writing letters of reconciliation isn't easy and there were a lot of semilegitimate excuses. When asked what I thought reconciliation was, I said that it isn't friendship, that it isn't necessarily any continuing relationship of any kind. Rather it is the ability to talk, if that is required, to others as an adult.

Lisa said she had sent her letter. "It was good. It didn't make all the problems go away, but at least I won't be a victim anymore. I began to realize that not writing the letter would have meant running away, being a victim. I am not going to do that again. It also helped me reaffirm my friends. They really are there for me."

Krista was extraordinarily anxious. "I started to panic at the prospect of sending this letter. I feel I am being pushed into sending it and I resent it, but I know I have got to do it. In fact, I did do it. I said it all at once. I broke all the taboos and secrecy and silence. There were eight single-spaced pages. I must admit that as soon as I had finished it, I didn't want to send it, and I wouldn't have if it hadn't been for the pressure from the group. I sent it to my father in care of his minister and I kept the telephone off the hook for three days. It was exhausting, but I have regained my right to speak the truth and I have got back part of me. I spent 15 hours typing that thing and it was a great release. Right now, I am feeling extraordinarily angry at my father, who was the perpetrator. My brother was just the surrogate. But acknowledging all of this has made me feel better. The truth has set me free."

Tanya looked sullen and then said, "I didn't send my letter. I worked on the letter to my father, but I am afraid that if I send it to him, he will turn on my mother. I am afraid that my mother will see it completely as my father's responsibility and that is not true. I am afraid he will kill her and then kill himself. On the other hand, I think that my father has suffered enough. I can't do this. Do I have to do this? It is dangerous."

It appeared that doubts were being created in all of their minds, and even though they had assured themselves, each other, and me that they would send the letters, now that they faced the perpetrator, all the childhood fears were coming back. Those fears were deeply ingrained in them, fears that if they did something like this, people would die, the family would break up, they would be punished or even killed. To break the hold that those deeply ingrained fears had on them took all the energy and determination they could muster.

After the three members had recounted their experiences in sending their letters, Lisa spoke again: "I feel very sad for the abusers. I can see how it must have been for them and it is good to know that there is a way out and there is forgiveness. Still, my mother is in denial and I don't understand it."

Tanya said, "It is letting go of hope. I'm afraid the revelation of Father and his family will affect the whole family. It will break up."

It looked as though their enormous fear of affecting the family might stop them all, yet with encouragement from the facilitator, Dr. Green, and myself, they renewed their determination. I told them that in order to make the letter as loving and as effective as possible, I would give them guidance. Otherwise, their words too easily could be governed by the anger and vindictiveness.

They were afraid of their vindictiveness. They realized how destructive it was. They realized that not only could they kill other people, but they could kill themselves. As homework, I asked them to look at the roots of the anxieties, and at the vindictiveness of their fantasies of what they might do, that kept them from sending the letters.

❖   ❖   ❖

Anna

Anxiety. Continual nausea. I want to cancel. Just go to therapy next week and mail this letter like everyone else is going to. I am constantly pushing away thoughts of anger and rejection. My family is sympathetic; however, like me, avoiding instead of facing issues is their solution, asking, "If it's going to cause you this much stress, why don't you just cancel?" Somehow I know that for me facing Mom is the best way, and it is this knowing that gives me the strength to proceed.

During my first few days in my parents' home, I missed opportunity after opportunity. Finally, Dad was planning to spend a whole day out and I knew that Mom and I would have enough uninterrupted time to read and discuss the letter. Handing it to her, I reassured her of my love for her and left her for an hour so she could read it alone. When I returned, I could see she'd been crying, but the hard shell of reserve was well in place. After talking for only a few minutes, her defensiveness, anger, and denial ruled the conversation. She went from one extreme to another, manipulating and condescending to outright insulting. I was reminded of the wisdom of Dr. Ney in insisting that we write out everything we want to say for surely I would not have been able to express myself any more now than in the past. I was crushed. I had secretly clung to the hope that she would weep in sorrow and anger over the abuse that I had suffered, dreaming in my heart that she was really different than she is. I labored to help her understand the difference between blame and responsibility. She couldn't hear me. She proclaimed her innocence over and over, declaring that if she didn't know, how could she possibly be at fault. Focusing on one or two points and refusing to see the whole, she strived to maintain control. Her emotional volleying was very uncomfortable; however, for the first time in my remembrance, I was not hooked in. Though I hurt, I was able to be reasonable, to listen compassionately to what she said, and really to try to understand her perspective. My uncustomary detachment in response to her behavior infuriated her. I was totally unprepared for the outburst of rage that declared I was "sick," that she wished I had never come, and that I should get out and stay out.

As I sat in my room thinking about how I would get home, she came in crying. She grabbed me, hugged me, and claimed that she was sorry for what she'd said, that she hoped I would get better soon, would get over whatever was wrong with me, and that she was happy just the way she was and had no intention of changing. When I didn't respond immediately, she went on trying to convince me to see, feel, and think her way. The right way.

We stayed on automatic pilot for the rest of the week. Longing for it to be time to go home, I wanted to hide, to cover up with a blanket and never get up again; this seemed so inviting. I'd only missed one week of therapy, yet I longed to be back in the safety of the group again. I wondered what I had missed and how everyone was.

Dad wanted to talk. I hadn't written his letter yet and so had sidestepped his several attempts earlier in the week. Well, letter or no, we were alone and there didn't seem to be any alternative but to tackle it. I began to outline briefly everything that happened. He listened, quickly showing a willingness to hear all I had to say. He asked pertinent questions. He wanted to know exactly what had happened to me. His anger that such awful things had been done to me was comforting. I must have wanted to hear those words from a parent for such a long time. Crying at the hard spots, his tenderness helped me go on. I had not planned to tell either of them such details of my abuse. When I shared my hurt and confusion about our relationship and the abuse in it, there were moments of defensiveness and anger, but they were brief. We worked through all the issues and resulting disabilities. He recognized and owned his behavior, asking me to forgive him at my request. We resolved all we could and agreed to disagree on the rest. I felt deep respect and gratitude toward him. We have truly reconciled.

Going home. All I did was bend over to move something and—bang!—my back gave out. I could hardly move. Pain surged up and down my lower spine like a knife. Medicine, bed rest, and "handle the stress that caused this" was the wise counsel my physician gave me. We talked. I felt safe openly sharing with this man. Afterwards he hugged me and requested that I check in with him often, just to talk.

❖   ❖   ❖

WEEK 21

Everyone but Linda was back in her usual place. Linda was struggling with some difficult situations at home. We all missed her. Lisa had brought the outline of the letter she sent to her mother. The group all concluded that she had done everything she could possibly do for her mother.

Tanya began reporting on her homework. She recognized that her vindictiveness was to keep her father in suspense. She realized that she was getting money out of him in this way. She also realized that her mother had used her as much as her father had. The little Tanya in her struggled continuously. Why couldn't she put her to rest? The little Tanya would assert herself and demand such things as ice cream. The more she thought about the little Tanya, the more she was frightened about her own tendency to dissociate. "I trust you, Group, because of all the benefits I gained from this. Don't take it personally about my stuckness. How can I let go of this child? I want to go on hating him. It seems to be good, but I realize that the bitterness and vindictiveness are beginning to control me. I am afraid of my anger, but I am even more afraid that he will take control. Anger at least stops that from happening, even if it kills me."

Amy was struggling mainly because of the turmoil in her marital life, but she also knew there were things that she could not bring herself to do. "I wrote the letter but I didn't send it to my mom. It's haunting me. I rewrite a little and then I don't finish. Then I start again. I think of stopping the whole group because you are leaving me behind. I am afraid of doing something that is going to make it worse. I don't know why I should send this to my mom. It wasn't her. Mom is there for me now and Sam isn't. Why should I drive her away? I am afraid she won't say she is sorry. On the other hand, maybe I am afraid to see how much she did know. I am afraid to hear her say that she is sorry because that would be acknowledging the fact that she did know. Right now I am feeling beaten up on, like a little puppy."

They felt a terrible sense of finality in writing to the perpetrators, acknowledging the perpetrators as humans with neither the extensive power of evil nor the potential for good that they had hoped for as children. To send the letters was a finality. After that, there would be no more unrealistic hope. They would become adults and they would be able to talk as adults. They would see the perpetrators as they really were.

Amy confirmed this. "I had a fear of finding out what my parents were really like. As a teenager, I felt vindictive toward my father. I gave him hell for wasting his life, but I recognize now that I was part of that. I am angry at you, Dr. Ney, for telling us to send these letters. I need my mother and I want to hold onto her. Please tell me I don't have to write to her."

Lisa looked dejected. "I am disappointed in my parents' reaction. There were all sorts of secrecy and denial. I can't read my letter. Do you need to hear it?" Eventually, Tasha, the facilitator, prevailed upon her to let her read the letter. There was a great deal of anger, but there didn't seem to be any vindictiveness. Lisa responded, "See, I do want my mother to come out of this denial."

Krista was becoming more and more angry at each group session, and it all seemed to relate to her determination not to let go of the angry six-year-old who drives her. The infant who had been given up by her natural mother had been put to rest, but the six-year-old was increasingly apparent, angry, and vindictive. "I sent the letter to my father, all eight pages, but I have heard nothing back. It felt good for a couple of days, but now I am falling apart. An old friend showed up and he treated me as a stranger. Apparently, he had seen my brother, who had told him I was a spoiled child. I hate my father. Is that vindictive? It is because he kept telling me how bad a person I was. Am I a bad person? I'm still looking for love. I can't stop it. That is who I am. I must be the most unloved person, and that will never change. It has been my entire life."

Anna agreed: "This is a disability both you and I have." Krista responded, "I am no better. I am still messed up. Am I alone? Can anybody tell me?" I pointed out that Krista seldom looked at the people she was addressing nor did she notice how they reacted, but because of the intensity of her emotions and the anger that lay behind it, she turned people off.

Anna was beginning to look increasingly peaceful. "I spent time in bed with my back injury and just to lie there was very helpful. I have confronted my mother and my stepfather. I gave my mother a letter of 13 pages. I covered everything personally with my stepdad and he said I was absolutely right. He asked to be forgiven and opened up to all sorts of things. I feel so good about it. I feel I have found a new friend. When I told him about the abuse I had suffered as a child, he was enraged and very affirming. My mother gave me a lot of pity, but I don't like what she does and I don't think she feels guilty about anything. She went from rage to guilt to abusiveness and started all over again. I felt such enormous frustration that I lost it once. I couldn't get through to her. It seems I never knew her and I don't think she ever knew me, so what am I supposed to do now? When I visited her at their expense, she said she wished I hadn't come. I have lost my mummy. She can't hear me, she doesn't know me, and it is very clear now: I don't think she ever did, but I am beginning to feel free from her. She is adamant that she was a good mother and didn't know anything about what happened. I think I did the right thing. My sister and brother were very pleased with what happened."

Shawna was also becoming determined. "I am not writing a letter to my mother or my father. I can see it all in my head. I know what is going to happen. I know something good can happen, but I can't do it. It would kill her. She has always been horribly dramatic. I am afraid she would do this again and I wouldn't be sure whether she was dying or whether she was just being dramatic. I have been having nightmares and I can't sleep with my husband. I would rather go crazy than be sane in this way, but I want to tell my mother that she tries to be the world's biggest martyr and I am fed up with her. What can I do?"

❖   ❖   ❖

Anna

Before I got here tonight, I had resolved not to read any more of my homework. I would scan it and share the parts I deemed important, thinking that this would stop the escalating problem over my writing. Discomfort and separateness engulfed me as I followed through with my decision. Excluded and different again. Sitting in my sorrow alone. They all proceeded as normal, oblivious to my pain. Why did this have to happen here? I want to be part of the group like everyone else.

Shoving aside my feelings, I concentrated on the process for tonight. "Anger has energy and strength but is blind." I diligently wrote down the insights as Dr. Ney gave them to us but I am not taking them in; they are just words.

It is my turn to share. I tell them basically what happened, without my notebook. Everyone acknowledged my bravery for facing my mother and felt hurt with me at her reaction, fearing their own mothers' reactions as well. They were genuinely happy for me and hopeful for themselves at my stepfather's remarkable response. Though I had completed the homework for the week I was away (to write to another perpetrator), I never shared this second letter to my genetic father with the group.

Dear Michael (*genetic father*):

I expect that this letter will cause you a lot of pain even though you have resolved with yourself and found a measure of peace and forgiveness. Our Lord has truly forgiven you, redeemed, delivered, and literally clothed and put you in your right mind. You suffered untold misery at the hands of doctors and institutions that were inadequately skilled or equipped to deal with your mental illness and demonization. I am also aware that you must have had some sort of abuse in your childhood to damage you so severely. Know that I feel great compassion for you and pray that you have the opportunity to work through your pain and be truly free from it. I, too, need to work through my pain and desperately want to be free from the compulsions, the addictions, and the pleaser mentality that drive me. After so many years, you may wonder, why now? Why would I pick now to stir up so many old painful memories best forgotten? Well, Michael, I just recently remembered the horrible way you sexually abused me. I was only one year old. You didn't even think I was yours, did you? You loved the others. Steve [*my brother*] shared the letters you wrote to him in the services. They tell exactly how you felt about me. These letters only confirmed what I already knew deep in my heart. You rejected me from birth, and then you abused me. I was just a baby when you stuck all those horrible things in me. You did sick things with my little body, and then when you were finished, you flung me by my ankle back into my crib. I relived the horror of that experience in a body memory. I felt like garbage, no good, thrown away. Years of fears of the unknown, a sense of deep unworthiness, as well as familiar demonic spirits were mine until now, 44 years later. The family curse, a demonic spirit, that was passed to me during that abuse incident, as well as my desperate need for love, acceptance, and approval, set me up for years of horrific abuse. The only other memory I've recalled that I think may have been you was when I was three. I couldn't see your face but I was crying out for my daddy not to hurt me, not to do this dreadful thing to me. Were you the shadow man? Did you rape me rectally when I was three? It was incredibly oppressive during this abuse. It was as though the demons were abusing me. Oh God, help me! The memory is so filled with terror. The remembering, reliving, and deliverance were so terrifying that it took three separate occasions to remember it all and become free. I was consumed with terror and even went into shock after one of the episodes.

Your obsessive love for my sister confirmed in me my feelings of inferiority. I am deeply damaged from the rejection, abandonment, and abuse. Some of these disabilities can never be rectified. I have suffered from obesity, bulimia, and anorexia. Set up for further abuse by the lack of basic needs being met, untimely sexual arousal, and demonic infestation, I became driven to find love at any cost. I am addicted to control, to keeping my environment safe so I don't get abused any more. However, I keep getting into abusive relationships. I am trapped into repeating the program. You are responsible for the destruction of the woman God originally planned for me to be. You need to ask my forgiveness for each area of my life that you have wounded. I would like you to make restitution for the years of pain, disabilities, and losses that resulted from the physical, emotional, spiritual, and sexual abuse. I wish to talk this out with you when you are ready. Please be willing, noting the cost, to sacrifice this for me by putting my needs ahead of your pain. I thank you for the soul searching this journey into wholeness will require.

Anna

Before leaving, I had another conflict with Dr. Green. I felt so alone.

WEEK 22

The seven patients, the two facilitators, and Dr. Green were all present and on time. That they had been coming so regularly through so much turmoil and were still ready to deal with more grief and pain was a great credit to their perseverance and commitment. However, I still worried that somehow they weren't going to see it through to the end, and they must. I was tempted to encourage them, but I felt that would be more insulting. After all, they were persisting and there was no need to doubt that they would continue to do so.

In the pregroup check, Amy, with her big, beautiful tummy, said that she felt she was "losing it" because of the conflict with her husband. As Amy talked about losing it, I listened carefully, because she had been hospitalized for a psychosis.

Krista reported that the child inside of her whom she had tried to put to rest would not go. She had a very strong attachment to the child and she wanted to continue nurturing it. She glared at me when I suggested that, painful as it might be, it was necessary if she were going to become an integrated person.

Shawna indicated that she felt 50 percent better, but she adamantly refused to write a letter to her father. She also glared at me when I urged her to take this difficult step. In fact, I remarked that some of the intimidating characteristics she ascribed to her father she seemed to have gained for herself.

We began going around the group, checking on how the homework had progressed. Amy said that she just could not face writing to her mother, that she depended on her. Now that she was in the last stages of her pregnancy and her husband was so unsupportive, she said, how could she possibly write a letter that might mean losing her mother's help and support? Writing to her father made much better sense, but he was dead. Even so, writing to somebody who was dead proved to be a great difficulty. The feelings she had toward her father were reactivated in her daily interactions with her husband. The lack of affection in her childhood, she recognized, had "crippled me. Only half of me got formed."

Amy was quick to note that she was feeling left out of the group. Obviously, much of her thinking was taken up with the baby who was soon to be born and with the fights at home. "I didn't want to come. I feel so uncomfortable here. I haven't written my letters. I can't do my homework because every time I start looking at the difficulties with my father, my husband is there and he triggers all of the old feelings over again. Besides, I am afraid of your reaction to my not doing my homework. I can't handle being angry with Sam. I am becoming obsessed with it. Sometimes I feel hope but I have to recognize that he doesn't really want to be a dad. I wish I could make him want to be a daddy. I feel I missed my childhood and now I am missing a chance with my marriage. I don't know why I am putting off writing these letters and why it is so hard to write a letter to a dead person."

She needed some guidance. The intensity of the conflict between her and her partner was affecting her ability to concentrate in the group and was having a deleterious effect on her health and on the health of the fetus. With backing from the group, I advised her to take some time off and to allow her husband, Sam, to be alone with their first child, Sheila. This thought frightened her because she was not convinced that he was well bonded to the child, but there was no other way in which she could ever find out whether, without her continually berating him, directing him, and urging him, he could relate to and nurture this child. I had some awareness that it would work but still there was a risk, and I acknowledged that. Later, Amy indicated that she had, in fact, taken a couple of nights off and when she returned, she was amazed to find her husband happily playing with their child.

With the urging of the group to pursue this, Amy accepted me as a surrogate father. With help and encouragement, she looked straight at me and said the bitter things she had felt about her father's neglect, why he had avoided her unnecessarily, why he had killed himself with cigars and alcohol, why he had made her feel so guilty. Like all the other group members, in dealing with reconciliation, Amy found it difficult to forgive even when I said, "I am sorry."

All the groups I have conducted find the following five steps useful when embarking on forgiveness. "I know I need to forgive you for the bitterness is killing me and trapping you. Part of me wants to forgive you but it is very difficult. It would be much easier if you:

1. "hear me out when I speak of all the pain you have caused me,
2. "acknowledge that you were responsible for the hurts and apologize sincerely for each one of them,
3. "promise that you will never do this again to me or anybody else,
4. "give an indication that you can carry out that promise by showing me some concrete changes in your life, get into counseling or in other ways indicate that you are trying to change and have changed to some extent, and
5. "help me to overcome,with additional assistance or compensation, the difficulties you have created."

When Amy went through this, I complied as best I might imagine her father doing. I apologized for each hurt, promised I would not do it again, indicated I was changing, and offered to help her. This offer was accepted when I indicated that I would spend time with her children, taking them to the beach, teaching them small things. When we had finished going through it, Amy's body was relaxed and her face was peaceful. She later reported that she had, in some kind of dream or vision, seen her father and that he looked different. Obviously, it wasn't necessarily the father who was different; it was Amy's perception of him. She had released him from the prison of bitterness.

Lisa, who was next, had watched the previous proceedings intently and said she yearned for something like that to happen with her, but, "I don't know what to say. I'm stuck and I am very angry with everything I have gone through. I am getting no answers. I cried all week. I feel like killing my mom. I have done everything I can do. I need to know what to do or else I will lie down and die. I am the victim, so if I don't die, I will just give up." The despair on Lisa's face affected the whole group and there was a solemn silence. She had written to her mother but so far there had been no response, apart from an angry telephone call. Was it possible that the mother might reconsider and write an apology? We all helped her to hope it might be so. I offered to see her mother, but Lisa felt it would be pointless because her mother would refuse. There was no way her mother could admit that she had been party to such horrendous ritual abuse.

Krista reported that she had written to her father but that her letter to her mother was unfinished. She began speculating on what she would like as compensation and decided that she would just like the opportunity to get to know her mom. Writing to her birth mother would be difficult, partly because she wasn't sure she ever had wanted to locate her. There was a deep yearning, but it was mixed with a terror that if she found her, she would find something very disappointing. These conflicting feelings showed themselves in the other struggles Krista was going through.

Anna was bothered by a dilemma about her letter. "When I read this out loud, I feel insecure and inhibited. Is it all right? Should I send it?"

As the group learned more about themselves, they recognized that insight could be a burden. It made them more responsible. And not only that, but they were becoming increasingly aware of a power that they didn't think they had because they had always responded as children. Now that they were adults, they began to realize that they could hurt people quite easily.

Linda was a model of tenacity and courage. She had not flinched even though she had some of the worst kind of reconciling to do. Having written her letters, she began discovering some very important things about her parents. "I discovered that they didn't know me. For the first time, I told my father what had been happening and that he had neglected to realize that I was being badly abused by two men whom he had always thought I should play with. Having told my parents what had happened and how it had affected my life, they both admitted they were very sorry. In addition, my mother finally admitted that she was not a good mother. Although this had created a rift in our relationship as it used to be, there appears to be some healing coming out of it. There is no resentment toward my father. In fact, the two of them are now having to get along with information they didn't have before and yet they are struggling with it. The compensation that I had asked for was for them to stop fighting and to treat each other as human beings, and they have actually done that. I have recognized recently that when I have gone to their home, they might be in the middle of a fight, but as soon as I walk in, they start to be more respectful and more polite to each other. Prior to this, I had always resented my father and mother's forcing me to take sides in their fights. I am really pleased to see the change, but I am not sure what is going to happen next."

Tanya said that the last week had not been so hard for her. She realized that something had happened to her at a very early age. "I lost my mother at the lake when I was two. Because I was so young, and because my development could not proceed, I realize now that I have to bury the baby. I buried two stones down at the beach. It was a soft evening, no wind, nobody about, and the two stones, representing two parts of me that did not develop, were laid to rest. I believe they are gone now and I feel much better. I began to recognize that my real parents have been my ballet teacher and my therapist. They have been bringing me up, but I realize that I can't hang onto them. I began to realize how I hated my mother all these years. We had so many logical discussions with no affection. I am beginning to realize that I can talk to her now as an adult. I am even calling her by her first name."

I had indicated earlier that one good piece of evidence showing that people have become mature is the ability not only to talk to their parents about anything and everything, but to address them as friends, using their first names. Most recoiled at the idea, feeling that to do so would be the end of any parent–child relationship, and even as adults, they insisted that they needed that parenting. Those who did do it, however, were pleased with the result. They could now see their parents more clearly; their parents could relate to them as friends, and most of the parents appreciated this opportunity. Still, some parents insisted that they be addressed as Father and Mother and were angry with me for suggesting otherwise. But gradually the value of the approach began to sink in and it was adopted by most of the group.

The group members were struggling hard with reconciling with the perpetrators. To facilitate this process, I wanted them to have some idea of what it would be like at the other end of the correspondence. As homework, I asked them to seek the forgiveness of their children. This idea was quickly picked up by all those who were parents. Shawna had no children and said she didn't know from whom she should seek forgiveness, but settled on her husband. It had been a long and difficult session. I could see tensions developing that needed to be dealt with, but everyone was too tired. It was almost 1 AM. I still had to get home, attend to some farm chores, get some rest, and be bright and reasonably alert at 9 AM for the next day's patients. I wondered if this was a good way to utilize my time, but I had concluded that when people travel such long distances, it is not fair to them to have short, incomplete group sessions. After the group, Dr. Green, Tasha, Shelly, and I spent half an hour discussing what was going on. Their insights and encouragements were invaluable. It was quite apparent, too, week by week, that Tasha and Shelly were benefiting by growing through the group a second time, this time facilitating others. This was helping them to gain a more objective view of themselves, to stop being so analytical of their own problems, and to reach out to others, thereby diminishing their own self-centeredness. As we were talking, we heard a noise in the hall. Later I found out that Anna and Krista had engaged in a very bitter conversation, the net effect of which was to harm them both and confuse the group.

❖   ❖   ❖

Anna

Grieving the loss of my newly found safety, I determine to chance telling the group how intimidated I am by the reaction to my writing. Although I am afraid of their disapproval and rejection, I value what is being lost more than I fear the challenge. After all, if I can't risk in the group, then chances are that I won't be able to anywhere. I am going to have to apply some of these principles that I've learned and to quit acting like a victim.

In group: "I have a problem that is threatening my openness in the group. So rather than lose what I can gain by continued vulnerability, I am going to risk asking you all to be very honest with me. If what I sense that Dr. Ney and Dr. Green feel is really happening, then I must face a blind spot and you, my peers, can help me. It started about six weeks or so ago when Shawna asked me if she could write down something that I'd written. I was happy to share it with her. Then Tanya also asked me. Dr. Ney said to her, 'You write it out in your own words rather than copy hers.' A few minutes later, I heard him say that we didn't want to start competition in writing out the homework. Later I really examined myself to see if my motives included my particular disabilities: being a pleaser, my need for affirmation and approval, as well as my drive to avoid trouble at any cost. I decided that I wrote out my homework at great cost to myself by repeatedly laying my fears aside and making myself as naked as I possibly could. Not once can I recall, no matter how difficult it was, that I avoided telling what I knew was the truth. I did this to get well, not to get approval. The only way that I feel this judgment could be a valid assessment of me is that I would not miss a class or not do my homework, not only out of a sense of responsibility to myself and you, but because I am also motivated by some fear of a man's disapproval—Dr. Ney, in this case. Two weeks ago, it came up again. I was genuinely panicked at the thought of giving my mother the abuse letter and asked Dr. Ney at break if he would please not make me go without checking it. He asked if I wanted the group's appraisal. I clearly told him that that wasn't necessary. What I needed was for him to assure me that the letter wouldn't destroy her, me, or my family. When we met again, he had me read it. Time for only one brief comment seemed available, and then Dr. Ney took over, saying 'Not all of us express ourselves as clearly as others. We are not interested in how well you write your letters, but only that you say what you need to, and in your own way. Isn't that right, Dr. Green?' She agreed immediately and moved on to Shawna. I didn't want to read my letter to find out if I'd written a structurally sound, grammatically correct essay. I wanted your support, your advice, and your reassurance. I felt inadequate to judge for myself the results of delivering such a letter. I was extremely fearful. On the way and at Mom's, I prayed over and rewrote it before I could give it to her. Last week, as I sat and listened to you all, I saw that I was not alone in my fear and insecurity. I didn't, however, share my homework out of my journal. I just told you what I could remember. At the end of the meeting, I carefully chose my words and asked Dr. Green if we were to bring the other letters we'd written to group or just send them. She said, 'This is not an English class. We are not going to grade your work.' Did I ever feel slapped! I said, 'I was just asking. I wasn't here last week and I wasn't sure.' She responded, 'Well, let's ask someone who knows.' She did, and Dr. Ney responded, 'If you feel confident, send them; if not, bring them in.' Dr. Green turned to me, 'Did you get that?'

"I sure did...I felt shut out, cut down, judged, just like she said I did to others. I really wanted help, guidance. I am not yet confident enough of myself and need the experience and knowledge and support offered in this room. I felt abandoned and judged wrongly.

"I don't think any of my peers has a problem or is threatened by my writing. Nor do I sense that they think I write to impress them or my facilitators. However, I could be blind to their feelings and am open to hear that now. I would like to have my freedom of expression back. You may recall that Krista said she had trouble following me in conversation at first and Linda agreed. Maybe they discovered, as I did many years ago, the benefit of daily writing in a journal; that the clearest method of expressing your deepest heart is in the written word. It pours out. Talking sometimes can find me bumbling and mixed up unless I am feeling safe. Thus I have written this instead of speaking off the cuff."

Immediately, Dr. Ney apologized. He said he was truly sorry. He asked for forgiveness. Then he said that he sometimes forgets that we still have these overwhelming childhood fears inside when we appear so mature and confident on the outside. He promised to be more sensitive to all of us as we labored to complete this very difficult part of our therapy. I was relieved by his response and greatly encouraged. Facing this tough issue not only had brought my freedom back for me, but had opened the door to more support and patience for the rest of the group. Dr. Green followed with apologies for her harsh words, stating that she hadn't intended to say it as it sounded. She had often taken the brunt of my anger. Posing as the "mother image" for us to work out our hostilities was quite a job. We all seemed to have intense and turbulent relationships with our mothers. Looking and acting nothing like my mother, you would have thought that substituting her for Mom would be impossible. On the contrary, however, her sometimes quick, direct comments pierced the same tender spot, and so she provided an excellent proxy.

Tanya was quick to ask for forgiveness for not responding more to my letter. She said it sounded so good to her she didn't think I needed to change anything. She was sorry that she hadn't seen my fear and need for reassurance. Linda said she always appreciated what I had to say, but at first had felt threatened when she had to follow me. She said she didn't feel that way any more. She added that I shouldn't change a thing. Shawna said she appreciated my writing because there had been times when it expressed what she felt but couldn't put in words. I had seen this before and been encouraged. As my desire had not been for a lot of focus on the quality of my work but to break through the lack of freedom of expression, I was greatly relieved when we went on to other things, that the direction of the comments was shifting.

Amy was telling us about her week. Boy, could I see a change in her. She was still struggling with her letters, especially with the one to her mother. Nevertheless, she was able to listen to us more consistently and her rescuing had almost stopped. I was beginning to really appreciate her. When she read her letter to her father, I could see the child, beautiful and wanting. Just love: that was all she needed and wanted. Even as an adult, she still so wanted his love. The compensation she asked of her father was just to play ball with her. Something clicked. I had been struggling with compensation, trying to justify it in some way. I mulled over Dr. Ney's exegesis of biblical restitution for sin in the Old Testament, and his explanation of the relief it provides for the perpetrator, but somehow I hadn't been convinced until now. Amy's simple yet profound choice of compensation put it all in perspective.

Lisa was sharing more often now. Sometimes she even read, or let someone else read, her homework. Still, she didn't altogether trust us. Afraid of disclosing herself completely, she kept us at a distance. Sometimes I felt as though she didn't think that our stories were as horrible as hers, and rightly so: ritual abuse must certainly be the worst kind. I think she thought we would be shocked by the perverse demonic stuff. Maybe some of the group members would have been, but I don't think so. We all were pretty bonded to each other and would have listened, supported, and believed her even if we didn't totally understand. Most of the time, we were at a loss to know what to say to her to draw her out. Dr. Ney was the only one who could penetrate the wall. Sometimes she worries me like Virginia did, and we lost Virginia.

It was Krista's turn and I am the subject. "Anna, you hurt me when you said I was 'your homework' just because I asked you to cut my hair. You implied that I was aggressive and overpowering and that you struggled with people like me. No one said anything about your flaws although everyone else's were mentioned. Anna, put away Anna's hurts and outrages for a few moments and try to hear what I am saying and feeling. You had your turn to talk about your conflict with Dr. Green, and now I want mine." I felt sick and threatened. "You overreacted to Dr. Green's innocuous statement. It is a fact that when humans are under pressure, especially extreme internal pressure, their minds tend to inflate the significance of any external pressure. This is well documented." Breathing deeply, I concentrated on listening and relaxing. The faces clearly showed support in my direction, and on several occasions, Tanya, Linda, and Shawna interjected on my behalf. Krista, however, continued, "Anna, I have a big problem with the 'feedback' you gave me on the night before you went to your mom's. I experienced pain from what you said, as well as from how you said it. I felt you were driven by an incredible internal pressure to get your letter perfect. You were in a very tense state of mind." Throughout the confrontation when insult and obvious distortion appeared, I wondered why Dr. Ney didn't stop it. Why didn't he protect me? "I didn't appreciate the way you came on board me, when we shared our letters. I don't care what you call it, sharing or feedback; that night it was full of Anna, not God. In front of the group, you stated that my letter was full of anger and to that I replied, 'Good!' Anna, you then covered and said, 'Oh well, I didn't mean that it is bad; I just sensed anger in it.' Then you stated that you didn't see much room for forgiveness. I told you I would be putting that in the ending, which hadn't been written yet. I had to exert a lot of energy to answer your complaints effectively. Anna, you were quite critical. I don't need that." Krista rehearsed the same charges several times, coming at them from various angles. I had no recourse. I hated this kind of haranguing, but I didn't know how to make it stop. What could I say or do to make her shut up? I felt that the accusations were way off base. I had understood them; I'd heard them often enough. Dr. Ney hadn't interjected, and I was certain that any defense on my part would just intensify the whole matter, rekindling rather than resolving anything. Finally, Dr. Ney said we had to move on as it was getting late. Krista was really annoyed, and made it clear that she was not yet finished and should have all the time she needed. After all, Anna had all the time she needed. We moved on.

It was after midnight. I was spent. Dr. Green and I hugged as I left for home. In the hall, Krista approached me, asking, "Can we talk for a few minutes?" Oh no, I thought. I can't do this again. I've got to get out of here. I answered, "Krista, I am exhausted. I don't want to talk about anything else heavy. Let's wait until next week and go over it then." As I turned to leave, she leaped toward me, screaming, "You selfish bitch!" Tanya was standing there. Somehow she was standing between us, holding Krista. I backed down the stairs and fled to my car. Shaken by what had just happened, I sat there. Calming down, I rationalized that she was going to hurt all week, that she had no friends, no one to talk to. She would just hurt all week. I got out of the car and returned to the building. Krista and Tanya were just leaving. I told her I was sorry for hurting her and asked her to forgive me. She was still angry, her eyes ablaze. "You should be!" Peace flooded me and a steadiness came into my voice. I quietly reassured her that I cared, that I hadn't meant to hurt her and was sorry. She accepted my apology and forgave me. They left. Returning to the car, I was immediately overwhelmed with grief. I had sold myself out. I had made peace with her at any cost. I hadn't expressed any of the anger or hurt I'd felt by her misinterpretations of my words and actions. I had just sat there letting her beat me publicly with her words. Then when she violated my space, cursing me and literally jumping on me, what did I do? I apologized for "my part of the problem." Very righteous, but not very honest. I had let someone victimize me again, and I took the blame to make the person "all better." As the truth revealed itself, deep, broken sobs gripped me. Tasha tapped on my window, "What's wrong? Anna, talk to me." I rolled it down and gradually was able to explain what had happened. She consoled me.

❖　　❖　　❖

WEEK 23

This evening there was great tension. Shawna and Amy were missing and, without any kind of introduction, Krista jumped right in. "Anna and I had a little tiff. I have had difficulty with Anna's feedback. She seems to be calling the shots all the time, and the wall went up. She wanted to control me, so I yelled at her. I sensed that she wasn't sorry for hurting me. She was just patronizing. Yes, I called her a bitch. I've written her a letter. I want you all to hear it. I want you to decide who is right. We must get down to what is right. Can't you see, this is just like my childhood? I was always wrong and you are going to tell me I am wrong again. I know you are going to tell me I am wrong again. I have always been wrong. Won't anybody stick up for me? Why isn't anybody on my side?"

Anna was in tears. "I knew you would make out that this was all my fault. I didn't want to create any unnecessary pain for you, but I didn't hear your woundedness and I am mad at myself for trying to make peace at any price. I have always done that and I am not going to do it again."

The intensity of the interchange between these two set the whole group back on its heels, literally and figuratively. They recoiled and sat as far back in their chairs as they possibly could, but having gone such a long distance together, they hated to see these two go at each other with such intensity. In fact, it turned out that, against the group rules, Anna and Krista had had an interchange after the group. I had been vaguely aware that something had been going on, but in the aftergroup sessions with Dr. Green, Tasha, and Shelly, I had not paid much attention. This incident reinforced the need I had indicated at the beginning that the group members must not have dealings with each other between sessions apart from those of the most superficial kind. In this instance, we were left having to deal with a very difficult conflict, the roots of which went back into both of their childhoods.

Linda and Tanya were the first to try to deal with the conflict. Linda, with her analytical attitude, wanted to know if they had had conflicts like this before. Tanya said she felt bad because she had watched this happening, and she admitted that she had just stood there when she should have been doing something. I attempted to point out the roots of the conflict, that Anna had a desire to be at peace with everybody and Krista was trying always to find out whether she was right or wrong. However, mere insight was obviously insufficient for them. I asked them to put it away because it was, at this point, taking up a great deal of time that we needed to deal with other things, but added that we would come back to it.

Linda reported that she had tried to write a letter to her father in which she told him how angry she was at his lack of being a father and how it affected her. She was also very angry at his violence and drinking. "I can remember his crude jokes. He said he was sorry. Sorry that he had felt lousy for many years and wished that I could forgive him, but I can't forgive him yet. However, he has changed his behavior when I am around and we are all benefiting. In addition, I sat down with my kids. My oldest son was very sensitive and upset that I should be so worried, but he told me what he felt about my yelling at him and hitting him and all the times when he was confused about my relationships with men. I apologized for all of these things and we went through the whole exercise, and I believe his forgiveness is real. It's amazing how good I feel now. It has changed our whole family."

With the joyful news of how well things had gone for Linda, there was encouragement for others to take a like attitude.

Tanya was keen to get on with the work. She had been talking with her children. "My children were touched when I admitted my faults. I can remember crying all night before my oldest child was born. Ernie told me how wrong my parents were in neglecting me. I'd like to give each of my children something symbolic to indicate my desire to make up for the things I didn't give them. It's very sad, as I think back about those things. I know there are plenty of reasons why they didn't get what they should have had, but I realize the awful importance of those lost opportunities. When I try hard to give my children what they need, it makes me remember what I didn't get. It makes me jealous. The worst thing my father did was to take me out of ballet class. You might find it surprising that after all the years of incest I could say that, but it is true. It had the most devastating effect on me. I am trying hard now to appeal to his good side, but I don't want to put myself in his power ever again."

The group members who had spent time with their children were beginning to realize what it was like to be forgiven. This provided greater impetus for them to forgive those who had wronged them. They realized that to a great extent they had to deal with their feelings of vindictiveness and desire for revenge, feelings that had grown out of their abuse and neglect as children. I pointed out that to forgive is to give away the power to punish a person and that is not an easy thing to do, but it is freeing for both the perpetrator and the victim.

Lisa was going through great turmoil. "I almost checked into the psychiatric unit. I am still struggling with some of the awful memories. After talking with Tasha and hearing how she had struggled with it, I finally let go of my mom and I feel a great relief. I don't expect anything of her so I shouldn't continue to be disappointed, but the memories of what happened are still terrifying. I sense that my mother attempted to take my life. How can I forgive her?" It was only later that Lisa gave me the list of memories that she had not disclosed to the group, and these indicated a time when she was about to be sacrificed and her mother had willingly given her up, although protesting weakly. At some point, she was shown a knife dripping with blood and told that this was her blood, that she had really died but had been brought back to life as a bride of Satan, that her life now was his. She also realized that there were secrets that she had been bound to keep that may have been implanted in her mind with an oath not to divulge or she would die. To let those memories out was to reinvoke those threats and make her feel that her life was in great jeopardy. "Maybe I witnessed some murders. I can't even know and I am not too sure if I want to remember. If I remember, what can I do with that information? I feel a great need to be protected when there is nobody there. I felt so terrified once I started screaming and I couldn't stop. I felt my mind would break. No one answered the phone when I called various people. Why weren't you there? On the other hand, there are some very positive things happening in my life. I wrote to my dead adoptive mom, asking her for forgiveness. I had a nice surprise. In the night, I felt her there, and she was accepting my apology."

Anna said she had written to her stepchildren and written and spoken to her own children, seeking reconciliation. Her stepchildren had been alienated partly by her husband's insistence and partly by their anger. She felt that she had not nurtured them as she should have, but there have been some very wonderful changes in their relationship. In dealing with her oldest child, there first had been denial and fear, but gradually a softening. With her youngest child, there was still considerable difficulty. She had been afraid to write to her husband asking for his forgiveness, but eventually she did so. Having done these things, she said she felt considerably freer regardless of their reactions. Initially, she had panicked at the thought that somehow they would all gang up on her. She had offered compensation. Some of the offers had been accepted. She wants to write a poem to her husband.

We spent some more time dealing with the intense hostility that had developed between Anna and Krista, but it looked as though there were transference issues here that ran very deep. Some of the difficulties were dealt with and some were unresolved. Anna went home tearful, while Krista went home furious. I had asked the group to write a letter to all the observers or bystanders in their lives who could have or should have done something during their times of abuse and neglect. Seeking an apology and wanting to forgive them: that would also include observers in their lives. When I mentioned observers, they looked around at one another. Obviously, there were times in all of their backgrounds when they had had some bad experiences, mainly because of what had not been done, rather than what had happened.

❖   ❖   ❖

Anna

This was a tough week of trying to focus on the homework with a constant yet vague sense of "truth sacrificed at the altar of peace" haunting me.

We were asked to write a list of all possible observers and to write one representative letter ("I wanted you to rescue me"). Also, we were to start to reflect on what it would take to forgive ourselves.

POSSIBLE OBSERVERS

(I have very little actual memory; this is only supposition.)

Ages one through six:
1. Medical doctors who treated my father. Surely they would have known that he could be violent and abusive toward his family because of the extent of his mental disorders.
2. Foster parents. How could they have not seen the marks of such violent and regular abuse going on in their own home?
3. Old woman on the farm. As with the foster parents, how could she not have known about the abuse right under her nose?
4. Woman in the upstairs apartment. She was concerned about our crying, yes, but why didn't she go further and find out for sure what was causing us to cry every night?
5. My mother. Where was she? Why didn't she wonder why I was so clingy and why didn't she find out where all my fears came from?

Ages six through 18 years:
1. Teachers, neighbors, relatives, doctors, club leaders. Certainly they must have noticed an extremely overweight, emotionally needy overachiever and wondered why. Yet as there were no behavior

problems and obligations were always fulfilled, perhaps they felt there was no need to pursue anything.

Adult:

1. Chief of police. When I confided my husband's use of illegal drugs and his sale of them to minors, there was no follow-up, protection, counsel, or help. Couldn't my danger be suspected here?

2. Doctor. When my second husband went to get his hand set, broken on my head, the doctor didn't ask me, "How is your head?" or "How are you? Are you okay?" Rather he asked, "What did you do to cause this?"

3. Pastors, church leaders to whom I/we went for counsel after the broken hand and again after the sexual abuse of the girls. Why wasn't I protected? Why weren't the girls protected? Why wasn't I told my rights? Even a "Christian" wife has to have the right to physical, emotional, and spiritual safety. Where was the counsel to have him removed and to leave all the children with me?

I chose to write to one of the people whom I can vaguely remember from my early childhood. She was in charge of my care during a short vacation.

Dear Auntie Margaret:

I am Sara's youngest, Anna. I know you haven't heard from any of us for years, but I am sure you remember us all. This letter will probably upset you, and for that I am truly sorry. Please think past the shock and guilt that my questions will undoubtedly bring up for you and try to focus on the freedom that truth will bring to me. You can't know the journey of pain a sexually abused child follows unless you have traveled it, so please bear with me, if for no other reason, for the sake of the close friendship you had with our family.

I was sexually abused many times in the first six years of my life. The memories of times, places, and people are jumbled, but the abuse itself is vivid. The therapy that I am presently undergoing includes the writing of letters to those involved. These are both to help set me free from the disabilities and to break the bondage of unforgiveness. You didn't abuse me; however, when I was in your care for the holidays, something happened to me. I am told that when I came home, I wouldn't go into a bathroom alone and I wouldn't let them shut the door. Margaret, I have some horrible memories of oral sexual abuse and physical violence, including a silence warning by near-drowning in the bathtub.

Please, I know you left us and went to the pub in the evenings, asking the motel owner to look in on us. Something went wrong. What happened? During the abuse memory, I recall the terrifying feeling that I'd been there before. It must have happened more than once. I don't know if this is where the oral abuse and violence occurred or if the trauma of waking up and finding no adult there tapped into the fear and memories of buried abuse.

You may well have the keys to unlock this mystery. My mom cannot tell me much more as she only knows the little you shared with her when she questioned you about my new fears on my arrival home. Please, for my sake, think back and even ask the other lady, Mary, who stayed with us. This is not about blaming you for leaving me. This is about setting me free from the past. I want to forgive all those who abused me, as well as those whose responsibility it was to take care of me. I cannot pretend it never happened. I am driven daily by the disabilities and compulsions produced by unresolved abuse issues. I intend you no malice. Please, don't push my neediness away. Your neglect of me in the past was most likely in all innocence; however, it happened and I am scared. Margaret, you may not have been able to help me much in the past, but now you have been made aware of an opportunity to compensate by giving me all the facts you remember personally and can find out from others. I wait with hope and anticipation for your response.

Thank you.

Anna

As soon as we sat down in group tonight, Dr. Ney says he wants Krista and me to update the group on last week's happenings after the session. Krista quickly responds, reiterating everything she had shared with the group last week, and then going on to say that she had approached me after the group just to clear up what hadn't been finished in group time. "Your whole attitude stunk! I just wanted to clear up a little problem with your feedback, to get it off my chest and settled once and for all. Yes, it was probably a fatal choice of mine to talk with you when you stated that you didn't want to talk about anything 'heavy.' But here is my point: I believe that you knew full well what I wanted to discuss, that it was a fault of yours, and I believe that you chose to raise yourself up in a controlling manner. You called the shots as to what we could or could not discuss at that moment in order to retain control over the situation. I was in a bind: On the one hand, I simply needed to have this issue dealt with. I felt that since we had spent considerable time listening to Anna's complaints, I should have time too. On the other hand, you took charge and decided what we could or could not discuss. Your tone was impatient and your attitude was condescending. You were trying to make me and my case seem as annoying as possible. You were and are in a position of dominance in order to squash my suit against you. You practically forced me to forgive you, being more concerned with my silence than with ascertaining that my hurts had actually been relieved."

Whipped, sickened, as on and on and on she goes. I hate this. Why does this follow me? Why do I keep getting people in my life who harangue me to death? Why does Dr. Ney let her go on and on like that? Do I defend myself? Aren't I supposed to let the Lord defend me? Do I answer any of her statements? I don't think any of them are true. I am not supposed to be defensive, but this is ridiculous. I am angry at her and at the others for just sitting there. I can see that they feel for me and that Krista has very little support for her accusations. Finally, I am asked to answer. I share briefly what happened in the hall, that I asked to discuss it at the next session and not then when we were both so tired. Also, I described her physical and verbal attack. Then I agreed that I had wanted her to forgive me and had quite likely pushed to resolve it before she was ready. Also, I agreed with her that I had said and felt like "I would have to pay for this later," even though it had the appearance of being cleared up. (What was happening now was living proof, but I knew that to say so would just stir up more strife.) I wanted the group to know that my silence and desire for quick reconciliation probably looked more "righteous" than Krista did. However, my good behavior comes out of my dysfunctions. I needed peace and was further motivated by my fear of aggression and anger. I asked Krista to consider forgiving me for hurting her. That much was true. I had caused her hurt and I didn't want to hurt her. She never saw that she had been aggressive or slanderous or had hurt me. No one suggested that she clean up her part. We just moved on.

WEEK 24

Shawna and Amy were back, but Krista was not present. I was concerned, so I asked Tasha to inquire. She was told abruptly on the telephone that Krista was not going to return. Lisa was in California on vacation. Shawna had spent some time in the psychiatric unit, where I had seen her. "It's not a four-star hotel. They never let you alone. The stress was awful. I'm not going back there. I'd just as soon be at home."

Tanya led off. "I wrote to the first psychologist I saw. He never did find out what was really troubling me, so I wrote and told him what it was and asked him to apologize. I think I'll send it. Maybe he will learn something that will be helpful to other people, but I am having difficulty knowing how to word it. I'm afraid he won't believe that I still respect him.

"I've been thinking a lot about my little Tanya who sounds so much like me. I have been listening more carefully to what she is saying and am recognizing more about myself. I think I have a job, a temporary full-time job. I'll be relieved to be thinking about something other than myself."

As the group struggled with forgiveness, it became very apparent to all of us that they were having difficulty giving up the power of revenge. I pointed out that when a person (perpetrator) injures somebody else (victim), it gives the victim a certain power over that person. Much of it is fantasized, such as the desire to kill when the other person is not looking. That fantasized power tends to inhibit the expression of aggression. They were so afraid that they might kill somebody that they wouldn't allow their anger to come to the surface.

It was also apparent that they wanted, by this time, to start helping others, and were beginning to reach out to their family and friends. I told them that there was a danger in doing this until they had resolved all or most of the difficulties inside themselves, because unless their conflicts were resolved, they tended to have blind spots. What they could not see in themselves, they could never see in other people, partly because they were unable to and partly because they were not prepared to. Their difficulty in recognizing the blind spots in observers was particularly apparent. They could recognize that the people who had injured them had failings and blind spots, but they couldn't recognize that the observers might not see because they didn't want to see. I believe that this had a lot to do with the fact that they also had been observers, not recognizing and not wanting to see the turmoil in others that they could have done something about, such as problems between a spouse and a child.

Amy was looking better. "Since I wrote that long letter to my dead father, there have been some improvements at home with Sam. Sam told me I was envious of his relationship with Sheila. Now I'm not so worried about it if he looks after her. I am beginning to recognize that he is the little boy who didn't get what he wanted and needed so badly. He has begun to play with Sheila. It is wonderful to watch them."

I had observed over years of treating families that a woman will often complain about her husband's lack of involvement with their children without recognizing some of the greater dimensions. The male's protectiveness is provoked when the family is under attack. In so many instances, I had noted that strong-willed women tend not to allow men to have enough responsibility; in particular, the responsibility of providing for and protecting the family. Threats to the family's security and provision evoke a nurturing response in men. By fulfilling all of the family's needs themselves, women never see that part of a husband, and so they continue to complain, while, at the same time, preventing it from surfacing. Amy was beginning to realize that there was a great deal more to her husband than she had first felt. He was, indeed, quite protective and nurturing now that she was allowing him the opportunity.

Linda was having to deal with a terrible situation—her molestation by a sexually abusive, murderous man during many of her teenage years. But she had written a letter to his mother and was waiting to see what the results might be. As for the observers who could have and should have done something to help her, she concentrated mostly on the teachers. "They didn't care. They could have, they should have known. I'm so angry at them. I know I need to forgive them. I can't remember who they are. How can I write a letter? How can we do this?" I encouraged her to pursue it as best she could with a letter and we would provide the opportunity for her to deal with it by being surrogate observers. She went on to talk about how much better things were between her and her children and how much they enjoyed her father as a grandparent. "It's a different atmosphere. My children like me. My children like my father, and my parents are treating each other with greater respect, at least while I am there."

Anna was still struggling in her mind with Krista, even though Krista, again, was not there and might not return. However, Anna was carrying on with the group. This was a process that I felt was necessary. Too often groups become so enmeshed in their internal struggles that very little is resolved, either within or outside the group. When this occurs, I insist on sticking to the agenda even if that means, to some extent, relegating the conflicts within the group to positions of lesser importance. That is not to avoid the obvious, that many of the turmoils within the group are a reconstruction of those outside, but it is an attempt to make sure that they deal with the outside situation. Anna stated that she had had a hard week. The letter from her mother seemed to have undone all the good that had happened when she had visited her. She said she felt depressed and had been weeping and that her back was giving her problems again. She had wanted to rip Krista's letter into tiny pieces. After the last group, she felt good when she left, but she began thinking about what she had done and wanted to do it differently. "I need to do what I am doing from a different point of view." To facilitate this, we reenacted, with Dr. Green's saying, "You are a selfish bitch," and Anna's appropriately asserting herself. Anna stated, "It's hard to see how often I have taken responsibility for others. Now I am awake, dealing with this as I should."

The difficulties between Dr. Green and Anna had, to a great extent, been resolved. Anna's determination and devotion had had a profound effect on Dr. Green. Speaking directly to Anna, Dr. Green stated, "I think you have brought me closer to God." Anna's response was, "I'll treasure that."

Shawna was again becoming stubborn. "I don't want to read my letters. Do you? The fact is that I am enjoying letting my father squirm. My mother keeps phoning me every day. I see some big changes going on there, but still my father won't admit what happened."

Dealing with observers is always very difficult. There is an interesting parallel between perpetrators and observers. The perpetrator would say, "I didn't realize what I was doing." The observer would say, "I didn't realize what I was seeing." Somehow it is easier for the victim to excuse the perpetrator than the observer. I believe this is partly because both the perpetrator and the victim appeal to the observer. "You should have seen what was going on. Why didn't you stop us? Can't you see what we have done to each other?" The importance of this, of course, is that the observers appear to be reasonably together and their complacency is hard for either the victim or the perpetrator to tolerate.

Dr. Green and I were also observers. We were part of the medical fraternity, even the larger one of helping people who could have or should have done more to prevent the abuse and neglect of children. We were part of the triangle and we needed to apologize. When we began, the group was astonished. "Don't be silly. You are our helpers. You've done more than anybody else to get us over this. Why would you apologize?" We said that we were apologizing on behalf of ourselves and our colleagues. They then began to talk about the times that various professionals could have found out what was going on if they had only inquired a bit more closely. People noticed but preferred to ignore physical illnesses, bumps and scrapes, poor performance at school, withdrawn behavior, and all sorts of signs that indicated that something desperate was going on in the child. I confessed that I had not always been as aware as I am now of some of these signals and what they meant. I had probably missed some important things. Dr. Green also, as a family physician, mentioned the fact that there were times when she suspected something but did not inquire.

Upon our having apologized, the group was quick to want to forgive. However, I responded that the whole process had to apply to us too, so we apologized further for all of the hurts, acknowledged the ways in which our behavior could have affected people, promised not to do it again, and indicated that we were changing to become more efficient and that we wanted to provide some kind of compensation in the form of extra effort on behalf of these people and their children. Having heard us out, the group readily accepted our apologies and forgave us. I always felt that forgiveness was vitally important. It was freeing and I felt better within myself. Dr. Green indicated she also felt forgiveness.

❖   ❖   ❖

Anna

Another week in the shroud of depression. I feel responsible for the break in group intimacy; the ongoing tension between Krista and her subsequent absence have destroyed a part of the safety and bonding of our group. I know that it can never be restored. We have all had a great fear of aggression and argument from our painful pasts and I watched as glimpses of confusion, hurt, anger, and fear shadowed the faces of my friends over the past few weeks. I wish I could turn back the clock and fix the problem. But in all of the intensity of this relatively simple problem is a cord that has bound me—my need to be responsible for all that goes wrong. I didn't instigate or fuel the rift between Krista and myself, and as I reread her letter, I am filled with anger at her false accusations and cruel judgments. I am responsible only for the pain that I caused her and nothing else. I don't have to own lies for the sake of peace. Just as Dr. Ney has pointed out over the months: "If you step on someone's toe by accident, you still stepped on the person's toe, caused pain, and are responsible to ask for forgiveness for that pain." I can do that and not give away my dignity, power, self. I can also apply this insight to Mom's letter. She invalidated my journey with her avoidance of my pain and the denial that I need to know and face the truth and pain of my past. I can recognize and apologize for the very real pain my search is causing her, and yet I can continue to pursue wholeness for myself.

Homework this week was to look at all those I would like to help, indicating how I would do it, and why.

WHO	HOW	WHY
Husband	Counsel	To improve our marriage, for his wholeness, to protect others and relieve my fears
Children	Counsel	So that they can be free while young and not pass on their dysfunctions
Friends	Support group	To give a place for growth, share what I have been given, provide a place for accountability for myself and others
Abuse victims	Writing/counsel	To give away what I have been given
Food-disorder victims	Counsel	To see them free from their bondage

A letter that came last week confirms my desire to reach out and see the positive effects my healing can have on others.

Dear Anna,

I thank God that he arranged for us to meet. In my workbook there is a section called "Create a light at the end of the tunnel" in which we are advised to ask a survivor who is further along to write a letter of encouragement. I had overlooked it until now since I didn't know whom to ask.

I want you to know that this is in no way intended to pressure you, but since God crossed our paths and since you have already ministered to me on such a deep level, I hoped that maybe you would be able to write me a letter. This would be placed in my book to be referred to during those deep, dark days. If this feels like too much, I understand, and I would be pleased to receive just a short, cheery note.

God bless you as you continue to walk into the light of his presence.

Cheryl

. . . .

Dearest Cheryl,

Thank you for your letter and your confidence in my journey. I hope that I can encourage you to face your long dark night, for such is the way to freedom he has chosen for us both. I don't pretend to know the answers to all your questions, but I can tell you that in my darkest hours of horror, confusion, rage, vengeance, blame, terror, shame, hate, grief, and self-pity, he never turned his face from me. I will give to you a precious treasure, share with you his sweet whisperings to me. During the release of an abusive memory, in the deepest torment known to my soul, I heard his grieving. After the memory subsided, I felt his arms around me, my little body curled safely against his chest, his loving comfort and reassurance surrounded me. He held me until I grew calm—safe, warm, and secure—as he whispered to me of his love. His grieving had stopped, but the compassion and knowing I belonged to him lingered. It was the most wonderful sensation I've ever known. He was not in a hurry; we cuddled for a long time. This experience is precious to me. I could never have felt the depths of his love except that I had felt the depths of man's depravity. We are not spared from man's sin against us when we come into this world but we do have a calling, a destiny, and a place of Love in him where we can run to and find comfort. He doesn't take away the pain, but he lives through it with us and then leaves only the scars, as reminders of his provision. How can I say that? Because now when I remember that abuse incident, I feel his arms and hear his soft cooing instead of remembering the abuse. I remember, but he has swallowed up the pain. Please, my friend, take courage, be willing, he will do the rest. If I can be of any other support to you, please write or phone. I know how sometimes I needed just to hear again and again that it would be all right, that the overwhelming feelings and memories would not consume me or destroy those around me when I let them come up. May God bless and keep you in the very palm of his hand.

    Lovingly,

Anna

Tonight, as I share my week and homework, Dr. Ney suggests that Dr. Green and I role-play my awareness and insights in the ongoing struggle with Krista. She surely plays the part well. All the feelings of shame and panic quickly rise and a great deal of effort is needed to overcome my desire to run. However, as I practice, owning only my part and allowing the other person (Krista–Dr.Green) to be responsible for herself, I sense the rightness of my response and my resolve to implement this truth and power into my life is strengthened. As I gather up my things to leave again, I am reminded that time is short and that soon this place of discovery and wholeness will be closed to me. I dread the passing of time and the upcoming loss of my world's stability.

WEEK 25

    Spring was coming and blossoms were appearing on the Japanese plum trees. There was a lightness in the air that could be seen through the small window in the room, but the feeling inside was anything but light. Krista and Anna were still at each other and there was a great deal of unresolved hurt and anger between them. Krista began with intense feelings of anger and sorrow. "I hurt because you looked down on me and that hurt me very much. You tried to make me out as a bad person. All my life, people have told me I am a bad person. I believe the truth is not being told here. I am feeling really awful. This is not just a problem of the child inside that I won't let go of. I believe you, Dr. Ney, are not being as direct with me as with Anna, and I think Anna has a bad attitude."

Every psychotherapist and counselor has had to deal with this dilemma. When being attacked, does one defend one's position or maintain the explaining or interpreting mode? Although we are trained in what to do, it is not easy, especially when the attacks are intense and eloquent and when any previous attempts to be helpful, supportive, and interpretive have met with vehement denial. Under most of those conditions, one counsels oneself to patience and persistence, but it doesn't help when one is being told in a group that one is unfair. In this instance, I tried to point out that Krista's feeling of intense sadness will always be there until she deals with that wretched little Urchin within her, a child who felt extraordinarily lonely and bad. The child always felt that it was being misunderstood and tried very hard to get people to understand, only to find that they were either repulsed or felt shaken by its demanding, whining, dependent pleadings alternating with vociferous accusations. I tried to point out that accusations traded back and forth inflame rather than reconcile.

Anna was doing her best to put into practice in the group the things that she was learning were effective in her family. "I am extremely sorry. I don't want to be condescending." That triggered a more contrite response by Krista and within a short while, there were mutual statements of, "I'm sorry, I forgive you."

Linda was ploughing ahead regardless of what was happening in the group. "I wrote a letter to my dad in which I told him that only recently have I begun to look at his role in my childhood. I never felt I was loved. My childhood was really awful. I told him that when he beat the boys, it was passed on to me because they teased and ridiculed me, and that he constantly put down other people. I wanted to do something but I was afraid of being responsible for our family's not having a father." Linda had just sent the letter and was trembling in anticipation of the response.

It was Krista's turn. She reported that she had written two letters and she had revised them so that they did not sound so angry. She desperately wanted her brother to tell her parents what he was responsible for so that they would have a better and more balanced view of the two of them. She listened to feedback, but her anger continued to boil. To protect and maintain a semblance of dignity, she said she felt she had to leave. She got up abruptly and left.

Anna, who was dealing with the observers, found out that the aunt to whom she had previously written was dead, but her mother gave her the address of the other woman who was with them and she wrote to her. She had also written to her husband, beginning by saying that she thanked him for encouraging and supporting her, but adding that she felt that he had tried to destroy her spirit. She wrote two and a half pages, indicating, among other things, that the kind of compensation she wanted was for him to become involved in treatment, preferably with me. She stated, "That's not an option. If he doesn't get help, I can't stay in the relationship. He first began by defending himself, saying how I had hurt him. Then he asked to be forgiven for things that he had done, but at this point, he won't come for treatment."

Tanya noted that they were beautiful letters. I reminded them again that they would desperately desire to change other people as they were changing, but that the only real power they had in changing others was to change themselves. I reiterated that if they tried to push or mold people, this would arouse a natural inclination to resist, a self-protective mechanism that is found in children. However, if they were willing to be the one person in the relationship to change, the other must. To transact in the same way would be impossible.

Shawna was looking particularly glum. "I decided not to come to the group. I am lagging so far behind. I haven't done my homework, and I feel that people are attacking me. I am always being compared. I do my best, but when I don't meet the group's standards, I feel my soul is being walked on. I expect my father is not going to help. He is just going to lie. He doesn't respond well to threats. I am not certain that I want to tell my mom how angry I am at her. I am not even sure what to tell her, except that I really resent being placed in the position of a surrogate wife."

I pointed out to Shawna that she was, in many ways, using the same kind of maneuvering her mother had used, pleading for pity but exerting considerable power. Shawna was particularly upset with Tasha, who had strongly urged her to complete her homework for her own good. Other members of the group apologized for any hurt they had caused Shawna.

Anna noted, "I didn't want my husband to land in jail," indicating that she, like Shawna, had felt a real problem in bringing the abuse and neglect to light. They all knew that there was a real possibility of making things worse for themselves, and they empathized with Shawna.

Dr. Green, who had been extraordinarily supportive and insightful throughout this particular group, apologized for putting pressure on Shawna. I backed this up by saying there was no need to apologize since Shawna knew what needed to be done. She was taking a passive/aggressive attitude that was harming herself more than anybody else. It was a mechanism that I knew that she used in dealing with her husband.

Shawna continued: "I sent my letters and now my parents are coming to visit. I don't know how I did it, but I sent my father's letter to my mother and vice versa. Now they both know what I feel about the other. It isn't what I intended, but I think some good will come about through it. I want to talk about helping others. I find people are drawn to me and I can't help them. I hardly know where to turn with the number of people who, with almost no prompting from me, tell me about the sadness, abuse, and neglect of their past."

I pointed out that there was a curious way in which people who had a particular hurt and had resolved it to some extent attracted others with similar kinds of hurt. This happened partly because the others saw in them some healing and energy that they wanted themselves. It was also partly because these people were particularly sensitive to similar kinds of hurts in others and could see them at a great distance. However, I stressed that it was very important that before they tried to help others, they resolved these problems in themselves. Otherwise, they could become enmeshed in a tragic triangle, where their attempts to help could result in blaming somebody else, upsetting dynamics, splitting up marriages, and alienating children. The old axiom that you cannot see in others what you won't see in yourself still applies. Insight and healing were required before they became too deeply involved in helping others. However, we were now at the seventh stage of our group, where I did want them to reach out to other people. There was already a natural inclination to do that, which partly that came from their improved health. In order to facilitate this, I assigned the homework of trying to analyze the problems that attracted them and were attracted to them, to think about why those particular issues came to their attention.

In the seventh stage of the group, it was vitally important that they begin turning away from their own problems and looking at those of others. Their unhappy past was a way of helping them come to know and appreciate the difficulties that other people encountered. Their rehabilitation required helping others, but they needed to know how to do it properly.

❖   ❖   ❖

Anna

Homework this week: What kinds of problems do people bring to you? And why do you pick up on people's problems? It would be easier to say what kinds of problems people don't bring to me! Since my early 20s, people have brought their troubles to me.

1. Marriage: women, a few men, occasionally couples
2. Sexual: homosexual, dysfunction, abuse—both men and women, but rarely children
3. Child discipline: women

4. Death of a child: one woman, two couples
5. Chronic illness: three women

Why did I pick up on these problems?

1. I was willing to listen, was compassionate and trustworthy.
2. We share a common pain.
3. There was a genuine desire to help stemming from my own unresolved issues.
4. My blueprint (natural ability) must surely include counseling.

Krista was not here again tonight, and Dr. Ney had Tasha phone her and encourage her to come. When she arrived, she and I were expected to clear up our conflict again. I owned only what I was responsible for as I had practiced with Dr. Green the previous week. It was still difficult: my heart pounded and my mouth was as dry as dust. Still, it was moderately productive. We had communicated at a reasonable octave and Krista did ask for my forgiveness, "*if* she had hurt me in any way." In my heart, I felt that the issues were covered more than they were resolved. However, we were able to go on with the group process.

When it came to Krista's turn to share, she attacked Dr. Ney vehemently, accusing him of unfairness toward her. It became uncomfortably obvious to the whole group that the angry, defiant Urchin within wanted justice. Dr. Ney acknowledged her pain, but pointed out that she would have to deal with the Urchin before she could let her hurt, anger, and unrealistic need for justice go. She raged at him. Nothing he said seemed to enter her understanding. She fled from the room, determined never to return. I felt relieved. Someone else, Dr. Ney even, had been attacked by Krista and had not been able to reconcile. It was hard for both of them, but sure helped me let go of my guilt.

When it was my turn to share, I told the group about my husband's response to my reconciliation letter: he had come in while I was writing it, and I had been so afraid of his reaction that I had begun to cry. He said, "No problem. It is probably true how mean I was. Just do it and don't worry." Then he said, "The truth will set you free." I thanked him and had the courage I needed to continue and to be totally truthful. Later, when I gave him the letter, he groaned, "Three pages." After about 20 minutes, he came to me and sat down, looking very upset. My stomach tightened in the old familiar knot as he related how I had hurt him, recalling incident after incident. I interrupted him, stating that we were discussing my hurts now and that I would be willing to hear his at a later time, but that now was my time and I wanted him to respond to me and my pain by letter. He became very angry and defensive, invalidating me, my pain, and the letter. He said he would never think like me, that he didn't love me, and that that was the only reason he had responded so cruelly to me in the past. He said that I had obviously not changed in my months of therapy and that we should think about dissolving the marriage.

After he left, I sat there staring at my crumpled letter. I realized that at this time he would rather leave the relationship than face the pain of change and responsibility. I was devastated. The issues he had flung at me were distorted and had festered and grown ugly with time. They had been mulled over and over and then buried alive. I allowed the recently discarded, helpless feelings to consume me: I knew this would happen, and here I was again. I felt so old and tired. After a short time, I was able to gain some emotional distance and look at what was really happening. I didn't fix the pain and tension between us by apologizing for the letter. I knew that my requests were valid and that I would not back down, nor would I pack and leave. I knew that at the right time I would be able to make any necessary decisions. I didn't have to have him tell me that he loved me, nor did I need his touch to let me know I was okay. I could live if there were tension. I could wait. I could even live without him, if necessary. I was not responsible for his choices regarding my letter.

A few days later, he said he was willing, although very doubtful of its value, to handle the letter, with Dr. Ney as a neutral third party if we could arrange it. As I finished reading my homework, I felt the hopefulness that others in the group felt for me and ultimately for themselves in their own painful relationships.

❖   ❖   ❖

WEEK 26

Lisa sat in her usual corner, but there was a great deal more animation on her face and even fire in her eyes. "Don't make me start. I can't. I am too churned up inside. I have been looking after this little child who has been screaming all day. I find that I can't tolerate it and I am going to have to quit." Indeed, this child was triggering in Lisa all sorts of memories and feelings that she was struggling to deal with. I told her that if she felt that she was losing control, then to quit was indeed the right thing. With that, she relaxed and agreed that at this point she would have to do so.

Lisa had still more to say. "I feel I can live now. I feel so very different. I did write that letter and I didn't know whom to address it to because I was such a small infant. I didn't know who ritually abused me, but I am beginning to remember more. So I wrote the letter anyhow and said, 'I'm not afraid of you even if you did try to kill me, even if you did marry me and give me as a bride to Satan. That baby I've now given to God; she is in the arms of Jesus. I belong to Jesus and Satan cannot touch me.' I kept gagging while I was writing this letter because it was so awful to think that that could be done to a baby. But I am free of it now; even though I keep remembering some things, it doesn't have the same power over me."

Krista had walked out of our previous group and it had taken a lot of effort to get her to come back. She was still sullen, but she was prepared to give it another try. "I've just received a letter from my father and I am not at all happy." However, when she read the letter, others felt that there was a good deal of hope and forgiveness in it. It wasn't entirely genuine, but it was a start. Anna said, "The letter sounds very hopeful. It sounds like he wants to reconcile." But Krista responded, "Don't you see it? He has yet to realize the truth."

Krista was doing her best to finish a degree in English but she had a particularly difficult teacher. "I'm being manipulated by my English prof. He insisted that the whole class come to his home for dinner, at which he presided like a guru. He then made a point of making jokes about my being in therapy. He's humiliated me in many ways and I'm going to take him to the university ombudsman." I tried to point out that although there was some real benefit in doing something official about instances of abuse and neglect, people cannot always expect to find somebody to defend them. It is much better that they take it upon themselves. There is also a tendency to seek vindication and retribution, in which case there are subtle ways in which they invite the continual putdowns. I futher pointed out that as she had described the event, there had been more than one occasion when she could have stood her ground, faced the professor, and told him in no uncertain terms that she did not appreciate what he was saying. Krista, however, took this as another putdown and became increasingly angry, with me in particular, feeling that I had not supported her desire to deal with the situation through official channels.

Part of my reticence came from my knowledge and experience in many countries where there are no ombudspeople and where there is very little sympathy for children who stand up to their parents because of abuse and neglect. I said that I wanted people everywhere to recognize that it was their own responsibility and that there was not always somebody available to defend them. I described that Solzenitsyn had written in his semiautobiography, *The Calf and the Oak*, of how the communists had written into legislation the provision that if anybody were arrested in the night, the neighbors could challenge the arrest and ask what was happening. This was an attempt to prevent what had happened during czarist times when no one would intervene on behalf of a person being arrested because they were afraid of being arrested themselves. In Krista's case, nobody in the class came to her defense because they also were afraid of losing their status as honors English students. I reminded her that relying on official channels meant long delays. It also means that some people who have been wrong are given no opportunity to deal with the victim directly, but instead have to deal with the authorities. This recourse has many faults, and I have never been particularly happy with the mandatory reporting of child abuse. In New Zealand, we established a crisis line for children that was maintained on a voluntary basis. We found that when children were encouraged to report their own neglect or abuse, there was little or no need for the authorities to intervene. In fact, the children were happier to do it because they weren't so afraid that they would lose a parent.

Anna had received a letter from one of her daughters in which this woman, now struggling in her own marriage, had indicated that Anna's letter was life-changing. Anna went on to say, "I need to forgive myself and learn to have fun. There are so many parts of this that have been helpful. Still, I need to tidy up some loose ends. I'm beginning to feel very tidy."

Linda was as determined as ever. "My father got my letter and stated that he just wanted to die. I was shocked at first, but I realized that although he felt terrible, he was not going to die. I found I had taken a great step in writing the letters. I don't feel that bad. I find that my son is so much more helpful and affectionate since he told me about how I had hurt him."

Shawna was looking disappointed. Her father had said that he apologized if he had hurt his daughter. Yet it wasn't a direct acknowledgment of what he may have done to her. Any lame apologies—like, "If I hurt you"—were not very satisfactory. Shawna was much more involved now, having dealt with some of her conflicts in the group. "I wrote my letter to my father. I told him how he had forced me into adulthood before my time and that it is a terrible thing when children lose their innocence. Children need to be free of worries, like how to please their parents sexually. I wish I could go back to a childhood, but there is nobody who will care for me now. I realize that I had let this go when I buried the Person I could have been but whose life and development were so truncated. I only wish I got half the admission from my father that Krista got from hers. I also wrote to my mother and told her I had to know how much she knew. It felt very good when I had finished the writing. I know, Dr. Ney, you want me to write to my aborted baby. That is going to be especially tough."

Tanya was looking considerably more peaceful. "I went berserk when my father was here. My mother said she was sorry and asked me how she could have known, but I knew she must have known. I was frightened of their reactions, afraid that they might die or attack me in anger and I wasn't expecting that they would try to appease me." I made a note to myself, reminding me for future groups that, in order to mitigate the impact, I had to help the group members estimate the kinds of responses to their letters they might get from their parents. They all expected some kind of dramatic reaction. They were not prepared for underreactions. Any ho-hum was more devastating than anger.

At this point, it appeared that we had to do some tidying up, and my hope that we could go on to deal with rehabilitation—that is, how to use the bad experiences of their past to help others—had to be set aside. There was one more part that needed to be dealt with. In fact, they needed to forgive themselves. We spent some time in the group doing this. Their role-play partners were their alter egos, telling them they were forgiven. I then assigned the homework of having them ask themselves if they had really forgiven the people who had hurt them. The best way to ascertain this was to record their own thinking to find out whether certain people and certain events kept popping back into their minds and analyzing what feelings accompanied the memories. It was my experience that when forgiveness occurs, the memory begins to fade, and the first indication of that fading is that the intense feelings disappear. I truly believe that one cannot forget without forgiving. The mind insists that the event be brought back for reconsideration. After all, they had to learn from the experience, and they couldn't do that if the memory had faded.

❖   ❖   ❖

Anna

I had been feeling a delicious peace and lightness all week. Being responsible for myself and trusting myself, owning my feelings and actions, as well as allowing others the same privilege, had certainly taken a huge load off of me. I had examined myself and felt that the only real need I had right now was the need to have fun, to play, to take myself less seriously, to laugh, and to enjoy the beauty around me. I also discovered the freedom to allow all the weeks of hard work to settle in and found I was not driven to dig deep into myself to produce this week's homework. I had done all the assignments to date, and even a few extra. Now I was going to relax a little, trusting that I could show up at the group knowing that not doing a written assignment was truly the homework I needed right now— to trust my own judgment and not be afraid of authority, such as Dr. Ney's disapproval or the disapproval of my peers.

Several letters added to the newfound joy of the week. Two very positive responses from my children affirming me and my hard work, as well as forgiving me, validated the teachings of reconciliation and the need for forgiveness and restitution. This letter from a friend also encouraged me.

Dear Anna,
How to find the words to say what it has been like for me personally to be the observer in your walk through to wholeness. You have caused light to fight its way through some of the darker questions in my mind and heart. Your perseverance and determination to be well have been an incredible example to me. I applaud you with my mind, heart, and hands.
Gratefully,
Shelly

Equipped with this encouragement, I entered the therapy room tonight. As I shared from my heart, not my notes, I was received and my victory acknowledged.

It was not such a lighthearted week for the rest of the group. Lisa's trip to California had obviously given her the needed rest from her excruciating emotional pain and turmoil and she had once again been able to allow memories to surface. She was even able to share them with us in detail. This was the first time I can recall her being that able to trust us with her pain. I don't know how she is going to be able to finish this process with the rest of us. She still has so much more to do. Surprisingly, Krista was back tonight. The tension between the two of us had dissipated, but she was certainly still caught up in her anger. This time, it was directed toward a professor. Dr. Ney again tried to assist her in recognizing her old pattern, but she was unable to let it go.

At this point in the process, we were all doing different homework. The group flow seemed disjointed. When I looked back, not so very far, I could see that we had all struggled with the same assignments and were comforted because we could identify with each other's pain. Now we were fragmenting, becoming individuals instead of a team.

As I listened to the week's events and the homework projects of Linda, Shawna, and Tanya, I realized that the disappointing responses to their letters, recurring memories, and relationship struggles didn't cripple them or prevent them from pursuing their healing. Truly, we were all getting much stronger.

❖   ❖   ❖

7

Rehabilitation: Using My Bad Experiences for the Benefit of Others

For the past 26 weeks, the patients have focused on themselves. This was necessary, but it tends to make them very self-centered and, to some degree, selfish. It is now time to turn their thoughts outward to helping other people.

Ancient wisdom and our experience have shown that it is not until people are reaching out and helping other wounded people that they really get better. This phase is devoted to teaching them how to mobilize their residual anger and frustration and to use this energy to help prevent child abuse and to heal those who have already been wounded. When they are focused on other people, their minds are not centered on themselves. As anyone in love knows, when your mind is concentrated on somebody else and you forget about yourself, your whole world picture changes. It is as if you were wearing rose-colored glasses. One of the real blessings of the "people treating" business is that, because you concentrate on others, it promotes your own health and sanity.

When people have been healed of their mistreatment wounds, they can see more clearly the wounds in others and the causes of those wounds. Thus they are in a much better position to help other people. Until this happens, they tend to perpetuate both their own and the other wounded person's problems in a reenactment of their early conflicts.

We encourage people to become active in various organizations that protect children and protest their misuse and mistreatment. It is important that they take a practical step and act immediately, rather than proclaiming that something should be done—by somebody, sometime. "Why doesn't the gvernment do something about it?" If they take one step, then all the other steps in the direction of helping children are much easier.

When one believes that one should do something and doesn't do it, a discrepancy between belief and behavior develops. That discrepancy is a tension that has to be sustained by energy. With many of those discrepancies, people can become tired, weak, lethargic, and more prone to illness. It would almost be better if they didn't believe that they should help, or that they didn't know that they could help, than to believe and not take some action. Thus we insist that patients do something positive before they complete treatment.

Until we see how we contribute to a problem, we cannot see how we can help to solve it. If people are not actively preventing child abuse and neglect, they are contributing to it. When they are unable to see how they contribute, they tend to blame some other agent and will scapegoat (usually the perpetrator).

Prevention is always better than cure. That is why we strongly advocate that the patients take it upon themselves to enhance the value of children and to stop any form of child mistreatment. Now they have to confront a real perpetrator (usually a profit-making institution or business, such as pornography). These businesses are powerful, and are run by cynical people who have few qualms about pushing the opposition out of the way. The patients have much more reason to be afraid of these perpetrators than of the ones they experienced as children. When they tackle these institutions and businesses, they gain a great deal more insight into what is really behind the mistreatment of little children.

In a study that we conducted on the causes of child abuse and neglect from a child's perspective, we were amazed to find just how often children implicated immaturity and marital difficulties. To them, these were more important than other contributors, such as alcoholism, drug abuse, or unemployment.

In order to be effective in preventing child abuse and neglect, patients have to clearly understand the needs of children and to see how vulnerable they are. By meeting those needs, they are learning to love. Often they have held the misconception that love is a "feeling." But it is clear that the most pragmatic definition of love is "meeting a person's needs." It is pragmatic because needs are definable, and, in fact, scientifically measurable. You can know when you are loving a person by how well you meet that person's needs.

It is important for me, as a model, to demonstrate my courage in dealing with institutions and businesses that abuse children. It is most effective if I can lead some type of protest. It isn't good enough for me to tell people to go out there and do it. I need to be at the head of the march.

By now I have recognized that there are a number of standard excuses for not becoming involved. I tend to deal with these quite firmly. Otherwise, people quickly start using them. The more often they use them, the more they become convinced of their validity. These excuses are:

1. "I can't do this by myself. I'll have to wait until we get a group together."
2. "I'm not sure that I know what to do. I had better take a course, otherwise I may be doing more harm than good."
3. "I've already committed myself to doing so many things. Besides, I can't resolve all the problems in the world."
4. "My family comes first and I don't think that it is right to take the time away from them or to endanger them."
5. "I don't feel my spirit is led to do this. I'll have to wait until I get a special message."

These standard excuses are not acceptable. Invariably they show how much the person is still afraid to confront a perpetrator. It is now time to stand up and be counted.

Each graduate is invited to become a facilitator in a succeeding group. Going through the whole process a second time while focusing on helping others has the effect of deepening the experience. A female facilitator states at the end of a men's group, "I used to hold men to be in only one of two categories. They were either wimps or sex objects. This experience has taught me to broaden my thinking about men and to see them as real people."

WEEK 27

I was absent for the earliest part of this group, attending a meeting of colleagues that only was held on this particular night of the week. I found I had to do this occasionally, just to keep in touch. It was gratifying that I had been asked to return and present some of my research data to the assembled group of psychiatrists.

It appeared I wasn't missed by everyone in the group. Being the only male and the one who kept pushing people into facing their conflict and pain, I knew I should expect some negative emotions, but it wasn't always easy.

The earlier part of the meeting with the group members was mainly facilitated by Dr. Green. Linda was talking as I came in, indicating how she had struggled not to be a passive observer in situations in which children were being hurt. Like many others, there was the tendency to enjoy vicarious vindication by watching instances in which the perpetrator was apprehended and punished. I reminded the group that it was impossible for them really to be a part of the solution if they didn't realize how they were part of the problem. That meant they must realize how they might subtly contribute to the continuing cycles of abuse and neglect by being either passive observers or vindictive observers. The trick was how to intervene. We did some role plays in which a group member would play the part of a parent abusing a child and I would follow with other members of the group as the observers. I suggested that the best response was something like this: "Excuse me, Mrs. Smith, I can see that you are really struggling with your baby and I can appreciate how irritating it must be, but I don't think that is the way to handle it. Let me give you a hand." To the child, depending upon the age: "I can see that you and your mom are being caught up in a bad situation. I think she needs a break. I know you are very angry and hurt. While she finishes her shopping, why don't you tell me all about it and then we will discuss it together."

Shawna was ecstatic. She was feeling so much happier with her husband. "This has been the most painful 20 weeks of my life and it didn't go unnoticed that you, Dr. Ney, were by my side. Thank you very much. Lately he has been so adorable. I haven't got a clue as to what I am doing that produces these changes in him, but I sure appreciate it and I feel a great deal calmer. Again, I noticed the enormous power of changing other people by being different yourself."

Shawna went on, "I like being in therapy. I'd like to be pregnant. I wish I had a child, but Alan doesn't want me to. I finally got down and wrote a letter to the baby I'd aborted."

Shawna then began to read the letter, which is included here with her permission. I noted the softness with which she read the letter.

> Dear Baby:
> This is the hardest of all the letters to write. I made myself believe you weren't a baby. I know I didn't have the right to rob you of your life. Your name is Sean and you are mine but I give you to God.

Shawna then went on to address the group. "I didn't want to write it, but once I started, I banged out that sucker in five minutes." Everybody noticed a very great difference in Shawna, and Anna particularly: "I was moved by the wholeness that you seemed to have gained in this area. You used to be so hard."

Tanya said she was pleased at the changes around her, although she wasn't experiencing all of them herself. "Incidents keep coming up in my mind now. I want to be free of my father but I don't want to hurt him. I am supposed to be pleased at my parents' responses. They both said they would be going to treatment. Mom said she was sorry and will see a therapist right away. Dad still insists that he doesn't remember anything. Is that possible, Dr. Ney? I feel my father would fall apart if he did remember. My mother is furious at herself for not noticing. I know I should feel happy, but I began vomiting when I got off the phone to my father. I just want to get him out of me. I can't forgive him, not yet. I'd like him to say that he recognizes what he did to me and that he is truly sorry. To say that he doesn't remember isn't good enough. I'm so angry at him, it is beginning to affect my marriage. If I didn't have children, I would just say goodbye and leave. I know my father is badly mixed up. His mother and his sister sexually abused him."

I have noticed how pathologically bonded children who were sexually abused are to the person who abused them at an early age. The abuse is humiliating and traumatic, but the worst features of it are that the child is bonded in a sexual union with his or her own parent and his or her sexual appetites are stimulated at an age when he or she cannot deal with them. Children who are sexually abused by a parent are bonded in three ways to that parent, and it is understandable why they have such a great struggle with undoing that pathological attachment. They are bonded in these ways:

1. As a child is bonded to a parent because of the need to depend upon them to survive.
2. As a husband and wife are bonded sexually.
3. By operant conditioning, whereby the parent becomes the source of sexual pleasure and so the child wants to return to the same source.

To help Tanya deal with this pathological bonding, we did a role play. I recognized only later to what extent the other members of the group became involved. With increasing emphasis, Tanya was encouraged to say, "Get out of my house. You don't belong there." I played the role of the father, responding with, "Of course I do. I'm your father. You enjoy having me in your house." As the role play went on, Tanya became increasingly angry and began shouting with great vigor: "Get out of my house. Stay out." As a metaphor, Tanya was attempting to act and thereby believe that the father had no right to be in her body or in her head, and she was now determined to keep him out. She ended up saying, "I wish you were dead, Father. You are dead. You are no longer in my house."

Anna understood the implications and said, "Those people had no right to be in my house, but I felt that I could not shut the door on them. Now I have done it and they will stay out." Linda also noted that having dealt with and forgiven the perpetrators of her past, she had fewer headaches and she was sleeping much better.

Amy was nearly due to deliver her baby, but she was still struggling with her mother and with her husband. She didn't like to see her daughter, Sheila, neglected, and felt that her husband, Sam, would never take up the slack. She then went on to say how she had struggled to say goodbye to her father, but it was hard because she had to admit that she had never let go of the little unhappy Urchin inside her. She said she wished she had had the courage to do that and to complete all the homework that she knew she must. She was afraid that in doing that she would lose her mother, upon whose help she depended. "I'm afraid that my mother is going to be sick and I am going to have to look after myself. But she keeps telling me how much she is doing for me and I hate it. She keeps rubbing in how much I should be grateful. I know I could cope. If my mother didn't look after Sheila, I wouldn't die. I have got to do it."

As often happened in the groups that I have conducted, things were getting a little disorderly toward the end. It was obvious that, although we had trucked through various stages, the patients were not all moving at the same rate. There was a lot of tidying up to do and we had to take time to do it. There was no question but that the members were still working very hard. I was a little disappointed that they did not get around to the most recent homework, but it was evident that they had been thinking about it. When we did the group exercise, they quickly itemized the people who had been forgiven and who had yet to be forgiven. Most of them had a greatly shortened list, but there were still a few key people who needed forgiveness. In most instances, this had not taken place because they either were dead, had not been written to, or had not indicated that they felt any culpability for abusing the child. This raises a very important question in this method of group therapy. Can you forgive a person who doesn't apologize? We struggled with this using role plays, and they helped, but it was clear that unless the person does admit to having wronged the patient in group therapy, the process will take much longer. I have had enough experience to know that it does happen eventually, but it is still a longer struggle than if it can be done directly.

❖   ❖   ❖

Anna

Last week we were informed that Dr. Green was to be in charge. Dr. Ney had a meeting that he couldn't put off. When he told us, I immediately regretted his need to be absent. Dr. Green seemed unconvinced that she could handle the group without him, while I felt the need for his "covering." I was glad that I'd worked through all my conflicts with Dr. Green so that I not only respected her, but could also submit myself to her leadership because I now trusted her. The relief I felt when hearing the homework assignment, which appeared routine and not likely to trigger anything too intense, revealed my deep need for male authority. Some of the group members had seemed genuinely pleased with this change in plans; I would comply, but was not at all pleased.

Dr. Green was obviously nervous as we settled down for our evening's work. With Dr. Ney, Krista, and Lisa away, the room looked unnaturally empty. Observing Lisa's absence, Dr. Green commented, "This indicates her need for male authority." She seemed a little defensive, and her quick evaluation of Lisa exposed her insecurity even more. However, as we moved into the homework, we all soon forgot our inhibitions.

Something I'd read during the week really struck me: "Centered in the self, not self-centered." This statement released a lot of guilt that I'd felt off and on during this long introspection. I had found it necessary to put away others' needs, except for the basics, and to focus on me to be able to get in touch with the buried pain, memories, and anger. Feelings of selfishness and guilt for my seeming self-absorption, as well as the well-intentioned warnings of others, "Just forget it and get on with your life," had often shaken my confidence. Knowing and accepting all of who I was and learning to live and give from within this being more than merely existing and giving to others were just what I'd been learning to do. Affirmation like this from a variety of sources seemed to appear just as I needed it.

Tanya's sadness seemed particularly heavy last week as she shared about the baby Tanya whom she had symbolically buried as two stones, one for each year of her life, in the sand. As she described her father, putting "things" up inside her, sadness and grief for what had happened to her, and similarly to me, bonded us. Later in the week, concern for her and wanting to reach out with comfort, these words came:

LITTLE TANYA
In the sand so deep, two precious stones,
Heart echoes, muffled sounds, low moans.
Like cheeks, the sand dries and cracks with tearlike salt.
Droning waves echo, Why? Why? Why? Who's at fault?
The child, nature's innocence, she's to blame?
Torn promises layered in a shroud of shame.
Crouching, in her mind, screaming, "I'm so bad!"
Lonely, aching, desperate, so needy, so sad.
Call it abuse—How? How do I dare?
Wholeness, through Hell? God, it's not fair!
Memories, pain, anguish, rage, wash daily out to sea.
With each passing tide, more and more, she is free.

I reported to the group that after writing my list of requirements necessary to forgive myself, I realized I had put myself in bondage again—proclaiming to them that I was learning to be relaxed, carefree, and accepting of myself and others, and that the homework I'd done reflected my old rigid expectations and not my growing wholeness. I had demanded of myself to be growing in the following ways:

1. Making amends to everyone I have hurt as far as is possible.
2. Learning new healthy skills in relating to self and others:
   a. Appropriate expression of anger
   b. Using wisdom—put purity over peace
   c. Putting away false fears, e.g.:
      Bathrooms
      The dark, night
      Fat\ugly\unwanted
      Anger\assertiveness\aggression
   d. Expressing love and patience for self and others
3. Developing personal skills to freedom:
   a. Mind—to be able to visualize, let go of the darkness, replace old destructive thought patterns, and release creativity
   b. Body—to develop healthy self-discipline in exercise and nutrition and to let compulsive behaviors go
   c. Emotions—to feel what I feel, let extremes go

True forgiveness for me includes genuine repentance and a change of behavior.

As you can see, these are all commendable and worthwhile goals. They are, however, goals and not necessarily requirements for forgiveness. I choose to forgive myself for the ways I have hurt and destroyed myself and others. I give myself permission to laugh, play, and experience the freshness forgiveness brings. The question that comes to mind now is, "Can I give the same forgiveness without demands to others?"

FORGIVENESS OF OTHERS

Regarding my father:
As I remember the abuse incident, I can feel myself curled up against the Lord's chest. His soft cooing and warm body comfort me. I weep with joy at how blessed I am to have felt and heard the Lord and to know his love for me so intimately. I have the scars. I remember what caused them, but God has swallowed up the pain.

Regarding the foster parent:
What he did was horrible. He must have been very sick. Yet, as I remember, what seems to be the most important element is the abused child's peace. I am so glad she is gone now, at peace at last. No more pain, hatred,

shame, rage, ugliness, and self-destruction. She is free and I rejoice. I can feel sorry for what happened to her but I am not overwhelmed, and I can remember her without my heart becoming gripped by fear.

Regarding my mother:

I am confused about my feelings. I feel sorry for her and I recognize her pain and fear. I wish I could help her but...how? I don't want to get pulled back into her web. I don't know how to be an adult without hurting her. I don't know how to respond when she chooses to be offended by my honesty and hurt by the enforcement of my safety needs. I don't want to hurt her, and I want to be free. I remember the pain she caused me and can forgive and even identify with some of her choices, yet I can't seem to breathe.

Regarding my stepfather:

I know that we have worked through and resolved much. Yet I am aware there will be things that he says or does that will not be okay for me. I am not afraid. I know that I can tell him and he will be open to hear me. We will always have our differences, but I know that I am respected and I treasure that.

Regarding my husband:

I am sure that I have forgiven him in many areas because of the positive changes in our relationship. I know, as I continue to confront many issues, as he answers my letter and processes his therapy with Dr. Ney, that there will be unresolved or unforgiven wounds on both sides. Even though this is hard and sometimes threatening work lies ahead, I feel quite confident that I will be able to work through any new discoveries. I wonder if he will be so willing.

Dr. Ney returned to the meeting. We were not expecting him at all tonight. I am really glad to see him; however, Tanya groans out loud and clearly shows her disappointment that he is back. She really wanted this night with only female leadership. All along, Tanya's biggest conflicts have been with him, and they have been just as intense as mine were with Dr. Green. Amy and Shelly seem a bit miffed as well. Shawna also had some strong reactions to Dr. Ney. One night, she actually hurled her notebook at him. There was some confusion as to who was leading and who was supporting the procedure, Dr. Ney or Dr. Green. Eventually, I asked. After that, we more or less resumed looking to Dr. Ney for direction.

Maybe feeling a little more separate and less needed tonight sparked Dr. Ney's discussion about the feelings and needs of a man. Again, Tanya's hackles were up. Amy was particularly surprised by his comments. The rest of us confessed that we didn't really know much about men's feelings, thinking that they usually hid them so well.

Shawna shared a most heartfelt letter. She had written to the baby she had aborted and asked forgiveness. As she read, a well of hidden tenderness unveiled itself. Calm and beauty seemed to settle over her. I resolved to buy her and baby "Sean" a copy of Frank Peretti's book *Tilly*, a heart-warming story of the reunion of an aborted child and her mother.

Word pictures always bring insights to me more quickly than does any other method. Such was the case during Dr. Ney and Tanya's role play.

DR. NEY: "You can't get me out. I am in your house. You invited me in and I belong there now!"

TANYA: "Get out of my house! You don't belong there! You were never supposed to be in my house!"

I could just feel the violation. "Get out of my house!" meant "Get out of my mind! Get out of my body!" They all just came into my house. Whenever they wanted, they came into my body and into my mind! That's why I let others violate my house when I grew up. I thought I had to let them. I owed them. I am overwhelmed by sadness as I look at my house. The doors are ripped off. Anyone could come in. I owe them and, anyway, I have no door to stop them. My mind flashes to another door. I pound on it and pound on it and it never opens. My doors are ripped off and their doors are locked. Now I am learning to build doors and I can say, "You must stay on the porch or you may come into my living room." I can say, "You can't come into my bedroom."

❖   ❖   ❖

❖   ❖   ❖

Lisa's Story

It is difficult to write my story, as I begin, once again, to face these memories so full of darkness and evil that are so very disturbing.

I know that as I tell my story I am breaking the oath of secrecy and silence that has imprisoned me all my life. I realize that this is an important part of my healing process. The isolation and confusion have brought depression and suicidal thoughts. There are more questions than answers but, as the pieces of the puzzle my life has been slowly fall into place, there is hope, and everything is beginning to make sense.

The signs of satanic ritual abuse have always been there. I have suffered the effects of these traumatic memories all my life, but I didn't understand that these feelings and images were memories trying to surface. I have always felt that something horrific had happened to me, and it was just beneath the surface. I always felt "something there," something wrong, deep inside, some horrible truth trapped in the feelings of forgotten memories.

As a child, I experienced terrifying nightmares almost every night for years. I remember some of the dreams vividly. They were so realistic. They were filled with Satan and strange people performing rituals and murder. I could smell and taste the sacrificial offering they were forcing me to eat. Human flesh. These dreams were also very sexual. As a child, these strange nightmares were so frightening that I would wake up screaming. I would need to sleep with my parents in their bed or I wouldn't be able to go back to sleep. I would cry and scream and be unable to relate the story to my parents. The occult symbolism was too confusing for a child's mind. I was unable to put a name to these strange dreams and, being preverbal when these rituals occurred, I had no way of making sense of what happened to me. Many times I said to my adoptive mother, "Mommy, something very, very bad happened to me." She would tell me it was in my imagination. I would insist something bad had happened as fear and terror gripped me.

To begin to tell of my earliest years will explain some of these details. My natural mother had six children, of whom I was the youngest. Each child was by a different father. She didn't marry until late in her life. One by one, we were taken away by Social Services and placed in foster homes.

I was told by my adoptive family that they fostered me for a year until I was two years old. Just before the age of two, they were told I would have to be put in an orphanage because I wouldn't go to my mother. I would scream and become extremely upset when the social worker would come to take me for my visits to see my natural mother. I also wouldn't let anyone touch me or I would scream. I believe the abuse happened before I went into the foster home at eight months of age, and during the visitations that went on for another year with my natural mother. Because I was so upset, my foster mother was told I couldn't be in a temporary foster home anymore. I was not to be going back to my natural mother and so I would have to placed for adoption. My foster parents had cared for me for a year by this time and felt that I was as their own child. So my foster parents adopted me and I was loved as their own child, and blessed with a very special family.

The effects of the abuse and the memories were forced deep into the subconscious mind, to be forgotten for a time, thus protecting my sanity from their intense horror. I also believe the security of having my adoptive family protected me from going through much more trauma, and so I was emotionally and physically healthy very soon and developing normally. Yet I never bonded to my adoptive mother, just as I had never bonded to my natural mother. I never wanted to be held or touched. I felt loved by them, but certainly never felt I belonged to them or was part of them.

I felt very bonded to this image of a man. He was always there; his image was burned into my mind. His memory haunted me. The image was of a man with long black hair and dark eyes who always wore black.

My first memories of this man (the high priest) were of being in this white crib and crying and crying. I was alone, it was dark, and I was crying and crying, but no one would come. Then I started to get images of this man. There was an open door and light would come into the room through the doorway. A man in a black robe with a hood and a white face (theatrical makeup) and dark eyes. When he wasn't wearing the hood, he revealed long dark hair.

On my birthday in 1989, I relived a memory. I could feel myself being held and carried in the arms of a man. There was an extremely evil presence coming from him. Words can't express how evil and horrible this presence was. The only way to describe it is that it was as if I were being held by Satan himself. This man was very tall with silver-gray hair and he was wearing a long black robe. Someone was walking alongside us in a long black robe with a hood, and I sensed that this was the man with whom I now have a bond. I could hear his robe dragging along the ground as we walked across a field of dry grass. There was a bright blue sky and it was a sunny day. We were moving toward a very large gray barn with patches of blue-green paint peeling off it. It appeared to be abandoned. I heard creaking as the barn door swung back and forth. There was mud on the ground in front of it and a very large puddle of blood in the entrance. I heard people talking, but I didn't understand what they were saying. He carried me through the entrance and then everything went black. I tried to see what was inside the barn but I felt horrified and the darkness increased. I decided I couldn't handle facing what was there and feeling what I had felt as that baby.

In July 1989, I had more flashbacks. During the first, I felt such an evil presence. It had never felt this horrible before. It was terrifying. There was blackness. There was something horrible happening. Why were these cries coming out of me? I didn't understand what was happening to me. Help me. It was dark and it was evil. It was going to kill me. No, I was not alone. God was with me. Jesus, You were there. That was why I was still alive. What was it? No. I couldn't face this on my own. It was too horrible. I wanted this out of me. I needed help. It was black. There was a circle. There were black robes. There was darkness, shadows. A white face, a black robe. My mother was there.

I could not continue the flashback; I was too terrified. Writing it down wasn't helping so I called Julie, who was my therapist at the time. She said that if I were too terrified, my mind would know that I couldn't handle it and it would shut down the remembering, not allowing memories to surface. That helped me so much because it was such a horrible experience—the feelings and the images. I could not face it on my own, not even with Julie on the phone. It finally all went away.

Later that month, the memory came back. I was inside the barn, being carried by the silver-haired man. I saw a man hanging upside down, a rope from the rafters tied around his feet. He was wearing very dirty jeans and a blue plaid shirt. His face was mutilated. At another time, about a week or so later, I saw his face up close, as if someone were holding me there, forcing me to see it. His mouth was wide open and it was very horrifying. Then I saw a procession of men in black robes walking around a large circle in the barn. I saw the man with long black hair. He laid me down in the straw and sexually abused me. I could feel him touching me.

When I finally allowed this to surface, the face no longer disturbed me and the feelings all went away. Later that night, a friend called and said she had been praying for me, and that she had seen these men in black robes walking in a circle in her mind's eye. I told her about the memory that had come up. She prayed for me. We thought that God had allowed her to see this image so that she would pray for me.

As the years progressed, the image became more and more real. I didn't know these were flashbacks of someone I had bonded to as an infant. I was very sexual as a child and I thought these memories were sexual fantasies. I always felt him touching me sexually at night. I didn't understand it and it wasn't frightening. I felt he loved me and I felt love for him, but I didn't know who he was or exactly what was happening. I felt a powerful bond to him and spiritual contact with him. I didn't understand the spiritual realm, but I was very sensitive to its reality. The nightmares seemed to end at about the same time that I began to have sexual experiences with this spirit.

My earliest memory of this was when I was four years old. I felt love for this image that would appear when this was happening. It was not frightening, and I remember telling him that I wanted him to touch me, that I liked it. I was not frightened of the image. I knew he was a spirit, but he never frightened me; he seduced me. It is strange to think of a little child's wanting sexual attention, especially from an apparition, but even at that age, I felt as though he were my lover. I know now that a normal part of coping with sexual abuse is for children to make it all seem good so that they are able to survive. They normalize the abuse, whatever it may be. Abused children often become deeply bonded to their abusers.

In my situation, this was the only parent figure I had. I believe this was a man with whom my natural mother was involved and he was a satanist. Satanists usually use babies and children in rituals as part of their belief that Satan gives power through the destruction of innocence. Therefore, babies are used as sacrifices, or they are dedicated to serve Satan and the cult group for which they are conceived. The rituals are very sexual and, as an infant, I bonded to this man when he sexually abused me. That was the only attention I received as an infant and so I interpreted sexual abuse as love. I didn't understand all of this as a child, of course; I just knew that there was a special bond between me and this spirit. He also appeared to me as a wolf.

As far back as I can recall, the bond between us has always been there. I felt him to be as a father and a mother to me, yet his presence was also very evil and unsettling. I knew he was a real person with whom I was in contact, but my adoptive family told me that the spiritual realm didn't exist: there were no spirits, no God, no devil, and the Bible was fantasy and fairy tales. We never had a Bible or were given any religious teachings. My parents were humanistic in their teaching and believed only in the material realm.

The image of this dark man was becoming more and more real to me. Over the years, his personality started to control me. I felt overpowered by his personality and I felt one with him. I didn't know where I ended and he began. The spirit sexually abused me for years up to the present. I can feel him raping me as though there were someone physically attacking me. It is very real and physical, not imagined at all. As the years went by, I became more and more controlled by him.

As a child, I acted out ritual abuse on other children, unaware of what I was doing. I dressed up in black material and made it into a cloak with thread from my mother's sewing box. I acted out things I know I must have seen, for I would not have known about them unless they had happened to me. Most of my play and fantasy as a child were centered on my natural family and this man. (I knew I was adopted.) In my games, they were all evil monsters. I felt a strange connection to them. They were in contact with me through this spirit. They would turn into wolves and vampires and they lived in this very old mansion. It is natural that a child fantasize about her birth family, but these fantasies were not at all normal. This role I played was very evil, and I believed it as well. It wasn't just fantasy in my mind. The characters also were all family members. In my childish way, I was acting out what had been experienced with my natural family. It was the innocent little child trying to make sense of the bizarre rituals and sexual abuse.

I also spent much of my time drawing pictures. They were pictures of people having sex. Animals were involved. Sadistic and masochistic sex was depicted, as were torture, murder, and death. This was definitely not normal, and not something I could have possibly known about unless I had been exposed to it. I did not watch violent movies on television as I was not allowed to, and I was terrified of horror movies and even of spooky cartoons, so they did not play a part in influencing me.

On my 13th birthday, this spirit, which was controlling my personality more and more, came to me and in a loving way asked me to give myself completely to him in a relationship. I had always known this spirit as a lover, but it seemed important to somehow give myself or commit myself to him. It was also to accept completely the bond between us as a relationship and not only as a sexual experience. I had many friends and a very close girlfriend, so it was not because of loneliness or being unpopular that I decided to accept this relationship. I just felt very different from everyone and this spirit made me feel so loved. I remember telling him that I would be his. For some reason, I had to decide that night. I decided to be his. I guess that is where my will entered once again and another door opened to the spiritual realm.

After this, he controlled me more and more. My personality changed drastically. I became very angry and withdrawn with my family (I ignored them most of the time), and I started to fail most of my classes at school. Though I had had many friends, they all rejected me when they found out about my involvement with satanism. To escape the pain and rejection I felt, I abused alcohol. My adoptive mother was always physically ill and needed me to take care of her. She was an adult child of an alcoholic and came from a broken home, and so was not able to provide mothering.

I became involved with different occult practices. I was experiencing unusual power and was psychic. I wanted to use this ability to control my life. I desperately wanted to change my life as I felt so depressed and unloved. Somehow, I knew about certain practices that I'd never actually heard of, but they seemed to be a part of me, coming out of me to direct me spiritually. I became involved with Wicca and fortune telling (tarot cards) to control my future and to try to create my own reality, which is the purpose of witchcraft. I never wanted to use black magic or to harm anyone to get what I desired. The spirit (he called himself Brian) told me that he was a high priest of Satan. In Wicca, there are many gods and goddesses, but one god and one goddess stand above all the others. I was a witch, but I did not desire to serve many gods. I was desiring to know the god that I believed was above all others, the creator of the nature I worshipped. I had never read a bible or been to church, so I had no understanding of God. The spirit, Brian, said the highest god (the horned god of the witches—Baphomet) was Satan. He was higher than the goddess and all others, and this was truth. Lucifer was the highest being and the bearer of light. He was the one I was searching for. I believed this with all my heart. I felt a bond with Satan that was very real. I sensed his presence and felt that I belonged to him, just as I felt with Brian. I believed he was God. At 16, I dedicated myself to him. I gave my life to Satan and became involved with a coven. I was already friends with some of these people, and was very attracted to a man who reminded me of the spirit. He and Brian were so much alike. I became involved sexually with different men in the coven. I was told that my conception and my birth were planned by my mother for Satan. Brian told me this. He said that my birth date was significant and that it was extremely important. The witches were very interested in communicating with the spirit, Brian, through me. He controlled me at will, acting and speaking through me. He had almost complete control over me. I would often fall into a trance and he would take control over me. I was told I was chosen by this spirit to be his channeler. I was given the name SweetLeaf by Brian as my coven name. I was told that I was a bride of Satan and married to him. I didn't understand this, except that I knew I felt love for Satan, a very deep bond that did feel like marriage.

In Satanism, evil is beautiful and good, darkness is light, and everything is twisted around. I didn't need to be brainwashed or indoctrinated. I already believed. The belief system of satanism was a part of me; it all just came out of somewhere inside me. I knew many things that no one had told me. I believe this was so because of the exposure and brainwashing that I had undergone as a child. It was an overwhelming control to worship Satan.

I listened only to music with lyrics that glorified Satan (Black Sabbath, Iron Maiden, Ozzy Osbourne, etc.). I had never experienced anything so exciting and powerful. This was the beautiful side of evil. My purpose in the coven was to be used sexually in rituals, and most of the time the witches used me to have sex with Brian, the spirit. He had sex with them through my body, and it was always in different rituals. Other demonic spirits used me as well. I was losing touch with myself as the spirit demanded almost complete control of me. I was used for ritual sex for a year, day and night, in various situations, from just before I was 17 to a month before I turned 18. It did not end completely until I was 20 years old. For a year, it was constant abuse and abusing sexually and being controlled by certain satanists.

While still involved with satanism, I became fearful and knew I was losing all control. I started going to a church and reading the Bible. Then the memories from my early childhood came with intensity. As I rejected Satan and received Jesus Christ, the memories seemed to be released. This all happened as I told God I didn't want Brian or Satan anymore. I didn't want the love, the bond, the sexual contact or control. When I was no longer involved with ritual sex and satanism, this seemed to open the door for memories to come flooding back. I believe I was acting out what had been done to me; the memories were controlling me. When I decided I didn't want to be controlled, the mind had to release these memories. I know victims of abuse often become perpetrators in the way they were abused and that it can be transgenerational. I didn't realize that these were actual memories. I didn't understand that I was remembering. I started regressing into a baby and remembering the rituals where the abuse took place. I was confused.

I started to make sense of it when more memories came up. I realized I had been acting out repressed memories. This man in a black robe—Brian—was a high priest who had abused me in rituals when I was a baby. He had access to me through my natural mother. I believe she gave me to him for a time. I don't know how long the abuse went on, but the memories were so traumatic, they were being relived and experienced again in all their horror. The feelings of the sexual abuse and the atmosphere, tastes, smells, sounds, images—everything the baby experienced. I was reliving the experience and I couldn't understand it. It was regression.

The spirit continued to rape me, and even though I was going through deliverance and prayer, he refused to leave. I was delivered from many spirits of demonic control, but Brian claims he has grounds or the right to stay. Most of the time, he avoids being confronted and will attack people during deliverance ministry to avoid being confronted and exposed. The attacks come as confusion and pain and vomiting. Usually people give up because the spirit will not leave. Concerning the memories, I continue to relive them and desperately need healing from their effects. I realize there are more memories that are repressed and trying to surface, and I struggle still with the personality of this spirit trying to control me. Sometimes I regress into the baby and her personality takes control of me at times. As memories have surfaced, I have experienced more and more healing. I know God is controlling my healing process and I believe that the spirit, Brian, is losing control over me as these memories are revealed. He has been losing power over me (my personality, thoughts, will, emotions, body) as the memories come into the light and their power is destroyed. They are then no longer a part of me. I believe this is the way God has been delivering me as the demonic spirits have had control through the repressed memories.

I did find all of my natural family members and made contact with them. My mother was just as I remembered her. I asked her questions, but she refused to tell me much about what had happened. She said she couldn't talk about it. When I met her, she was distant, cold, and emotionless. She persisted in wanting to be friends with me, but the more I asked her about the past, the more she became nervous and secretive. I told her about the memories and she became abusive and threatening. She even tried to turn the family against me. It became a very abusive situation and I had to cut myself off completely from contact with her. I went through many strange head games with her and I realized she was trying to control me. She knew I was needing answers and she refused to be honest with me. I got a lot of information from my sister, who was the closest to me in age. She told me about some horrible times when she saw our mother being violent, and when I mentioned sexual abuse, she said that all my sisters had been abused, as had she. Their abuse went on for years.

I have found it very helpful to be in therapy now. It has helped me to confront the pain and the identity I have as a victim. I no longer accept that as my identity. I know that it is not who I really am, and I am getting in touch with the person I was created to be. She is beautiful and powerful, and she is struggling to be free, to be who she is. I am becoming her more and more.

I believe God did much healing in me through the group therapy process. I was separated from the baby who was abused. Before the group, I was that baby. She was so much a part of me. She was the biggest part of my personality. I was able to let her go, to give her to God and place her in Jesus' arms to be with him. Then I saw the shadow of someone beautiful coming toward me. Not long ago, I saw her and we ran to each other. She was smiling and very beautiful and pure, and she embraced me. It is part of accepting myself and becoming and living as I truly am, the real me who had been trapped in the darkness and the abuse, afraid to live, afraid to be. Now, as a result of the group therapy, I have confronted her fear and inability to live. I am able to trust my secrets to others so that I no longer am alone in the abuse, isolated and ashamed. The acceptance was very healing. In sharing some of the experience of abuse with others, I was not ridiculed or blamed or told I was crazy. I needed a safe place to bring my memories and there was a lot of remembering that happened as a result of feeling the support. I remembered the abuse when I was alone at night (not with the group), but I tried to share as much as I could. This helped me tremendously. This was my hope in the group most of all: to be able to begin to share and to have support in what I was remembering. That was the most difficult and most rewarding part of the group. I wanted to share more, as I held many memories inside that I had never told anyone about, such as the more recent memories of ritual abuse and satanism. But I know that to share as much as I was able to helped me very much. I still don't feel that I told enough, but I was able to disclose some of the most disturbing memories and my struggle with the feeling that I had to return to satanism. Everyone seemed to believe me when I said that I wanted to be healed and not sick, that I didn't want these memories to control me, and that I didn't want to be an evil person. They told me many times that they didn't think I was crazy, that they believed me and accepted me. I used to feel so alone, but I identified with them in many ways. Our stories connected, as it seemed others were telling about the same feelings of guilt, shame, fascination, and repulsion. Many of the stories touched me deeply and helped me to share.

❖   ❖   ❖

8

Rejoice: Accepting the Fascinating Fullness of Life

It is amazing how hard it is for some people to look at life and rejoice in being alive. Life is replete with vagaries, inconsistencies, stupidities, and anxieties, but it is also full of humorous anecdotes, lovely sunsets, good meals, warm beds, and quiet countrysides. For so many of the adults who were abused as children, it seems impossible to enjoy life. They don't know how because they did not enjoy their childhood.

There are a variety of other reasons why people don't or can't enjoy life. These include:

1. They don't believe that they deserve to enjoy life.
2. They can't enjoy life because they expect that very soon it will turn sour and it would have been better not to enjoy anything than to be badly disappointed.
3. They can't enjoy life without other people enjoying it with them, and the other people in their family or their close friends don't seem to know how either.

Having gone through the depths of their inner hells and come out again, there is great cause to rejoice. We plan a champagne party, with plenty of good food and fellowship. However, we believe that it is important not to place too much emphasis on food or fun, but to note how the group members can exchange words, poems, pieces of art, and the like that are really important mementos of the time that they have spent together.

Part of rejoicing in life is to climb mountains. One climbs a mountain not to find out what it is like, but to find out what "I'm" like.

As they enjoy this time together, we ask them to imagine a wonderful celebration. To this, they invite anyone they wish and have at their disposal any facility. Everybody picks up on that image and happily contributes to it.

It was so important to maintain confidentiality that we forbade them to learn the other members' last names, addresses, phone numbers, and so on. Now is the time that they can exchange this information, and with warm assurances that they will meet again. This many do, joking about the harsh times that they have had—much like soldiers returning from the front. It is also a time when they can encourage each other's further growth and development.

There is no question but that, although this therapy is designed to put away the child abuse and neglect once and for all, no treatment can be 100 percent effective. We hope, however, that the patients have learned the skills that will help them to continue being helpful to themselves and to other people.

I have always looked forward to the end of treatment with mixed feelings. It is sad to see people whom I have come to know so well leave for the last time. I wish them well and try to give them a final word of instruction. Usually, they are chatting so happily that they take no notice of me. How much gratitude does one get? Well, I am human, and it's nice to hear a hearty "Thank you." In fact, when people are well treated, they tend to credit themselves for their improvement. It is not that they are ungrateful, but that they can see their own accomplishments in a better light. They are not nearly so dependent on me, and I consider that a good omen.

Once people can face the hardest issues in themselves, the world is open to them. They can look at any harsh reality. But other people will become afraid of them because (1) they are not afraid of any truth, (2) they cannot be manipulated, and (3) they cut through their facades and tend to become impatient with false relationships. People cannot see in others what they will not see in themselves. Therefore, when one takes a hard and truthful look at oneself, one can see the truth in others.

Now that our patients have looked deeply into their own pain and ugliness, they can look into almost any harsh truth. This makes them very good observers. When they become honest with themselves, they can see dishonesty in big chunks all around them. However, I warn them that other people may not appreciate this truthfulness. The knowledge of good and evil about ourselves, and the world around us, is a blessing and a curse. It brings sorrow and joy. My friends in this group are about to find this out.

WEEK 28

The next evening everybody but Krista was present. The group obviously was concerned about her continuing absence. She had left in great anger and distress. My attempts to bring her back, the urgent calls of Tasha coaxing her to return, have failed. When one group member fails, it worries the rest because it could happen to them also. They wanted to know if there were any way that Krista could be induced to come back and whether they could help. I pointed out that all my attempts to analyze, interpret, placate, and apologize only resulted in her continued anger. There was a difficult transference problem, which I could only resolve if I saw her individually. She wasn't prepared to see me. I hoped time would change her attitude somewhat. I certainly would contact her again.

This evening, Lisa was dressed in black as usual and looking very glum. "I'm not doing well. I quit my job, but I can't afford to. I was becoming very afraid that I might hurt the little boy I was looking after. I began to realize that his helplessness and dependency represented something in me that I could not tolerate. His screaming reminded me of the screams I've never been able to express. Dr. Ney, during a private session, helped me see that to repress those terrifying fears in myself, I had to suppress the screams in him, and I might be desperate enough to become violent with him. I accepted Dr. Ney's suggestion that I quit my job. I know I sound like I am whining. I have to deal with my memories, but I don't have the support to let them come up. It takes so much energy just to fight to bring them to the surface. Then I panic and I fight to keep them down. There's no safe place. I have millions of people to call, but I don't have the real support I need when I need it. I need someone there when the memories come up, and I can't predict when they will. I dreamed about having a husband, but I don't believe a husband could handle me. I have a friend, but she is going through the same experience of dealing with her ritual abuse." There was a long silence and then, mostly to herself, Lisa said, "I almost went to see him." She was talking of a friend in a city not far away and the group by this time had some idea of whom she was talking. Now they were all very curious. "He's a real sweetie," Lisa shared. The group members all urged Lisa to pursue the relationship, knowing that he might be a man who would be there with her, particularly at night, when the memories and the visions were most terrifying. This "sweetie" might be able to handle her outbursts and help her deal with her anxieties.

As we went around the group, Anna began talking. "I've been battling all week. There's been a deep sorrow in me ever since I saw Dr. Ney hold Amy's baby. I need to talk to you about something, but I'm terrified of what you will think of me." The group members all began to express sympathy and concern, saying that there was nothing she could say that could shock them, not after all of the horror they had heard from one another. But when Anna said that she had been a perpetrator herself, that she had sexually abused two little children, mild though it was, the group was shocked into stunned silence. "I feel so ashamed. I need to apologize to you because the children aren't here and I don't think I could find them. Please accept my apologies." Through her tears, she couldn't see the looks on the faces of the other group members. She didn't see their shock turn to anger, then to dismay, then to sorrow, and finally to sympathy.

Tanya said, "I forgive you, Anna." Anna responded, "Thank you." The rest of the group followed suit, some reluctantly. The other members murmured their sympathy. Representing the children who had been abused, they told Anna that she was forgiven. Anna reluctantly began to forgive herself.

"I can be so much more understanding toward my husband. I'm much less judgmental since I have accepted what I have done."

Linda looked haggard. "I am cranky and tired. I'm not sleeping enough. I quit one job and now I am really worried about money. My mother won't lend me any. I would like to ask for help, but I could never do that." She couldn't even role-play by saying, "I'm broke. Please help me."

As a group exercise, we asked Linda to address each of us in turn with, "Please help me." Initially, it was mechanical, but eventually it became much more sincere. One by one, as she went around the group, Linda heard them each say, "Certainly, what can I do to help you?" With greater practice, she became much more confident. Later, we found out she did ask her mother for help, with gratifying results.

Shawna stated that she was in a foul mood and had a headache. Her parents had come to visit her together. There had been a curious mixup or, more probably, because of subconscious reasons, Shawna had sent her father's letter to her mother and vice versa. This mixup had opened up the whole story to both parents. She was pleased that they had responded so quickly by coming to see her, but she was still convinced that her letters would do no good. Her worst fear had been that her letters would kill her mother and enrage her father. This didn't happen, but she wasn't happy with the results. Her father implied that the incest was all a misunderstanding, saying, "I apologize for anything that you thought I might have done." For Shawna, this was insincere and totally unsatisfactory. Her mother denied that she knew anything about it. Her father was very worried that Shawna would leak the information that might embarrass him in his work as an army officer. She had longed for her parents to be genuinely remorseful and repentant. She was angry at their superficial responses. To cover her anxiety and deal with her failing hope, she responded with, "Who really cares what they think?"

Tanya was calm and certainly much more peaceful. "When I brought Leanne to see you, Dr. Ney, she really didn't want to come. It is a compliment to you because she said that if she were ever going to see any psychiatrist, you would be the one. She seemed to have no trouble talking, though she had said she wouldn't talk."

Tanya went on to explain that her son, Paul, had a sore stomach. Somehow Paul represented her father. She noticed that her stomach was also sore. "It is as if my father were in my stomach." Her double bond of daughter and lover still kept the father within her, but it was beginning to loosen. Tanya couldn't explain why she was so unhappy. Her parents were reacting in the way she had always thought would be most beneficial to her and to them. They were both willing to go for treatment. But, like Shawna, she felt that her parents' apologies, and even their desires for treatment, were insincere. After such a long period of hoping that their parents would apologize, seek forgiveness, and change, it was very traumatic for both of these women to find that their parents were dealing with their daughters' attempts at reconciliation through forgiveness in such an insincere manner.

Tanya's thoughts were always very complicated. She must have spent much of her day trying to iron out the extensively intertwined complexities of her own conflicts. She said, "Sometimes I wish I didn't see all these things. Sometimes I wish I didn't have to keep thinking. It is very tiring. Sometimes I have difficulty knowing the difference between my children and me, but I'm working at it. We've got to be separate."

Dr. Green and I asked if the group felt there was anything for which they should apologize to us. We asked not because we felt hurt or needed them to acknowledge their occasional aggression toward us, but because we wanted them to begin to realize that we were, in fact, humans. This would help develop their independence. Because we had been reasonably patient, empathetic, and wise, having insights when they were suffering most, they were very attached to us and had an idealized view of our capacities. It was important for them to realize that, like their parents, we were also humans. As humans, they would have to deal with us. In general, they said, there wasn't much for which they felt that they should apologize, except that sometimes they had not shown up for a group or had not done their homework. Sometimes they had not participated as fully as they felt they should. Dr. Green and I had no difficulty in accepting their apologies. We did remind them that part of our forgiveness, just as they required of those who mistreated them, was a commitment not to do it again.

There was considerably less tension, less pain, less sorrow, less anger in this group now. In fact, this group ended on a very calm, almost emotionless level. They all commented on the fact that although they had realized so many benefits from their treatment, they were feeling rather blah. It appeared that after experiencing such pain, sorrow, anger, and fear over the course of 26 weeks, they now almost missed those emotions. After all, they had engendered hormones that kept them very alert and alive. It was this lack of pain, resulting in a lower hormonal level, that seemed to produce the lack of intensity that they now felt was anticlimactic.

As homework, I suggested they ask themselves how they would like to enjoy life and what was keeping them from it. We were now facing the last two sessions. We were going to really rejoice, to fully grasp all the vagaries, inconsistencies, joys, and sorrows of life. Now that they could honestly look at life, they could see it as something about which they could really rejoice. "Next week, bring balloons, cake, poems, paintings, party hats, and cards. I'll supply the champagne."

❖   ❖   ❖

Anna

At the end of last week's session, I wept in brokenness for the sadness of the door metaphor and the impact that seeing Amy's baby sleeping peacefully on Dr. Ney's arm had on me. Dr. Green sat with me as I wept and shared my sorrow. I had been haunted by a word picture created by Dr. Dobson when he described what he saw as he wrote for the Surgeon General's report on pornography. The horror of that mental imprint returned tonight as I watched the baby, oblivious to the rest of us, with his sleeping head nestled in Dr. Ney's hand, legs dangling on either side of his arm, limp and trusting. Dr. Green understood immediately and shared a burden of hers that has motivated and empowered her many times over the years.

At home, I wept until I was spent. The sadness prevented rest, let alone sleep. Troubled, I pulled myself out of bed and began to write. Again the pen unlocked the deep burden of my soul.

"I grieve the loss of innocence—mine and the world's. I grieve the loss of total vulnerability of babies, children, teens, and adults. To be open and not afraid. To be open and not wounded. To be open and not violated. To be open and fulfilled. To never taste shame. I grieve the loss of man's innocence. I bear the cross of my fallen humanity. I see what we have lost. I weep with him who has lost the most, my Heavenly Father. I long with him for our restored trust, love, purity, and oneness. I purpose to fight the sin he hates, that swallowed me and then I swallowed. I will cling to him and all that bears his fragrance and I will fight all that rapes his children. As he leads and empowers me, I am willing to join the fight to stop child abuse and exploitation." Completing this, I fell back into bed, sleep coming immediately. In the morning, as I reread this, I knew the sadness would never go away completely. It was the Father's heart. He would call on it from time to time to remind me of where I've been and to encourage me to do his work.

Later, as I drove to a very timely appointment with Dr. Ney, I recalled the line, "The sin he hates, that swallowed me and that I swallowed." Shame climbed hotly, claiming my chest, neck, and face. I was 12. I had been baby-sitting with two small children, one baby and one toddler. I had wanted to see what it felt like to have a baby suckle and had held the infant up to my own chest. Later, when I checked on the sleeping toddler, I touched her; it was through her panties and only briefly, but I touched her just the same. I was sickened by what I had done, then and now. I fought with myself all the way to my appointment, knowing that this was what I needed to share. Many times he had reiterated "that unless we were willing to see our part in the problem, we couldn't be part of the solution." I was so ashamed of myself that I couldn't look at him. After a while, he said he suspected what I was going to tell him, and that whatever I told him would not alter what he thought of me. Even after that reassurance, it still took ages before I could mumble out my confession. We talked for quite a while and then he intimated that I should share my shame with the group. No way! I had never flatly refused to comply with any of his requests before, but this was too much and I wasn't going to share it with anyone. I had managed to confess it to him, and that was sufficient!

Homework: What was I going to do to help others? Well, I knew where the line was. I wasn't going to share with the group even if he thought it might be a springboard to free the consciences of some of the others. I wasn't going to!

"Tonight I must ask you to stand in for some children whom I abused as a teenager...." After going over the whole shameful story, I asked them to forgive me. "Would you please forgive me?" Never looking up, I recognized Dr. Green's and Dr. Ney's immediate responses. Tanya, and then Lisa, responded, with others following. Linda shared the way she had abused her own children, and she and Shawna both admitted to trying to get a baby to nurse from them when they were teenagers. Dr. Ney had been right: my confession did open the doors to healing for others. Shelly and Tasha both protested that it was just teenage curiosity and not abuse and that it had harmed no one. Dr. Ney countered that it had apparently harmed me judging by the amount of struggle I'd had over sharing it. We had a break then, and after the break, I could look at my friends again, feeling forgiven and accepted with the worst of myself known. Tasting just a little of the humiliation and shame of a perpetrator was going to be invaluable for understanding and forgiveness and compassion. What an oppressive burden they carry.

Dr. Green was asked to share something about each one and ask for apologies that she felt were necessary. Once again, she said that I had brought her closer to God than she had ever been before, that she really saw and believed my desire was to be a godly woman. Nothing she could have said would have filled me with more joy, especially after my earlier confession.

Exhausted. We were all exhausted and looked it. I left wondering why we were finishing up the group. Party next week? Unless I was blind, we sure didn't look like a group of graduates.

❖   ❖   ❖

WEEK 29

I'm sitting in my usual corner close to a door of our group room, which actually has two doors. I lean back and I feel mightily pleased. In front of me are some extraordinarily beautiful women. It's hard to imagine the drawn, sallow faces, the tense shoulders, the dowdy dresses, and the frightened stares that were so characteristic of these same people 29 weeks ago.

Yes, 29 weeks. We're at the end, and we have arrived there on schedule. There is, by popular request, one more group to come, and it will be the second time we are going to focus on the eighth stage of therapy, rejoicing. The coffee table in the center of the room is crowded with flowers, cookies, crackers, chocolate cake, and two bottles of champagne. Everybody is ready to get on with the partying.

"Wait a minute. We still have homework and business comes first. I hate to be the 'party pooper,' but rejoicing is not the same as partying." I hope that these wonderfully courageous women can differentiate between trying to make themselves happy and really enjoying a peace that only comes from freedom from internal conflict.

At the end of the last week's group, I had suggested some guided imagery. "You're in a large, empty room of your house. There's a knock at the door, and when you open it, if you open it, there's a stranger. You must decide whether or not to let that person in. The person has a gift for you. If you allow the person to come in, he or she presents the gift and you must decide whether you are going to accept it and whether you will open it. When you do open it, it's something that fills your room and makes your life different."

Anna is particularly anxious to share her vision. "It was a big box, but I knew it would be empty." Everyone looked at her and they almost started to cry. The thought of an empty box after all that she'd gone through didn't seem fair. "But when I opened the box, I found it was filled with laughter, which filled the whole room."

Linda had moved closer to the corner where she characteristically sat, and from that position she looked across the room. She had an enigmatic expression, but she seemed terribly tired. "I've been exercising and going to bed regularly on time and sleeping the whole night, but I've never been so tired. Maybe I've been catching up on a lot of sleep that I haven't had for years. When I opened my box, it had one flower in it, but the scent was so beautiful that it filled the room. However, this week was hard. I cried for three days when I began remembering why I could never accept money." It appeared that among Linda's desperate financial difficulties was that she could never ask her parents for money or approach a bank for a loan. She then described how, during the time when she was being sexually abused by the two older boys who lived across the street, one had brought her money. When she had accepted it, he used that to entice and intimidate her. Having worked this conflict through, she now went off to the bank and negotiated a loan.

Linda continued, "I sat down with the kids and discussed the way in which I have been relating to them. In the past, I've never given them a choice. They had to do what I told them. So now I began giving them alternatives. They responded quickly and gladly and have since been much healthier. I've started looking into pursuing an education. I've also turned down the offer to go back to my second job. I've found that getting rid of my car and taking the bus has reduced the stress in my life. When I'm on the bus, I can chat, make friends, and enjoy the trip. When I drove the car, I was always late and always pushing myself and the car too fast in order to be on time."

Shawna, ebullient as ever, with a mischievous twinkle, said, "My box had a pop-up thing of a carnival scene." She also told of coming with her mother to a joint appointment in my office. She was impressed with how her mother had handled the revelation of her incestuous relationship with her father. "When you became ill, I became mother and wife." She was frightened of what might happen when her father found out how much her mother now knew. The letters she had sent to her parents had been sufficiently ambiguous that, until the time she spoke so candidly with her mother, her mother could have interpreted the statements in a variety of ways. She again related, "I had expected my mother to die, but she took it very well. Now Mom is struggling with whether she wants to remove her husband. I hope she begins to realize her part of it, but I guess she hasn't had the 29 weeks I had to prepare her for this information."

Tanya looked distraught and seemed to be regressing in some ways to her earlier self. "I feel so sad these days. I don't want to, but I know I must. I have to stop hanging onto the desire for the childhood that I wished would have been." She was mourning the loss of her father as a father, but was determined to say good-bye to him. "Maybe my son is sick at his stomach for me." She brightened up and talked about her present being an aura that gradually engulfed her and filled the room with warmth. She was also determined to begin saying good-bye. "I have a present for all of you." She brought out a bag of stones. "Where I come from, there aren't stones like you have here on the beach. It's so wonderful. I've got a separate stone for each of you. This is for you, Dr. Ney." It was a smooth brown stone that neatly fit into the palm of my hand, and like a good worry stone, if properly caressed, was quite comforting.

Amy had again brought her baby, who by this time had quite skillfully endeared himself to everybody in the group. He showed no anxiety even when there were loud peals of laughter or angry outbursts. It was almost as though he had heard it all before and he was right at home. On this occasion, he was sitting in his little chair beside me, holding tightly to my little finger. The sight of the affection he showed me was creating strong mixed feelings in all the women, but for Amy it was very comforting to know that a man could show affection. This was particularly poignant for her because her husband showed little and her father, as she could remember, showed none. She shared, "The person at my door had a repair kit and was going to repair our hearts, Sam's and mine, and he did. The living room was filled with peace."

For the first time in many weeks, Lisa was not wearing black. Her face showed great relief and she was very happy to talk about the fact that she was looking at life differently. This was partly because the man she had known some months before had phoned her to apologize, stating that he had changed in his attitude. They had met and she had found that, true to his word, he was much less aggressive and, consequently, she was much more interested. "Mine was a really big box. In it was a huge bouquet of dried flowers. They seemed to leave the box on their own and to rearrange themselves all around the room."

Lisa also talked about the disturbing memories. She had begun to realize that many of these memories were not from her infancy, but from her adolescence when she was living with a satanist. They were hard memories to face, but gradually she was able to recognize that she was part of and party to some grotesque satanic rituals that involved being possessed by a male spirit who used her to have sex with a female. In a later conversation with me individually, she was able to talk about how disturbing it was not to know where her boundaries were. She couldn't quite decide whether it was her or the spirit or whether she was male or female. What was most disgusting was that it appeared that this male evil spirit was using her to have sex with a child, the part taken by another woman who was in the coven, and who later also struggled not only to leave the coven, but also to remove its terrible effects. But for tonight she was definitely wanting to rejoice, so who was I to bring up some of the yet-to-be-resolved conflicts stemming from her unhappy adolescence living with a satanist?

Our graduate, Tasha, also had a beautiful visual image of opening the box and finding in it a cross, and it filled her life and her room with peace.

She went on to describe with great gratitude how, by being the graduate facilitator, she had vicariously participated in many of the pains and sorrows of the group. It had been a privilege for her, but it had wounded and healed her at the same time. "You guys helped me complete my own healing."

Anna responded with input: "You are a bridge between the doctor and ourselves. Your contribution was invaluable."

It had taken a short time to collect these lovely descriptions of their thought lives, and each one clearly indicated that something very beautiful had come into her life and filled it so that she felt very differently about herself. But now was the time to get to more serious homework, even though it sounded considerably less serious when it was given. "All right, now, I would like to hear from everybody what it is that you would really like to do with your life and so really enjoy it, and what might be keeping you from that."

Linda had obviously provided the answer: "I want to bring greater peace and security and spend time with my children."

Shawna: "I would like to go to school, but I'm afraid of the grading." This fear of failing had its roots in her childhood and like so many other persistent fears, had apparently started quite innocently. However, it had grown as she, throughout her life, had become increasingly afraid of submitting her homework or her exam to find out whether she had failed or not. Characteristically, she did her homework assiduously and always passed, but there was still a faint possibility that she might fail. Various members of the group assured her that failing wasn't such a terrible thing. I described an incident from my own life where I had attempted to tackle a double set of examinations, which were normally taken six months apart, and had, to my great chagrin, failed part of it and had to rewrite them. But the assurances were of no avail: she was still convinced that she couldn't return to school because she'd have to take an examination. I passed her a clipboard and told her, in a professorlike way, "You are now about to take an examination." She became flustered, handed the clipboard to somebody else, and protested loudly, "No, I won't do this. Nobody is going to make me." The group provided the support and eventually she sat poised with pen, paper, and clipboard, ready to take the first question. "One. What is the circumference of the earth in kilometers?" "Oh, no. This is not fair. I don't know. Does anybody know?" She began checking to see if anybody might have the answer. "Two. What is the name of the sixth pair of quarks?" "This is ridiculous. How can I possibly pass?" Various people suggested names, and Dr. Green eventually cheated, giving her the correct names. I glowered across the room. "Three. Is an electron a wave or a particle?" "I don't know. Why are you asking me? I don't want to do this. Can't we stop now?" "Four. Name two essential fatty acids." "Ha, that's easy." "Five. Where does the flexor polycis longus insert?" "That's stupid. Why are you doing this?" I proceeded with the remainder of the 10 questions and then asked Dr. Green to mark the answers, as I had provided some of those she didn't already know. "All right, I'm sorry to inform you that you have failed your examination. Do you understand? You have failed your examination." Although Shawna joked, it was obvious that this was having quite an impact on her. She began to laugh a little bit and then began laughing more outrageously. It had suddenly occurred to her that she had, in fact, failed her first examination. Hopefully, from this point on, it won't be so bad to face examinations and the thought of failure, and she'll go back to her pursuit of higher education.

Tanya was still looking distraught, and she alone of the group appeared not to be able to party or prepared to rejoice. "I don't want this group to be over, but I don't want to come anymore. I'm mourning the death of my father. He took a piece of me with him. I can never forgive him, but I'm not going to pretend anymore." Tanya was struggling. She was struggling hard to remove the father who had been imprinted in her as both parent and lover. I pointed out that parent bonding is an almost indelible imprint that is hard to change. If to that is added sexual bonding, it makes it very confusing and even more difficult to change. She was trying to get her father out of her, and in doing that, she was losing part of herself. It was a horrendous struggle. She then began to realize that, as she was having to pull away from her father, so she had to let her son pull away from her. I explained a little about the process of separation and individuation. "I'm afraid that if he pulls away from me, there won't be anything left of him. He won't be able to exist without me." She understood the process and now appeared to be strong enough to engage in it.

Amy was clearly anxious about contemplating the future and enjoying life. "I want to get on with my writing. I should be sitting down and doing some experimental writing every day. But maybe I should take another course. No, that's foolish. I'm taking plenty of courses. I must start my writing, but I feel that until I deal with all the stuff in my family, I can't concentrate. Maybe I'm chicken." It appeared that Amy had not yet sent the letter to her mother. "I'm afraid she'll get hysterical and then I'll get angry at her. She's such an airhead. Even my husband says so. I'm afraid I will become like her." It appeared from her anxiety that although she was terrified that she would in some way become like her mother, there was another fear, and that might be associated with the fact that she had at one point been psychotic and was afraid that it might happen again. When I suggested this, she protested vehemently: "No, that's not so. I know now that it's happened once, it won't happen again, and I'm not afraid that it will." But she did agree. Amy had to admit that since she had an infant, and while her husband was struggling with studies, poor finances, and his own difficulty with fathering, she really wanted her mother to be there for her. She was the only piece of solid reality that she had, and yet she also knew that it was an illusion, that her mother never had been very solid, and she was afraid to face it. I suggested that it was like stomping on the floor on which she was standing. Eventually she had to know how firm it was or else she could never step further along down the hallway of her life.

Lisa was quite adamant. "I want to dive into school and finish my grade 12 English. I'm very excited about it." There was approval from the group. They had all worried about Lisa and the deep darkness that seemed to envelop her, the heavy oppression that weighed her down. It was hard for them to imagine from the basis of their own experience what it would have been like to be ritually abused as an infant. That she had improved so much was, in everybody's opinion, quite miraculous. Yet they knew that she was still struggling.

Anna had always been the leader. It was apparent to everybody that she was truly free of the awful memories and the deep conflicts that had so plagued her life. "I've always had an overactive conscience, and it has kept me from so much, but now my conscience is clear. There's nothing in the way of enjoying life. Even though my husband is very depressed, I'm not trying to fix him and that's wonderful." I then described the joint project that Anna and I had agreed on—to undertake writing this book. I invited the other members to contribute if they wished, and if not, asked if we might use their stories. This produced a certain ambivalence, and yet they all understood how much benefit it would be for others to learn about their experiences and to realize that there was a way through. Eventually, all agreed to allow us to include their stories.

Now was truly the time to celebrate the joy that they were experiencing. Joy is not something that is easily understood or frequently realized. It has very little to do with laughter or partying. It has much more to do with seeing the world through different eyes, looking at someone else and knowing there is a real person there, a person who is not going to threaten you, a person whom you can get to know and understand. I pointed out the real benefit of knowing and loving another person. Jesus Christ was very clear that people must love one another. He knew it was for the benefit of the lover, as well as the one loved. When your mind is focused on somebody else, your physiology arranges itself so that it is much better harmonized: your blood pressure drops, your pulse rate goes down, and your bloodstream is not filled with catecholamines, those hormones that tighten up and make your heart pound.

So we popped the cork on the champagne and drank to each other's health. As soon as the first champagne was downed, it was quite obvious that our joy had to be tinged with sorrow. This was the last group for Dr.

Green. Her husband was adamant. Twenty-six sessions had been planned and we were already on week 29. At the end of the partying, when all the champagne had been drunk, the cake eaten, and only a few cookies remained, everybody stood to leave and lined up to throw their arms around Dr. Green. I had acknowledged Dr. Green's contribution to the group as being much more significant than she herself could accept. She was wise, persistent, loyal, and insightful. She had borne the brunt of various members' ambivalent feelings toward their mothers. Many tears had been shed over those feelings, and she had endured it all to come up smiling and to return to the group. It had not been easy for her. Her husband knew how much it had taken from her.

After the session, characteristically, Tasha, Shelly, Dr. Green, and I discussed how everybody was doing. Tanya was our greatest concern. She seemed to have regressed, but I was convinced that she was working through something of great significance and that she would endure. We were impressed with Linda's sudden finishing up of business. Anna had always been determined to tidy up, and was radiant in the beauty of the peace that she was feeling. I reported how Lisa had recently slashed her wrists, carving a deep cross. I pointed out that during the time that she was so anxious, she felt that she was losing reality, but the pain and the blood had brought her back into contact with a painful reality, which was better than losing contact. Amy, with her baby, was still struggling to know how much she should push the final business with her mother. Shawna was doing well and was quite determined to come in with her husband to see me. Both Tasha and Shelly had benefited by being the graduate facilitators. There was no question but that it was an important part of their continuing recovery to be helping other people. It had always been my hope that the graduates of these groups, healed in their hearts and minds, would be able to face the hard reality with a fresh honesty that would shock and confound the world. They knew they had a great blessing and with it, a heavy responsibility. I was convinced that at least half of those people would go on becoming more healthy, and many would contribute to the necessary healing of our society. If nothing else, they would stop the transgenerational transmission of neglect and abuse in their own families.

I said they were beautiful women, and I mean that, but it has a connotation that they were beautiful to look at. Certainly, they were lovely in their newly found freedom and joy. That was expressed on their faces, but some were overweight and none of them were particularly comely, yet there was a joy radiating that expressed itself in many other ways. How does a man feel when he can see deeper and more clearly into the heart of a woman than the woman can herself? There were aspects of their lives I knew nothing about, but how the pieces fitted together made much more sense to me in most instances than it did to them. It's an awesome responsibility and it can be so easily used to manipulate people. I thank God, I really thank God, that I have not been extensively tempted to use this knowledge for my own gratification. Moreover, when I have been tempted, He has given me the strength to make sure that it didn't go very deeply into my mind. But there is no doubt that the knowledge that I had about these women could so easily have overpowered them. The fact that they could, with so little difficulty, say good-bye to me, provides me with very little credit for all the change in their life. More particularly, the fact that they thanked God, and not me, is a testimony to God's working through me. Even in saying that, it almost sounds as though I were patting myself on the back. But it is a fact: God has used me to help heal these women. God only knows that I didn't deserve to be used in this way. It is a privilege. It is a gift. It is an enheartening, embolding experience, and I thank him very much. May the glorious name of Jesus be praised. Amen.

❖   ❖   ❖

Anna

The last few weeks, I've dreaded the arrival of this night, thinking I'd never be finished on time. The group would end and I wouldn't be healed. I would have tasted wholeness, but not had time to acquire it. Abandonment would be mine again, losing the safety of the group, the intimacy and the freedom to know and to be known. And yet now I was so excited. I felt like a kid on Christmas morning. Even though I'd had to have my dress altered to fit the extra pounds, I felt beautiful, full of life and anticipation. The celebration.

I remembered our first night in group therapy. Scared, sitting stiffly, listening to the explanation of the horrendous journey that we were about to begin. The balloons and streamers that adorned the room were in a sharp contrast to the grim faces, clenched hands, and awkward conversation. Dr. Ney commented on the decorations, saying, "These are left from the celebration of the last group. This is what you'll have at the end: a celebration with champagne, balloons, food, and fun. But we can't have the celebration without the hard work. You have begun a journey that will cost you more than you can know right now."

I had looked longingly at the balloons, my thoughts lingering on the promised party, wondering if that day would truly come. Up until this very week, I never really believed that I would complete this program on schedule. Yet here I was and the day had arrived, and I was ready to say good-bye and move out into life. Victory! I had been a victim and learned to survive. Now I was a woman and learning to live. Only recently had I begun to regard myself as a woman. Acknowledgment of years of lost womanhood grieved me, but I was determined to make the best of the ones I had left.

We were asked to bring in poems, stories, flowers, food, decorations— anything we wanted to enhance our celebration. We all participated by bringing either music, food, or flowers for everyone to share. Dr. Ney supplied the champagne. Some of us felt a need to be more personal in our good-byes. Lisa and I made everyone cards expressing our love and gratitude for their part in our healing. Shawna presented carnations, choosing colors that represented how she felt about each recipient. Tanya expressed her love by giving each person a stone that she thought particularly beautiful.

Krista was still missing, and even though Virginia had been invited and had responded affirmatively, she, too, hadn't come. Amy felt that she didn't belong or deserve to celebrate because she hadn't sent her letter, and Tanya was extremely sad. Shawna was impatient to get on with it. Celebration seemed to have an edge of loss and sadness. Dr. Ney insisted that we must have business before pleasure and finish up some last details.

Listening to the group members share their "box" presents, I rejoiced that we all had hope and beauty in the place of such sorrow and despair. We would have been afraid of the boxes in the past, knowing they would be filled with disappointment and pain. Today we not only were able to open them, but we also allowed ourselves to fill them with treasures. Amazing! Sure, we still had stuff to deal with, but we had all come a long way. I saw such growth in everyone who had persisted to the end.

We left behind mountains of anger, vengeance, despair, unforgiveness, bitterness, rage, sickness, compulsion, self-pity, and self-hate. In their place, we were learning self-respect, trust, vulnerability, balance, and hope. Truly, it wouldn't be long before we would be strong enough to stop anything from getting in the way of our happiness.

At last, the call to celebrate. We ate and drank and reminisced over the hardest parts, the most rewarding times, and the saddest moments, as well as the laughter and the fun times. We lingered on the memory of our moonlit walk, savoring its mystique. With each sharing her own special memories, we soon covered almost every part of the journey. Following are my reflections as shared with the group that night.

CELEBRATION—ENTER LIFE

Longing to hear God's distant voice, yearning for life, seeking answers in the everchanging face of the forest's fall, winter, and spring. Endless hours wandering through the trails, beckoned by the stillness of the woods, as if somehow its peace, power, and life could permeate the roar of emotional anguish and quiet its ever-present companion, physical pain. My known world dissolving all around me, family skeletons pounding on closet doors, shattered dreams based on claimed promises for my now nearly grown babies, gray fog settling on the remains of youth's promised intimacy, and in the distance the last beat of the heart of my existence, church ministry dying in a shroud of questioned integrity. Prayer? Yes, I used to pray—every day. Quiet times, the mark of who I was becoming and the guarantee of all that I am. And now no voice is heard toward the heavens, and yet the sound of the soul's cry cracks the heavens wide. Incarnate Truth deposits his wisdom, nothing appears changed, yet nothing will ever be the same again. The seed, Wisdom, germinates, producing trust and hope that cannot be reasoned, only cherished. And so I enter therapy....

Unknown faces, fear rising in my throat, expected nakedness. Turn back? Nowhere to go! Pushing forward, feigned strength. Stay in the room, hear the hurts, feel the anguish behind each story. Ride the waves of communal pain, a sisterhood of losses. Forgotten days dredged into today's light. Hope, a faint echo as darkness enters each memory. Run before it's too late. Shouting angry voices, victim's senseless abuse, worlds rage in one small room. She's stumbling, help her up, we'll all fall—she cannot stay. Fading, she's gone. Weeks blur until...death comes and a promise of life echoes across the child's watery grave. Nothing hidden, everything lost. Insurmountable cost. Truth released, confrontation complete. Bittersweet road to freedom. No, another leaving our path to wander, again alone. Learning, relearning, testing, failing, rising, falling, up again. Emotions soar and subside, energizing weekly vigils. Lightness seeps on the horizon like an early dawn. Tranquillity, soft joy, laughter. Yes, still tears, but also laughter. Gifts, fragrant successes mount. The shell that encased the room cracks and each unique shining seed of promise spills. And so we enter life....

We all said our final good-byes to Dr. Green. As I hugged her, I reminded her that she had played a significant role in my healing. She had taken an incredible amount of flack, anger, and rage from me as I worked through my mother issues. There were no words to express my gratitude to her for standing by me, loving and accepting me when I was the most difficult. Her glowing face testified that our appreciation and growing wholeness were payment enough for the many long hard months of work. None of us wanted to leave. We dawdled over the cleanup, thankful that next week we would meet again.

❖   ❖   ❖

WEEK 30

Except for Krista, who left with great anger and hasn't been back since, even though we have coaxed and urged her to return, everybody is here tonight—everybody, that is, except Dr. Green. I really miss seeing her sitting in her familiar spot with that serious young face that quickly breaks into a smile just when I need it. But she had to leave; her husband insisted that 29 weeks were all there could be. She had done more than she had agreed to do. "Dr. Green, I really miss you."

For reasons I can't quite explain except that I believe they are healthy, the group doesn't seem to be taking me very seriously. I feel that I ought to leave them with some kind of lesson, a final message that will sustain them in the future. This is the last group. I won't be seeing them, except individually—and that infrequently. "You have been given a blessing. You have looked into hell and you haven't flinched. Now you can look into any truth. Because of your enormous honesty and courage, you have something that very few people in the world have. To be able to look at hard truth is a blessing and a curse. You won't always be appreciated for your truthfulness."

There was a chorus of agreement. They already knew that. Shawna was most emphatic, saying, "You have no idea how true that is. My family doesn't appreciate me. They don't want me. They don't want to hear the things that I've got to say about us all. I feel so alienated." This began a discussion of alienation.

Linda agreed that she had felt very alienated from her family, but she didn't seem to be bothered by it.

Shawna stated, "I don't have any friends anymore. My friends all want me to go back to the way I was. They are convinced that you, Dr. Ney, have deliberately subverted my thinking. They can't figure out why I don't want to spend time with them. I'm alone, but I'm not lonely. In fact, I really enjoy my own company now. Yet I miss my husband when he is away. He has been away before, but I really miss him this time. I think I really love him." She reflected, "Yes, in many ways, I miss what I was but I wouldn't take it back—any of it."

Linda said, "The people who really loved me still love me. My father came over the other evening for a good chat. It's the first time we have had one in a long time."

Lisa, sitting very still in her usual corner of the couch, smiled her own peculiar Mona Lisa smile: "I have good friends and family, but I don't get all the help and support I need." Then she became increasingly solemn, and eventually she broke into tears. All this serious talk was obviously disturbing the rejoicing that was to be part of this last group. To me, it appeared that Lisa was giving contradictory messages. She wanted us to be concerned and she wanted us to hear all that was bottled up in her heart, but she would go only so far and then stop. I decided that this evening she was not going to stop, so I kept pushing and prodding. Eventually she poured it all out in great fear and trembling. It appeared that there were still memories coming back from her early ritual abuse mixed with memories of the abuse she had received from the satanist with whom she had lived as a teenager. She found that she needed somebody to be close to her when the memories started surging to the surface of her mind, but she was still living alone. She didn't know of anybody who could sustain her through the emotions associated with the memories that she had to talk about. The group sat and listened to all her despair and horror. They murmured quiet reassurances and intimations of understanding. After Lisa had dried her eyes, she looked around and said, "Thank you. I'm glad you pushed me. I feel better now." Finally she had realized that caring people were not going to be alienated, even by the most horrible revelations of what was hidden in her heart.

Anna looked beautiful. There was such a serenity, such a peace, about her. "I have a God-given sense of being, of life. I don't feel any particular alienation, but I do feel strange. I find I am getting along well with children. I used to avoid them; they frightened me. I feel so healthy. I do feel alone, but I certainly am not lonely." She then revealed that after years of not being able to bathe or wash herself with water, her skin had remarkably healed so that she was enjoying both water and bathing. There seemed to be a definite connection with understanding the roots of her near-drowning experience as a child. Having dealt with the memory and conflict, it appeared that her skin was allowing her to be immersed. She could enjoy water once again.

Tanya was looking very uncomfortable, and eventually she admitted to the group that she had something to tell them that she had kept hidden all these weeks. She described her last individual session with me and our discussion about whether she should see another therapist as well. Even though I had advised against it, she had found one whom she felt was helping her. The group members seemed rather taken aback, but one and then another assured her that they didn't feel particularly insulted. I still thought that it had diluted the impact of the group process.

Amy came late with her baby, who was growing rapidly. Remarkably, the child was calm through the noisy expression of strong emotions. He was obviously at home with the group. The child was passed from one to the other. Linda particularly wanted to hold the baby. "At least let me hold him with his eyes open this time." She looked totally at ease with the child. Having resolved many of the conflicts with her own children, and having, like Shawna, mourned the loss of her aborted child, it looked as though she was in a much better state to hold and enjoy children. It confirmed once again in my mind a belief that a mother has difficulty making and maintaining attachment to a new infant until she has mourned the loss of any other who may have died during or after her pregnancy.

I asked the group members to deal with any unresolved conflicts they might have with each other. Though they had hurled strong accusations at one another and had had many difficult confrontations, there appeared to be no bitterness or rancor. They accepted each other with remarkable grace and good humor.

I asked them if they would comment on what changes they saw in each other.

Shawna was looking wan because she had a viral infection, but she sat very peacefully and had a ready smile. The others in the group pointed out how much she had changed, how much more ready she was to talk about herself. She admitted that with the resurgence of her love for her husband, she was thinking of having babies. "I wouldn't hurt them now. I'm sure I wouldn't."

The group pointed out that Amy had learned how not to continue trying to rescue people. She appeared to be more relaxed and looked very healthy. She no longer put herself down and she communicated much more directly. I noted that she was not wearing the usual outrageous combination of colors. She felt hurt by this observation, but admitted that somehow that didn't seem necessary anymore.

The group noted that Lisa was less of a mystery. She was talking more and revealing much more about herself. There didn't seem to be the helpless whimpering that the group had noticed when she first arrived. She had regained her sense of humor and had stopped wearing black.

According to the group, Tanya was much calmer. She was clearer and more direct. Her thinking seemed to be better formulated, and for some of the group, she was much less intimidating. She again stated that she felt very sad that the group was ending. She also felt sad about her mother and father when she should have been glad that they were doing exactly what she wanted. It was as if a very tumultuous chapter in her life had come to a close. Even though it was a tragedy, she said, it was the end of a book, and as an avid reader, she always felt sad about closing a book.

To everybody, Anna was very peaceful. She said she felt that she had gained a quiet enjoyment of life. The fact that her skin disorder had been gone for a month was a real blessing. "I'm heavier than I've ever been in my life, but I'm beginning to accept my body."

To the group, Linda was observably much happier. Her humor still shone through, but without the sarcasm. She was quieter, but very insightful and thoughtful. The group remembered how she had been aggressive and sometimes quite mean. Now she was bold. This helped her a great deal in her interactions with people. Humor was no longer a facade to cover anger. She was genuinely funny.

The two graduate facilitators also contributed from their own experience. They had changed as well, and the group could see it. Tasha was happier, but more apparent was the fact that she wasn't crouching, pulling her legs up underneath her in an attempt to ease the pain in her back. She walked straight, she could sleep in her bed, and she was without pain. "It's the best thing I could have done, working with you guys. You have completed my healing. I feel great."

Shelly was always energetic and had conquered her bulimia. She now felt a sense of assurance that was obvious to everybody. She noted that she was asking questions and talking about things that nobody else in her family would dare to mention. Although she felt that she had to deal with those forbidden topics in spite of her family's objections, she was not afraid of the outcome. She noted that in this second time through the group process, she was much more objective. "For the first time, I feel like an adult. I feel like a woman and not a kid."

It appeared that Tasha and Shelly had gained vicariously by participating in the group in a way that they hadn't when they were group members themselves.

So this was the end of the end, the last session of the last stage of the group therapy. I felt a deep yearning to communicate something very significant. I did try, but while I was talking, most of the group members were chatting with each other, ignoring me and happily exchanging addresses.

It had been a rule during the group that they were not to communicate with each other outside the group. They knew each other only by their first names. They now found out who the others were and where they lived, and certainly were going to keep in touch. To avoid being totally ignored, I mentioned the problem of gaining weight. There was silence. Then they wanted to know why some of them had gained. I said I thought that it had happened because while they were in the intense conflicts stemming from their mistreatment, they had relatively high levels of catecholamines, powering a higher metabolic rate. Now that their conflicts were resolved, they were reverting to a lower rate of metabolism. Consequently, they would have to cut back on their calories. In addition, they were now better able to accept themselves as they were, including their bodies. They didn't have to appear beautiful. It was quite possible that their genes had intended them to be plump. When I pointed this out, they generally agreed that they were very much the size and shape of their mothers. We didn't discuss it very long because most of them were saying good-bye, hugging each other, and shedding a few tears.

Well, they are all gone. Here I am sitting in this group meeting place, looking across an empty room, and wondering exactly what had happened. It was miraculous. Unquestionably, these women had changed remarkably. I could pat myself on the back, but I really didn't deserve it. They had worked so hard—the facilitators and Dr. Green were very much a part of the process. Besides, all treatment comes from God. He heals us and we are privileged to be part of that process. But still I could be very pleased about one thing: the order of events, the process, the homework exercises, and the group exercises seemed to fit the treatment needs of these terribly conflicted adults. I could say, "It worked. It really did."

❖   ❖   ❖

Anna

For the first time, I entered the room with a sense of detachment. I had grown to love these women, women who, in the regular course of life, I would probably have never come close to. For me, the group was over last week. I'd known it then and it was reconfirmed now. Dr. Ney was in his usual spot, notepaper on knee, leaning back, surveying us. He must have been proud of us and proud of himself.

Several times he tried to get started, but the chatter stopped him midsentence. Watching him, I realized his humanity. A healthy, loving, compassionate, counselor, leader, and teacher—yes, but still a man. A human being with frailties and strengths just like the rest of us. He seemed smaller and no longer all-knowing. I observed his features, his eyes, nose, mouth, his frame, noting his actions and reactions. We are going to write a book together. I'll be his coauthor and maybe his friend, but no longer his patient. It felt good.

Tonight we were going to be taught and given some of his wisdom, as a gift, to take with us:

- Notice, in counseling, what you are feeling about what the patient is saying. This is a good indicator of how others are feeling.
- Unforgiveness affects you as much as them.
- Don't treat your own family!
- What is good for your neighbor is good for you. Maybe it can't be seen immediately, but it will become apparent in the long term.
- God wants friends, not babies. Moses questioned, reasoned, and even argued with God. He was a friend. Adam walked with God; God did not carry him. He provided friendship.

- Good built into a child will be with him or her forever.
- Love is commanded; therefore, it is not an emotion, because emotions cannot be called up on demand.
- Love is commanded; therefore, we must be capable of performing it. That means we must already have the basic understanding that we need to love.
- God so loved he gave us his son. Love is meeting someone else's need.
- You'll know when you love because someone's needs will be met. You'll know when you are loved because some need has been met. These needs are definable and measurable.
- Is meeting the need of someone with resentment love? Yes, the need being met is a gift of love. If it were done with joy, it would be an additional gift. Take a child who needs a drink of water. The mother is harried. She stops her million tasks in frustration and impatience to give the child a drink. Yes, she loves the child: she is meeting the child's need.

The partying is more subdued than last week. We all look tired, low on energy and drive. We know that this group can never be re-created. Tonight is the final good-bye.

Epilogue: A Follow-up of Patients in the Group

No hypothesis is worth considering unless it is tested. No clinical observations on patients are valid unless they are made on the same subjects before and after treatment. It has now been approximately two years since the women in this group finished their treatment, so we contacted them to see how they were doing. The following summary is written mostly in their own words. Their self-assessments have been corroborated with the observations of myself and Anna.

It is always difficult to assume that any improvement or any worsening is attributable solely to the treatment, but there does seem to be some causal link. To determine more accurately whether this type of group therapy is effective in dealing with abused people, we are now collecting data in a more controlled fashion. I think that it is fair to state that the clinical evidence indicates that this type of treatment, and the hard work put in to it by these patients, is sufficiently encouraging to warrant further use of this program.

I (Philip Ney) am writing this part so that Anna (pseudonym) will not have to write about her own improvement. Anyone who knows her readily attests to the remarkable change in her life. Although she is struggling with a very serious medical illness, she is full of vitality, hope, and a determination to help others gain the opportunity she has found so useful. She states:

"Group opened up the doorway of life for me. I successfully completed my first year at the university, continue to facilitate in group therapy with Dr. Ney, am involved in prayer counseling, lead a codependency group, and volunteer at a local school to talk to students when they first disclose abuse, as well as work part-time at a transition house for battered women and their children. Life is good and the healing process goes on in my life as I continue to give away what I have learned.

"I have been rewarded for my hard work by seeing my children and stepchildren make strides toward personal growth. My siblings are in counseling and I have a growing relationship with my parents. My husband and I have had some time apart, but have developed a very open relationship with a solid base of communication. I can truly say that abuse and neglect can be stopped, old patterns broken, and the most devastating hurts healed."

Anna is a very effective cotherapist. From her studies, experience, and natural inclination, she is accurate in her observations, perceptive about when to encourage, and phenomenally determined that no one will drop out of treatment or fail for lack of trying.

Tanya was always full of energy. This seems to have become much more directed and better utilized. She states:

"Since the group finished, I have had a series of temporary jobs. I think that I have sabotaged myself by not allowing myself the benefit of a full-time position, because it brings up old issues. However, as a graduate in one of Dr. Ney's follow-up groups, and as an employee in several temporary jobs, I have found success and fulfillment. There is more of me, my mood problems are relieved, and I am much stronger. I am changing little by little in a positive direction. I catch onto old patterns much more quickly. I am more specific and can identify problems rather than just get angry.

"I fight less with my daughter and catch old triggers more quickly when reacting with my son. I am more honest in my marriage relationship. I don't automatically do what my husband wants and we are able to communicate better than prior to the group. My parents and I have an unstated agreement not to talk about the past. The result of this agreement is that I do not allow my children to be alone with them."

Shawna has moved with her husband, who was posted to a city close to her own parents, where she continues to work out very difficult conflicts. She states:

"The group really helped me become more assertive. I can say 'No,' tell people when they hurt me, and ask for help when I need it. I can listen to constructive criticism and grow from it, but still react if it is not well put. I am not daily driven to distraction by my body, but recognize that I still need to take charge of it. I was able to quit smoking right after the group and not gain weight...a real victory for me.

"My biological clock is ticking. I am finally ready to have a baby. I hope it won't take long. Relationships are generally going better with Mom. We are talking more. I don't need my husband around all the time anymore. I actually enjoy and look forward to some space when he is away. As for Dad, it is no better, no worse.

"I miss what we had when the group was all together and wish that I had somewhere like it to go at times. One negative thing that has happened to me from group is that I think too deeply and see too clearly, and sometimes I would like to turn it off."

Virginia, who dropped out of the group, continues to struggle in her relationships, especially with her partner. She knows that she needs further treatment, but it continues to be a problem to stick with anything. Virginia returned to begin treatment once again, and although there are still many obstacles for her to overcome, she is determined to finish the group process this time.

Lisa, who had struggled so hard with such terrible conflicts arising from her ritual abuse, obviously needed further treatment and was referred to a competent psychiatrist. She states:

"I am still in the process of healing from my past, but I am handling my life so much better. I can particularly see my personal growth around controlling people. I am more assertive and far less fearful. I have been able to let my family go, realizing that they are neither able nor willing to take responsibility for the abuse.

"I went to a three-month ritual-abuse youth support program after finishing our group. It allowed me to continue confronting my memories, and because of Dr. Ney's group, where I was accepted regardless of my story, I was able to trust and open myself up to others. I have finished high school and have applied for the first year psychology program at the university, starting next fall."

Amy, who had been pregnant through most of the group, did not complete the group and struggled with some components of it. Initially, her partner showed an interest in obtaining treatment for himself, but when it was offered, turned it down. When Amy was contacted, she made it clear that she was better, but did not believe that all of the improvement was a result of the group, as there were parts with which she did not agree. She states:

"Since the group finished, I have taken a one-year life skills program where I focused on parenting skills. I have separated from my partner, and although we can now communicate better than ever, I still have difficulty expressing my deep feelings to him. He has grown as a person and a parent and wants to reconcile, but I am not yet ready.

"I am still dancing, and will dance for the rest of my life. It is a very important part of me. As for my future, I am entering a two-year career-planning program and I am really excited about it. My mother and I have a more relaxed relationship, and I am able to confront her with hard issues when they come up."

Linda not only worked hard at the group, but had held down two jobs and looked after her parents and her children. She now states:

"I am a much more secure and social person. I have fun. I play ball and bowl regularly. I can manage with only one job and I spend the rest of the time at home. This has allowed me to get closer to my children and I am much more involved in their lives.

"My dad passed away this year, making it very difficult for my family. I was able to maintain my personal growth by not taking care of everyone, especially my mom. I did not and do not allow her to depend on me. Amazingly, we are becoming friends. My attendance at an AlAnon group has helped me to maintain this distance. As three of my family members have faced their alcohol problems, I have been able to see traces of my previous codependent behavior patterns and let them go.

"I am in the same relationship, but it is much healthier as we can communicate so much better. I feel just great about it. I am much more relaxed and not so caught up with my body image. Life still has its ups and downs, but I am much more able to cope."

Krista is a determined woman and ploughs along with her rehabilitation. She still has to develop many close relationships, but that is not for lack of trying. She finished her education at the university and began recognizing that she has talents in helping others. She had some good and some bad experiences in volunteering. As time has progressed, her anger about parts of the group experience has subsided, and she recognizes what she gained from it. She is sorry that she wasn't in a better position to hear and utilize the feedback that she was getting. I think we all admire her for her intensity and tenacity.

Anna and I have often reflected on the very important part of the healing process provided by first being a patient and then a facilitator. The facilitators go through the same process, but from a very different perspective. They find that in helping others through the wide variety of role plays and so on, they themselves benefit. They become much more able to see their problems from a more objective point of view. Both Shelly and Tasha have gone on to fulfill their career dreams. They are successfully using the tools learned in group to face life's challenges. This includes further education and looking after their families.

What about the venerable psychiatrist? It would be foolish to say that I didn't need to change, and incorrect to say that the group had no effect on me. It is not easy to participate in the excruciating suffering of other people. I must say that each time I plunge into despair along with the patients, I wonder, "Do we really have to do this?" However, to see them emerge with a much more definite sense of who they really are, with insights into their psychodynamics, with new behaviors in their interpersonal relationships, with old bitterness and angers put away, and with a new capacity to develop and enjoy their lives, I realize that I also participated and vicariously enjoyed their remarkable change. Obviously, identifying with them in their sorrows and joys, I had to change. I am extremely grateful for all that I have learned as they have shared their sorrows and insights with me. I thank God that he has used me as an instrument of his continual willingness to hear and his determination to heal the sufferings of humankind.

From our experience over the years, it has become increasingly apparent that there is a natural flow of the sequence of events in the progression of treatment: (1) It begins with the gradually increasing trust and confidence of the patients in each other and the therapist; followed by (2) the memories of their pain and the expression of all the vast variety of feelings; (3) the expression of anger and fear that arises from their pain, which now must find both expression and proper channeling; (4) the guilt that comes from their aggressive fantasies, children's tendencies to blame themselves and their portion of responsibility as victims, perpetrators, and observers; and then (5) finding that there is no possibility of recovering the childhood that they should have had or of becoming the people they should have been, they quickly become despairing. In that despair, they find the basic defense of splitting into three self-images. (6) Once the two shriveled and demanding false images are relinquished, buried, and mourned, they are in a position to reevaluate their relationships, negotiate realistic expectations, and come to terms with the people they really are. (7) With the strength of that knowledge, they can engage in the difficult work of reconciliation—being forgiven by those they have hurt and forgiving those who have harmed them. (8) Having become reconciled, they can start reaching out to help and heal other people. (9) With their increasing ability to love others and thoroughly enjoy life, they can rejoice in their newly found awareness and strength.

It appears that some of these stages are more difficult to negotiate than others. Those who balk at letting go of their false images stay angry and defensive. Clinical evidence indicates that the patients who respond best to treatment are those who are able to participate in that treatment and to utilize every aspect of it.

Resources

BOOKS

Brody, S., & Axelrod S. (1993). *Anxiety and ego formation in infancy.* Madison, CT: International Universities Press. A classic treatise on the factors that influence a child's fears and self-awareness.

Crowder, A. (1994). *Opening the door: A treatment model for therapy with male survivors of sexual abuse.* New York:Brunner/Mazel. Designed to assist clinicians working with male survivors of sexual abuse, this book focuses primarily on the personal and psychological aspects of recovery from sexual trauma.

Dickstein, L. J., & Nadelson, C. C. (Eds.). (1992). *Family violence: Emerging issues of a national crisis.* Ontario, Canada: Times Mirror Professional Publishing Co. Multidisciplinary approach to the identification, prevention, and treatment of violence in the family. Includes bibliography with contact agencies.

Flanigan, B. (1992). *Forgiving the unforgivable: Overcoming the bitter legacy of intimate wounds.* New York: Macmillan Publishing. This book discusses the phases of forgiveness and provides practical therapeutic exercises to help clients move through the phases to forgiveness.

Gilbert, K. R., & Smart, L. S. (1992). *Coping with infant or fetal loss: The couple's healing process.* New York: Brunner/Mazel. The essential purpose of this book is to delineate the steps of an effective grief resolution process. A mixture of equal parts scholarship and compassion.

Ilse, S. (1990). *Empty arms.* Maple Plain, MN: Wintergreen Press. This practical and encouraging book for those touched by miscarriage or infant death includes a list of available resources.

Kaufman, B., & Wohl, A. (1992). *Casualties of childhood: A developmental perspective on sexual abuse using projective drawings.* New York: Brunner/Mazel. The discussion focuses primarily on the essential link between childhood sexual abuse and specific developmental problems.

Malchiodi, C. (1990). *Breaking the silence: Art therapy with children from violent homes.* New York: Brunner/Mazel. Chapters consider art evaluation and art intervention with abused children, and the difficult and sensitive area of child sexual abuse.

McAll, K. (1982). *Healing the family tree.* London: Sheldon Press. A British psychiatrist examines intergenerational brokenness and its healing. The text includes fascinating examples in support of an unusual hypothesis.

McCann, I. L., & Pearlman, L. A. (1990). *Psychological trauma and the adult survivor: Theory, therapy, and transformation.* New York: Brunner/Mazel. In this remarkable book, the authors' extensive clinical experience with traumatized clients, as well as their profound awareness of the limitations of existing paradigms, have directed them to construct a new heuristic theory that can be applied effectively across different victim populations.

MacKenzie, R. (1990). *Introduction to time-limited group psychotherapy.* Washington, DC: American Psychiatric Press. This book describes the phases and required skills for therapists new to this field.

Ney, P. G. (1974). *The law and the essence of love.* Victoria, Canada: Pioneer Publishing. This book provides a unique view of human nature, emphasizing relationships to spiritual realities.

Ney, T. (1995). *Allegations in child sexual abuse: assessment and case management.* New York: Brunner/Mazel. Through the use of everyday and legally relevant examples, complex principles are translated into comprehensive and feasible recommendations for practice.

Nichols, W. (1992). *Treating adult survivors of childhood sexual abuse.* Sarasota, FL: Professional Resources Press. This book can enhance a therapist's understanding of the effect and treatment of incest.

Nouwen, H. J. (1979). *The wounded healer.* New York: Image Books. This little book should be required reading for all who walk with another person through emotional pain.

Piper, W. F., McCallum, M., & Azim, F. A. (1993). *Adaptation to loss through short-term group psychotherapy.* New York: Guilford Publishers. A thoughtful book rich in clinical material but based on a research project. It relates the issues of loss to the basic principles of short-term groups.

Schetky, D. H., & Green, A. H. (1988). *Child sexual abuse: A handbook for health care and legal professionals.* New York: Brunner/Mazel. This highly comprehensive manual examines child sexual abuse in the context of normal psychosexual development; provides a survey of current literature; describes the process of psychiatric and medical evaluations of the child; and covers false allegations of sexual abuse.

Smedes, L. B. (1986). *Forgive and forget: Healing the hurts we don't deserve.* New York: Pocket Books. A book on forgiveness and why it is so important for healing.

Stanford, S. (1987). *Will I cry tomorrow.* Old Tappan, NJ: Revell Publishing Co. Powerful description of one woman's journey from the effects of pregnancy loss to healing.

Trepper, T. S., & Barrett, M. J. (1989). *Systemic treatment of incest: A therapeutic handbook.* New York: Brunner/Mazel. Based on the premise that therapy can succeed in halting incest without dissolving the family unit, this volume presents a three-step treatment method that has been used successfully with hundreds of families touched by incest abuse.

van der Kolk, B. A. (1992). *Psychological training.* Washington, DC: American Psychiatric Press. Describes the role of the group in the origin and resolution of the response to trauma; a stress-management approach.

Worden, J. W. (1991). *Grief counselling and grief therapy: A handbook for the mental health practitioner (Second edition).* New York: Springer Publishing Co. A handbook for learning how to address grief issues.

ARTICLES

Chamberlain, D. B. (1992). Is there intelligence before birth? *Pre- and Perinatal Psychology Journal*, 6: 217–237. A review of scientific and clinical data on the development of intelligence before birth.

Crittenden, P. M. (1992). Children's strategies for coping with adverse home environments: An interpretation using attachment theory. *Child Abuse and Neglect*, 16(3): 329–343. One of a series of articles by a well-established researcher, showing the effect of neglect on children's development.

Crittenden, P. M. (1984). Sibling interaction: evidence of a generational effect in maltreating infants. *Child Abuse and Neglect,* 8: 433–438. This article describes observations of how children imitate their parents' treatment of other children in the family.

Kaufman, J., & Zigler, E. (1987). Do abused children become abusing parents? *American Journal of Orthopsychiatry,* 57: 186–192. Describes the chances of child abuse becoming transgenerational.

Kestenburg, J. (1985). Child survivors of the Holocaust—40 years later: Reflections and commentary. *Journal of the American Academy of Child Psychiatry,* 24: 408–412. Discusses from a psychoanalytic and developmental point of view the impact of the Nazi Holocaust on child survivors.

Kipper, D. A. (1992). Psychodrama: Group psychotherapy through role-playing. *International Journal of Group Psychotherapy,* 42: 495–521. Described are the neo-classical approaches of psychodrama, action methods, and clinical role-playing.

Korbin, J. E. (1986). Childhood histories of women imprisoned for fatal maltreatment. *Child Abuse and Neglect,* 10: 331–338. Case studies of the backgrounds of women who have killed their children.

Lyons-Ruth, K., Connell, D. B., Grunebau, H. U., & Botein, S. (1990). Infants at social risk: Maternal depression and family support services as mediators of infant development and security of attachment. *Child Development,* 61(1): 85–98. Research that demonstrates the connection between neglect and a child's delayed development and difficulties forming human attachments.

Mullan, H. (1992). Existential therapists and their group therapy practices. *International Journal of Group Psychotherapy,* 42: 453–468. Instead of the usual interpretation, members of the group are to be brought up to the threshold of their self-knowledge so they can choose.

Ney, P. G. (1985). Mandatory reporting of child abuse. *Community Health in New Zealand,* 1: 32–43. This discusses the pros and cons of mandatory versus voluntary reporting of child abuse and neglect.

Ney, P. G. (1987). Helping patients cope with pregnancy loss. *Contemporary Ob/Gyn,* 29: 117–130. This article describes practical techniques to help women understand and deal with the major conflicts and intense emotions following a pregnancy loss.

Ney, P. G. (1987). The treatment of abused children: The natural sequence of events. *American Journal of Psychotherapy,* 41: 391–401. Describes phases in the usual unfolding of conflicts that have arisen from childhood mistreatment.

Ney, P. G. (1988). Triangles of abuse: A model of maltreatment. *Child Abuse and Neglect,* 12: 363–373. Shows how most if not all tragedies of abuse and neglect are comprised of a perpetrator, a victim, and an observer forming a triangle that rotates with time and place.

Ney, P. G. (1989). Child mistreatment: Possible reasons for its transgenerational transmission. *Canadian Journal of Psychiatry,* 34: 594–601. This is a scientific and philosophic hypothesis describing why and how child abuse is handed on to succeeding generations.

Ney, P. G. (1992). Transgenerational triangles of abuse: A model of family violence. In Emilio C. Viano (Ed.), *Intimate Violence: Interdisciplinary Perspectives,* Hemisphere Publishing Corporation, 2: 15–25. Describes how tragic triangles of abuse and neglect develop in families.

Ney, P. G. (1994). The worst combinations of child abuse and neglect. *Child Abuse and Neglect,* 18(9): 705–714. Less than 5% of mistreated children experience only one type of abuse or neglect.

Ney, P. G., & Barry, J. E. (1983). Children who survive. *New Zealand Medical Journal,* 96: 939–940. Describes the conflicts of children who survive the death of siblings, particularly those in hospital.

Ney, P. G., Fung, T., & Wickett, A. R. (1993). Child neglect: The precursor to child abuse. *Pre- and Perinatal Psychology Journal,* 8(2): 95–112. These findings indicate that neglect makes a child more vulnerable and more susceptible to abuse.

Ney, P. G., Fung, T., & Wickett, A. R. (1993). The relationship between induced abortion and child abuse and neglect: four studies. *Pre- and Perinatal Psychology Journal,* 8: 43–63. Reviews their research into a possible connection between child abuse and induced abortion.

Ney, P. G., Fung, T., Wickett, A. R., & Beaman-Dodd, C. (1994). The effects of pregnancy loss on women's health. *Social Science & Medicine,* 38(9): 1193–1200. Presents findings from a large study that correlates various types of pregnancy loss with a woman's later health.

Ney, P. G., & Herron, J. A. (1985). Children in crisis: To whom should they turn? *New Zealand Medical Journal,* 98: 283–286. A report of findings from a study to determine who a mistreated child is most likely to turn to for help.

Ney, P. G., Johnson, I., & Herron, J. (1985). Social and legal ramifications of a child crisis line. *Child Abuse and Neglect,* 9: 47–55. Describes the working of a volunteer-manned distress line for children in New Zealand.

Ney, P. G., McPhee, J., Moore, C., Trought, P. (1986). Child abuse: A study of the child's perspective. *Child Abuse and Neglect,* 10: 511–518. This article reports findings from a survey of mistreated children and how they are affected.

Ney, P. G., & Mulvihill, D. (1983). A case of parental abuse. *Journal of Victimology,* 7: 194–198. Provides a case study of parent abuse and discusses possible underlying factors.

Ney, P. G., Wickett, A. R., & Fung, T. (1992). Causes of child abuse and neglect. *Canadian Journal of Psychiatry,* 37: 401–405. When surveyed, children indicate the most important cause of their mistreatment is parental immaturity and conflict.

Smith, J. A., & Adler, R. G. (1991). Children hospitalized with child abuse and neglect: A case controlled study. *Child Abuse and Neglect,* 15(4): 437–445. These authors found abused children were more likely to have been separated from their mothers during the first year of life.

VIDEOS AND FILMS

Pipes, W. E., & McCallum, M., et al. (1993). *Short term group psychotherapy for loss patients.* New York: Guilford Publications. Video for therapists and graduate students who wish to learn the basic techniques.

A chain to be broken. (1980). California: F. M. S. Productions. A short video that covers all kinds of abuse and emphasizes a coordinated community approach.

Yes, you can say no. Seattle, Washington: Committee for Children. Useful to those helping children deal with abuse and intimidation.

OTHER RESOURCES

Foster Parent Training, Indicators of Abuse and Neglect. Nova University, Regina Park, Saskatchewan, Canada: Florida and Saskatchewan Foster Parent Association.

Ney, P. G., & Peeters, M. A. (1993). *Deeply Damaged: An Explanation for the Profound Problems Arising from Infant Abortion and Child Abuse. Second Edition.* Victoria, Canada: Pioneer Publishing. The first of two manuals for group therapists interested in using these techniques, this manual provides the theoretical framework.

Ney, P. G., & Peeters, M. A. (1993). *Hope Alive: Post Abortion and Abuse Treatment; A Training Manual for Therapists. Second Edition.* Victoria, Canada: Pioneer Publishing. This manual provides detailed instructions for group therapists about techniques used in this book.

Pearce, A. (1989). *Working with Sexually Abused Children.* A Resource Pack for Professionals. Bristol, England: Childrens Society, Purnall Distributing Center.

PROFESSIONAL ORGANIZATIONS

American Group Psychotherapy Association, 25 East 21st Street, New York, NY 10010. Professional membership organization.

Canadian Psychiatric Association, 200–237 Argyle Street, Ottawa, Canada K2P 1B8. Professional membership organization.

Pre- and Perinatal Psychology Association of North America, 2162 Ingleside Avenue, Macon, GA 31204. Does innovative research and writing in a new field. Relevant to anyone interested in personality development.

Index

on expectations, 113, 122
and inner child, 153
letter of, 140, 146, 155
picture of, 97

Letters
disappointing responses to, 183
to perpetrators, 135–36, 139, 143–45, 146–47
sending of, as part of reconciliation, 131–32
Life, lack of enjoyment of, 202
Linda, 16, 31–32, 36, 40, 47, 62, 67, 96, 97, 121, 187, 209–10, 215, 220–22, 228
anger of, 58
on blame, 83
on expectations, 114, 123
on inner child, 92, 111
letter of, 175
Lisa, 16, 22, 40, 76–77, 93, 96, 155, 214, 215, 217, 221
as adopted, 58
on demons, 48, 53
guilt of, 72–73
on inner child, 103–4
letter of, 146
memories of, 123–24, 183, 204, 211
on mother, 111
on perpetrators, 84
picture of, 97
ritual abuse of, 29–30,113, 140, 160, 164, 179–80, 227
story of, 193–201
Loneliness
as phase of reconciliation, 131
as symptom, 23
Love, definition of, 185

Male authority, 138
need for, 189
Man, feelings and needs of, 192

Maneuvering, 176
Marital difficulties, 149, 154
as cause of child abuse, 185
Masturbation, 75
Maturity
lack of, *xiii*
signs of, 156–57
Media, vulnerability to suggestions of, 110
Memory(ies)
process of, 22
release of, 199–200
Miscarriage(s), 103
Mistreatment, intervention in, 35
See also Abuse
Money, problems with, 210
Mother(s), 192, 210, 213
in conflict with, 37–39
letters to, 143–45, 155
protecting, 42
Mourning, for inner child, 92, 102–4, 109

Neglect
child's perspective on, 185
correlation of, with abuse, *xiii*
emotional and intellectual, *xii*
first experiences of, 35
physical, *xii*
transgenerational transmission of, *xi–xvi*, 215
See also Abuse; Child abuse; Mistreatment
Nightmares, 194
Nonacceptance, 60
Nonresponse, 8
Nonverbal expression(s), 54
Nourishment, effect of, 6
Nun's Story, The, 94–95

Objectivity, need for, 5
Observer(s), 12
emotions of, 133–34